PAUL MARINER

My Rock and Roll
Football Story

PAUL MARINER

My Rock and Roll Football Story

Reach Sport

What an amazing dad you were. You were my hero, someone who I looked up to and admired so dearly, such a selfless and loving soul. You were the life and soul of the party, so charismatic and full of energy. You had this aura that attracted people who wanted to engage and listen to your stories. You would do everything and anything for anyone, even if you had just met them, and you were always there to help someone else out and not think anything of it. This was a quality that I really admired about you, Dad, so generous and caring.

Your sense of humour was unmatched, no one was safe around you, and you could give it as much as you could take it. Your one-liners regularly had people in stitches. There was never a dull moment being in your company, and quite often my friends wanted to hang out with you instead of me!

Despite being a superstar and a hero to many, you were so humble with your achievements. It fills me with pride that you made so many people happy with what you achieved on the pitch. You represented a group of fantastic football clubs as well as the England national team, and we couldn't be prouder of you as a family. Your legacy will live on forever.

I'm so glad I was able to look after you and care for you. You were a fighter and you still had that incredible sense of humour until the very end. Sharing all those moments with you and being there for you means the most to me.

I know life won't be the same without you, there isn't a day that I don't think about you, but I know you're in a better place now. I'll miss everything about you, you were so special to me.

Love you forever,
George Mariner, 2021

Reach Sport

www.reachsport.com

Written with Mark Donaldson

Published in Great Britain and Ireland in 2021 by
Reach Sport, a Reach PLC business.
www.reachsport.com
@Reach_Sport

Reach Sport is a part of Reach PLC.
One Canada Square, Canary Wharf, London, E15 5AP.

Hardback ISBN: 9781914197284
eBook ISBN: 9781914197291

Photographic acknowledgements:
Reach PLC, Alamy, Mirrorpix, Paul Mariner personal collection,
Getty Images, Greens On Screen, ESPN
Every effort has been made to trace copyright.
Any oversight will be rectified in future editions.

Typesetting by Danny Lyle

Printed and bound by CPI Group (UK) Ltd,
Croydon, CR0 4YY.

CONTENTS

INTRODUCTION

To know Paul Mariner was to love Paul Mariner. We all did. Couldn't help it. We loved his personality, his kindness, his stories, his humour, heck we even tolerated his constant noise – there was no option for an 'indoor voice' with Marrers. But most of all we loved his love. Would do anything for anyone, that one.

The process of encapsulating Paul Mariner's life story actually began way back in 2010 when Brad Feldman – commentator for New England Revolution in Major League Soccer – sat down with Paul, his close friend and subsequent work colleague, and they spent several hours chatting about PM's life and his career. Respective work commitments meant the project was put on hold and, alas, they never managed to restart it.

I had no idea the pair had even discussed the idea when I sent Paul a WhatsApp message on 16th February, 2021.

'Morning darling. Quick question – does writing a book interest you at all?'

'Tell me what it entails. Seems a lot of graft... but yes I fancy it. I'll be guided by you.'

'If it was something we went ahead with, would you be able to spare a few hours a week to do it via Skype or Zoom?'

'Yes. Because of this illness I can spend more time on it.'

Introduction

No mention of any previous chats with Brad. But at that stage Paul's health wasn't the best, his memory starting to become affected by regular radiotherapy and chemotherapy to try and treat his glioblastoma.

Then, out of the blue in mid-March 2021, an email from Brad Feldman offering all of the transcripts from their various sit-downs more than a decade before. Nearly twenty-five thousand words. The only thing Brad wanted in return was a guarantee that I would be able to use the content provided for Paul's book, which we both hoped would be a fitting legacy to our good friend. An incredible gesture from Brad and without which a lot of the in-depth stuff from Paul himself would never have seen the light of day. I'll always be grateful for your generosity, Mr Feldman, and a huge thanks to everyone else who subsequently took time to chat to me about Paul. I appreciate it greatly.

As Magnus Magnusson used to say on Mastermind... 'I've started so I'll finish.' Completing the book became an obsession. Due to the severity of Paul's condition we knew it was a case of 'when' and not 'if', so I was determined to finish the job for Paul and his family even though I only had four months to put everything together before the publisher's end-of-July deadline, as well as arranging and carrying out nearly forty interviews with those who Paul knew best. The patience of my wife, Lainey, cannot be underestimated, looking after our young daughter Ava Grace while Daddy spent hours locked away working. I love you both as much as Marrers loved the Deep Purple song 'Smoke on the Water'.

On the evening of 9th July, 2021 I was sitting at my desk at my home in Connecticut writing the music chapter of this book – with tears of laughter rolling down my cheeks while recounting some of the nonsense that Paul Mariner and Ian Gillan got up to – when Steve Nicol sent me a text containing just two words... 'Paul's gone'. The tears of joy were immediately replaced by tears of sorrow. We knew it was coming but that didn't make it any easier.

Chapter 20 is as far as I got with Paul when writing this book. We never did get the opportunity to finish it together. We didn't have the chance to talk about all those memories from his many years with us at ESPN headquarters in Bristol, Connecticut. We didn't get the chance to talk about why he and Stevie, when both were on ESPN FC together, would share the same small cubicle at work before the show, huddled together like they were back in the Revs dugout during a New England thunderstorm; Nicol, wearing a makeshift napkin bib while slurping his wife's home-made lentil soup, and Mariner, eagerly demolishing Eleanor's homemade beetroot and managing to avoid getting any bright purple drips on that day's pristine immaculately-ironed white shirt, with the elbows of two great friends practically touching. And we never will.

The world is a poorer place without Paul Mariner and his irresistible effervescence. But memories of the great man will last a lifetime and nobody can ever take them away. We loved his love. And we always will.

Sleep well, Marrers x

**Mark Donaldson,
writer and friend, 2021**

FOREWORD
BY IAN GILLAN

W hen I look back at my long career in music there are many names from the past that are brought to mind for one reason or another, and they gravitate naturally to either the smile or frown department in my brain lobby. Paul Mariner always appears at the smile desk – he has never once failed to make me laugh.

We first met in the late 1970s, back in the day when it seemed that every footballer wanted to be a rock star and most rock stars thought they could kick a ball. I stayed at Paul's house whenever I was in the area and we certainly used to enjoy life. Days merged into evenings. Evenings got longer and longer. Only God knows what time we returned home some mornings.

There was one memorable occasion when it was snowing heavily. Leaving our eye-rolling girls in the car, we jumped out, stripped off and played in the snow like kids without a care in the world.

The nights out were also a bit special. My favourite one was in March 1983.

It started with us going for a boozy meal at an Indian restaurant in Ipswich. After we had finished eating, Paul suggested

a challenge – so we put together a spontaneous and sophisti-
cated dare, requiring us to drink this awful concoction which
contained almost everything that was left on the table after the
meal, including beer, wine, spirits, food scraps and the contents
of the ashtray. It was absolutely disgusting but Paul was up for
doing pretty much anything, so we did the dirty deed without a
second thought. He would have acquitted himself very well as a
wild rock musician. He was always game for a laugh. He would
look you straight in the eye and challenge you to be boring.

One of the boys with us in the restaurant that night
mentioned that Van Morrison was playing at the Gaumont
Theatre in town and asked if anyone fancied going. I was up
for that, as was Paul, so we all trooped along to the venue. I had
performed there a few times and knew the manager – in fact,
Paul had actually been on stage, singing the chorus to 'Smoke
on the Water' with me and the Gillan band a few months
earlier – so we were sorted out with posh seats in the Gaumont's
equivalence of a Royal Box.

The venue was only one third full, and it seemed more
like a prayer meeting than a rock concert. The congregational
euphoria was shattered as Mariner, myself and the rest of the
gang sat down as quietly as possibly, which, considering the
amount of alcohol that we had just consumed at the Indian
restaurant, was not quiet enough for the band and assembled
audience. They all turned round to glare at us and shout-whis-
per SSHHHUUSSSHHHH. We were only there briefly, but at
the end of the only recognisable song we all stood up, cheered
and whistled, making a heck of a racket. That was all too
much apparently – members of the audience really shouldn't
be louder than the headline act – and we were thrown out for
being 'over-enthusiastic'. Van Morrison's manager was furious

and came steaming round, chin first, threatening us with all sorts. He was quickly followed by the worried venue manager who uttered a rather more serene *'Please, please – would you mind…er…leaving??'* while gently shaking his head.

No Van Morrison encore for us, but the night was still young and deserved an encore of its own.

Our next destination was Jonathan's party barge, which was moored against the Ipswich Waterfront. A feast had been laid out on the table by a friend of ours, the very generous owner, Jonathan Crisp. Plenty of drinks, just not enough food. Despite our earlier intake we were hungry again, so Paul and I went to the local fish shop where we placed an order for fifty 'fish 'n' chips' along with similar numbers of plastic knives and forks and an industrial sized jar of pickled onions. The owner put up the closed sign and after twenty minutes we returned to the boat and laid out everything on a long table in the luxury saloon, with the hugely impressive jar of onions as a centre piece.

Feeling uncomfortably hot after a few more drinks – and several very tasty, pickled onions – I decided that a swim would help me cool off, so I took off my clothes and, leaving behind a startled tableau of onlookers, jumped overboard into the Orwell estuary, completely oblivious that the area down below was full of sharp poles, discarded bicycles and a few gasping fish.

I hadn't really thought it through properly as I discovered that, in the absence of steps, the only way back to the dry stuff was up a bow rope. So, up I went, buccaneer-style, to be grabbed by the bulwarks and hauled aboard by Paul and other startled guests.

Stark bollard naked and dripping weedy brine I was suddenly depressed, because, during my piratical rope climb, I had forgotten to have a weapon clenched in my teeth as traditionally required by those attempting a bit of 'swash', in the category 'buckle'. So, I skipped into the saloon, grabbed a plastic knife, shoved it in my mouth and rushed back out to the deck heading for a dive back into the Orwell. Only to be tackled heavily and wrestled to the ground by defenders Butcher and Osman, then sat on by centre forward Mariner. A word of advice...if you ever see those three coming at you, abandon all plans and find a quiet corner, which is what I did, I think, although, to be perfectly honest, I can't remember what happened after that.

Paul was a brilliant and brave footballer (his best goal for me was against Scotland; watch how he terrifies the keeper) as well as a regular guy, and just like a lot of our peers, was immortal and omniscient...we all know better now of course. I think that was true of a lot of footballers in those days, with most of them from humble beginnings, ill-prepared, as they are today, for intimate public curiosity, living life to the full, blissfully unaware of the media traps and the self-discipline that was needed to move on in life.

Then there was the banter, of course, which was hilarious. One of the great things about making jokes about each other was that it immediately defused and took the edge off any brittle moments. Unlike the ways of some of the top players in my game (music), footballers had to play as a team and so I felt good in the company of Paul and his mates with not one megalomaniac among them, apart from me maybe.

You know where you stand with Paul. No airs or graces, he is what he is...an incredible guy. A friend for life. Nobody wants a bullshitter for a friend. You want someone who will tell you what's what and someone you can trust. Everyone in Deep Purple adores him. I cannot think of anyone else that we have had backstage over the years — celebrities or otherwise — who is more loved. Paul Mariner is up there at the top table.

This is one hell of a fight that Paul is going through right now. I've read and thought about this and written a lot about it over the years — there are some things that just turn a little wheel in your mind and set the cogs whirring.

I remember hearing once about doctors trashing the efficacy of homeopathy. Well, I had distant relations who were homeopathic chemists and herbalists. So, I knew a little about the subject, but had little faith in it myself, particularly the logic behind it. Then I heard another doctor talking about a miracle patient 'Clinically, we really made very little contribution to his survival, it was simply the man's will to live that got him through'. So that got me thinking about this homeopathy thing; to me it's just like your chosen God...If you believe, it really can work. I don't know how it does that; it's nothing to do with science or hocus-pocus and everything to do with belief and commitment. To my mind, if anyone is going to beat something with grit and determination then it is Paul Mariner.

But... I went to see him today for a hug and a beer. His candle was flickering. Mother Nature takes her course and what can we do about that?

I am reminded of a song called 'Above and Beyond' and the line that says...

'...souls, having touched, are forever entwined...'

Paul leaves the field. There is no substitute.

We stand, we smile and cry, all of us improved by knowing him.

We applaud.

Ian Gillan
Saturday 1st May, 2021

1

A Question of Sports

I've looked up to many people in my life. None more so than when I was sixteen years old. But that was only because I'd grown just half an inch in the space of two years. Five foot three on my fourteenth birthday and five foot three and a half when I turned sixteen in May 1969.

I was a mouthy teenager but decent at football: captaining both the Horwich schools' side and the town's youth team. Scouts were paying attention and there was a fair bit of gossip that certain clubs were showing an interest in me, but that was when I was nearer fourteen than sixteen. Those scouts soon turned their attention elsewhere as the bigger and stronger players with similar talent became more noticeable and started to take centre stage.

I was soon just another kid playing football and I wasn't enjoying it nearly as much, so I decided to pack it in. To play cricket.

Billy Beaumont — or Bill to those of you familiar with a certain BBC television sports quiz — was my former teammate at Chorley Cricket Club and one of those people I looked up to, both physically and metaphorically. A year older and several inches taller, he took me under his wing when we spent the summer of 1969 travelling all over the north-west playing for Chorley's second team in the Northern League. We had a blast. I was a wicketkeeper – and actually went for trials at representative level – while Billy used to bat near the top of the order. He was also rather proficient at a certain other sport, a proficiency that led to him signing for Fylde Rugby Club later that year after his father – who'd played for the club – wrote them a letter asking for his son to be given a trial (in which he played full-back).

When I look back now, that summer seemed to last forever. Those were the best days of my life, as Bryan Adams might say. Thankfully the autumn and winter of '69 weren't bad either because not only did I finally start growing again – I was up to five foot eight and a half by Christmas – but football was also back on the radar thanks to a chance encounter with someone I used to play against for my school team. Just like Bill Beaumont, Steve Walsh also went on to make an impact in his chosen career. He was the scout who recommended N'Golo Kante to Leicester City before going on to become Director of Football at Everton.

Steve and I were both under-agers in the Mitre Pub in Chorley when he approached me one night and asked if I was the guy he used to play against when he was a defender for St Augustine's and I was a central midfielder for Horwich Secondary. I explained that I'd given up football because of my lack of height and decided to play cricket instead. By this stage, however, I was roughly as tall as Steve after growing five inches in a matter of months. He asked if I still had an interest in football and mentioned he was playing for St Gregory's, an under-18 team playing in the Chorley and District Alliance

League who were affiliated with the town's working men's club. And was I interested in joining him?

I had a decision to make. I'd been enjoying my cricket, but Billy had switched to rugby and it wasn't quite as much fun without him around. I also knew there wouldn't be as much travel involved if I was playing football locally in Chorley for St Gregory's. In the end, I didn't need much persuading from Steve – the cricket was great fun while it lasted but the timing of this just seemed right.

That particular St Gregory's team was put together by a fantastic guy called Alan Jones, whose job it was to assemble the best local players to complement the boys he already had in the squad. Alan wasn't terribly knowledgeable about football, but he was excellent at getting people he knew or players that played for him to persuade other players to come and join. Steve Walsh approaching me in the pub was the perfect example of someone doing Alan's work for him. The gaffer was like some kind of Lancashire Godfather with all his contacts and he'd namedrop new signings to attract potential signings – *come and join us because Paul Mariner has just signed and we're going to do this, that and the other.* Alan knitted everything together, but on a matchday he basically put the kit out and said: 'There you go lads, now go and get on with it!'

We trained on a pitch right beside Victory Park, home of Chorley FC, and used to play there on a Saturday morning before Chorley played next door in the afternoon. It wasn't uncommon for scouts to take in our games then watch Chorley a couple of hours later – especially so when we went on a run in the Lancashire County Youth Cup in 1970-71. In those days that particular competition also included teams from Liverpool and Manchester because the county boundaries weren't realigned until 1974. We went on to win the trophy – quite an achievement for a bunch of local woollybacks like us – and in the summer of 1971 I received an offer to join Chorley Football Club. I signed for our local semi-professional team for a tenner a week.

What turned out to be a long and eventful football career was up and running.

* * *

Football and education. In that order. Growing up on a council estate in Horwich – between Chorley and Bolton – my early life pretty much consisted of those two things and very little else. I was usually in charge of organising the football in the playground, and that's where skills were honed, but the real fun was had after school. There were a lot of young families on our estate and I grew up with loads of kids of a similar age who, like me, were football fans and also loved playing the game. I'd come home from school and the first thing I wanted to do was have a kickabout with my friends. I may have been an only child but they were like brothers and sisters to me. It was a fantastic upbringing.

Everything is different these days because parents, under-standably so, want to know where their kids are at all times. Life was far more simple back then: we finished school and went home for a quick bite to eat, got the gear on and went straight to Slater's Field in Horwich to kick a ball around until it got dark. Then we would move the coats or jumpers we'd used for goalposts and relocate them in the middle of Longworth Road, the action continuing under the street lights outside our homes, interrupted only by passing cars.

The final whistle was always Mum shouting that it was time

to come inside. We usually tried to sneak some added time at the end of normal time, but Peggy's second yell always seemed more forceful and none of us were brave enough to try for extra time before supper. The penalties weren't worth thinking about.

My dad, Jim, was a manager in a cotton mill – how stereotypically Lancastrian. He would get on the bus every morning and work a full day. We couldn't afford a car, and I was around six years old when he was finally able to afford a 1959 Norman Nippy, a little 49cc moped. It was hilarious watching him come home from work. There was a steep hill going up to the house where we lived and we used to laugh when we saw this white crash helmet bobbing side to side as he got closer to home – but the moped moving slower and slower as the hill got steeper and steeper! It was definitely a no-frills upbringing, but I made the most of it and look back on that time fondly.

I suppose we taught ourselves how to play football. You had to work out on your own how to get the better of a particularly good defender, or how to beat someone who was faster than you. There was a fair bit of trial and error, but it was a great way of coaching yourself. And if your pals were still doing their homework, or weren't allowed to come out until they'd had their dinner, you'd just bang the ball against the wall yourself and practise controlling the ball.

Living in Lancashire meant I had the choice of several clubs to go and watch, but there was only one team I wanted to support – Bolton Wanderers. Going down to Burnden Park on a Saturday was one of the highlights of the week. I've since travelled the world and, after finding out where I grew up, many people have asked me why I wasn't a fan of Manchester United or even Liverpool. I never considered going to watch any other team apart from Bolton.

I also had a soft spot for Tottenham in those days because they were the big, successful team at the start of the Sixties, doing the double in 1960-61 then signing Jimmy Greaves the following season. He was my first footballing hero. When I was young I loved watching goalscorers, and Jimmy was just sensational. God-like even. The star striker was the hero more often than not. I liked the sound of that. My father used to tell me about Puskas and Gento, he tried to educate me about the world game and not just Bolton Wanderers, but strikers were always the main topic of conversation. Especially Jimmy Greaves.

I remember asking Dad to take me to watch Tottenham play at Bolton for my tenth birthday. He agreed, but with my birthday being in May I had to wait nearly seven months to get my present. Fast forward to Saturday, December 7, 1963 – watching those Tottenham players come out of the tunnel at Burnden Park in the whitest shorts, the whitest socks and the most incredible, spellbinding, almost-metallic blue shirts, I had never seen anything like it before. And, of course, getting to see Jimmy Greaves in person for the very first time was incredible for this particular ten-year-old.

I used to stand at the embankment end at Burnden where the old steam trains used to pass right behind us, a mode of transport I had a particular affection for. Sometimes when the engine driver wanted to watch a bit of the match he would deliberately slow the train down. And depending on which way the wind was blowing, the steam from the engine would come over the embankment which meant some of the fans couldn't see the game. This happened on that particular day and it was a good few minutes until it cleared up!

Bolton had a couple of full-backs – Syd Farrimond and Roy

Hartle – and the pair of them loved to put their foot in and make a tackle. It was a regular occurrence that Syd and Roy would take it in turns to target the opposition winger and try to force him out onto the gravel at the side of the pitch. But they had a hell of a job that day against Welshman Cliff Jones, and I remember being mesmerised by him and Jimmy Greaves. It was a very muddy pitch, as they all were in those days at that time of year, but they could have put Jimmy's kit straight back in the hamper after the game because it hardly had a mark on it. His balance was unbelievable and the Bolton players couldn't get near him.

Although Wyn Davies equalised for Wanderers after Syd unfortunately opened the scoring for Spurs with an own goal, Jimmy scored to put Tottenham ahead and Bolton ended up losing the game 3-1. Despite the result, that was the day when I properly fell in love with the game of football and its great goalscorers.

* * *

Football was my first love but the importance of a good education was drummed into me by mum and dad. I did okay at school in the early years, but my teachers and my parents both agreed I wasn't quite clever enough to get in to Rivington Grammar, so it was a comprehensive education instead at Horwich County secondary school. In fact, I still couldn't get in to Rivington even after I'd just turned 24…

SOCCER star Paul Mariner is playing for England against Northern Ireland today, which has caused problems for his old school. Bolton-born Paul was due to open Rivington and Blackrod High School's annual fete, but his international call-up meant organisers had to find a replacement. Deputy Head Teacher Mrs. Anne Sharples joked: "We're rather annoyed with Don Revie, but we're obviously very pleased for Paul." Ipswich striker Paul was a pupil at Horwich County Secondary School, which became part of the new comprehensive high school in 1973. The fete will instead be opened by Mr David Brown, chairman of the parent/teacher association.

The Bolton Evening News, 28th May, 1977

I'm sure the staff and teachers at Rivington were of a high standard, but I doubt any of them could have helped me more than Alan Smalley, my sports master at Horwich Secondary. He was in charge of the school football team and someone I always looked up to. I learned so much from him and he eventually made me captain of the side, so I owe a huge debt of gratitude to that wonderful man.

The mid-Sixties was a period I look back on fondly. I was doing well as a central midfielder with my new school team and the World Cup in England in 1966 was generating a huge buzz. Mr. Smalley told us to watch every game we could and try to learn from the players we were watching – Pelé, Eusebio and Jimmy Greaves were the three I wanted to pay particular attention to. This was the kind of homework I didn't mind!

Mum and Dad didn't have too much money when I was growing up – we certainly couldn't afford tickets for any of the World Cup games at nearby Old Trafford or Goodison Park – but we did have a black and white television and I pretty much spent most of July sitting in front of it watching the games. Pelé and Eusebio didn't disappoint, although some of the treatment dished out to the Brazilian genius by opposition players was an absolute disgrace. Unfortunately Jimmy Greaves didn't make much of an impact in the tournament, failing to score in the group stage then missing the quarter-final against Argentina because of injury. Geoff Hurst scored the winner in that game and the rest is history, but Jimmy Greaves remained my favourite player.

I may have been mouthy as a kid but I never challenged authority. Not even in 1967 when Mr. Smalley said no to a youth coach from Bolton Wanderers, my boyhood team, who'd been in touch enquiring about a certain fourteen-year-old.

"You can go to a better club than that. You should aim higher than Bolton," he told me. I had no reason not to believe him.

Over the next couple of years, however, I used to think 'What if?' with more regularity as time went by as my growing pains, or lack of, were giving me serious doubts that a potential career as a professional footballer would ever materialise. I was disheartened, having convinced myself the opportunity may have passed me by. I left school at sixteen having got my CSEs, but not enough qualifications to secure a place at university. That's when I spent my 'Summer of '69' playing cricket. I just needed some time away doing something different.

With football pushed to one side − albeit reluctantly but thankfully only for a few months − I had to decide what I wanted to do with my life. I was keen to get a further education, so I signed up for night school at Leigh Technical College on Mondays and Thursdays, and day school on Wednesdays, to study mechanical engineering as part of an OND, an Ordinary National Diploma. But I still needed a job to make some money.

Initially I wanted to be a joiner because I enjoyed working with wood. Unfortunately for me we had about three or four joiners, or carpenters, in our family and Mum and Dad weren't overly keen on that idea. And I didn't fancy becoming an electrician, one of their suggestions, because I was convinced I would blow myself up. So just before I returned to football and signed for St Gregory's, I started a four-year apprentice-ship working for the Metal Box Company at a local factory in Westhoughton, helping to manufacture various types of cans. I loved it, but it didn't love me – I didn't realise until a few days in the job that I was allergic to certain types of metal! I ended up with this horrible rash on my hands and had to use all sorts of special creams. At least the manual labour helped me bulk up as I sweated in an oversized boiler suit while wearing dainty gloves to protect my 'allergic-to-certain-types-of-metal' hands.

Ted Facey was my gaffer at Metal Box, a lovely man who was a big football fan so he would cut me a little bit of slack if I needed to get off work early when St Gregory's (then latterly Chorley) were playing midweek games away from home. However, if I didn't change a part correctly I'd get dog's abuse, just like anybody else. It was pretty arduous and things had to be done on time, there were no excuses if jobs were not completed.

My schedule for the week was tough. On Mondays and Thursdays I'd go to work at seven in the morning and finish at four, come home for dinner, catch the five-thirty bus to Leigh – a journey that took about an hour – then go to the technical college from seven until nine. I'd then catch the nine-thirty bus and get back home about ten-thirty. Tuesdays were the same, except I had training at night. And I'd go to college during the day on a Wednesday, start in the morning at eight and finish at six, getting home around seven. Friday night was the only chance I had to put my feet up before playing football on a Saturday.

A Question of Sports

I've often thought about how things might have panned out if I'd not gone to The Mitre pub that night and bumped into Steve Walsh again. Right place, right time and all that. The cricket was fun but football was my first love and what I really wanted to do. I just needed a few months away from it to realise what I was missing. The Bolton Wanderers ship might have sailed when I was fourteen, and who's to say if anything would even have come of that if I'd had the opportunity, but I was given a second chance by St Gregory's and it was one I was determined to take. It might not have paid any bills, but I was back in the game.

If you were looking for the glamorous side of football then you would not have found it at St Gregory's. The pitch next to Victory Park that we used for training didn't have any goal-posts, the club did have its own but they were stored round the back of The Mitre pub – half a mile away!

I'd love to say we took it in turns to carry them to and from training and games but I'd be lying, although I did manage to exhaust my list of excuses before it was eventually my turn to help.

We also used to get changed at The Mitre, in a room upstairs from the bar. We weren't even allowed to use the entrance to the pub to go upstairs, we had to go round the back and through a small door that looked like it had been borrowed from a bloody barn. The only thing that was missing was some straw and a few chickens!

In spite of the rather underwhelming facilities, my first season with St Gregory's was decent. We won the league and cup double, and with local cup finals being played at Victory Park, home of Chorley Football Club, there was usually a decent crowd in attendance. Over the summer Alan Jones used his contacts to add a few more of the best local youngsters and in my second season I can't remember us losing a single game in the league, we were virtually unstoppable. It was a disappointment if we didn't score at least four or five goals in every game. We actually beat Ecclestone Youth Club 26-0 in one game – I think I scored six or seven and we had to be told the score afterwards because everyone had lost count! But the Lancashire County Youth Cup was the one we really wanted to win. We were up against some of the top under-18 teams in the country, never mind the county, including Lancaster City and Kirkby Town, two of the best and well-funded clubs.

Lancaster City was a non-league academy team. Their players turned up at our place in a big posh bus wearing all the gear and accompanied by a whole staff, including physios, masseurs and all sorts.

They waltzed onto the pitch with shiny numbers on the back of their immaculately-ironed jerseys and the name of some well-known sponsor across on the front. Meanwhile we got changed in the barn above the Mitre Pub having removed our crumpled strips and stained shorts from a couple of black rubbish bags. After carrying the goalposts from the pub to the pitch and putting up the nets we thumped them 6-1.

Our best result was beating Kirkby Town. At the time they were seen as one of the best youth teams in the whole country and they had some real hardy boys with plenty of talent. That area of Liverpool produced the likes of Phil Thompson and Dennis Mortimer and I wouldn't be surprised if a number of the Kirkby team we played against that day ended up going professional.

With Lancaster City and Kirkby Town both dispatched, St Gregory's went on to win the trophy. A truly remarkable achievement, just a bunch of boys playing for a parochial little team from Chorley taking on and beating far more established sides. It really was quite the feat, although when you look back at what some of our players subsequently achieved in the game then maybe our cup win wasn't as big a surprise as it appeared at the time.

Mickey Walsh went on to join Blackpool – where he scored the goal of the season on BBC's *Match of the Day* – and he also played for Everton and the Republic of Ireland. But one of his biggest achievements was featuring for Porto against Juventus in the Cup Winners' Cup final in 1984. And Brian Parker, our goalkeeper, played for Crewe Alexandra, then later joined Arsenal.

Steve Walsh and his central defensive partner Steve 'Kipper' Wilkinson – a ginger-haired butcher from Brinscall – also made the step up from St Gregory's to join Chorley, just like Mickey and Brian did. And that's the route I took initially as well.

We started off in the reserves, playing in the Lancashire League – in one game, Steve Walsh and I came up against Joe Royle of Everton when he was coming back from injury – and the standard was decent. Then, if you were good enough, you'd graduate into the Chorley first team and thankfully I was able to do that pretty quickly.

I made my debut as a substitute against Macclesfield Town on Saturday, October 16, 1971. It was goalless at half-time and at the start of the second half I was told to go and warm up. Shortly after came the call to get stripped. I managed to provide the assist for our opening goal and the game finished two-all.

Thankfully I did enough during my time on the pitch to impress, and the reward was a first start for Chorley against Morecambe the following Tuesday in front of 775 supporters.

And after starting a game for the club my weekly wage increased from three quid to a tenner. I was now on the second bottom rung of the footballing ladder, although not quite high enough just yet for a case of acrophobia.

2

Looking Forward

Did they mean it? I've got no idea. I certainly hope not. Those two Lancaster City players who were responsible for breaking my leg in December 1971 could easily have ended my career full stop – a simultaneous scissor tackle, one from each side, which snapped the bone just above my right ankle – but what they did do, as a result of their reckless actions, was keep me out of the game for long enough to signal the end of my time as a regular central midfielder.

There's no way that match against Lancaster City should have gone ahead, there was ice on the pitch at Victory Park in Chorley and conditions were treacherous for the FA Trophy third qualifying round fixture. But the referee gave it the green light, and that game ultimately turned out to be the last one I played for the first team that season. The injury kept me on the sidelines for about five months but thankfully my recovery was without any drama, mainly thanks to the wonderful staff at Chorley Hospital.

I tried to return in a reserve fixture against Crewe Alexandra just before the end of the season. We lost 5-2 and I managed to play about an hour, but Steve Walsh said after the game that he'd noticed I still had a slight limp at times. I definitely felt ready to return but I was clearly still a fair bit away from full fitness, so the decision was taken to rest up and get myself properly ready for pre-season training.

A lot of things changed at the football club that summer. The team was no longer playing in the Northern Premier League – the fifth tier of English football – having resigned its position, despite finishing mid-table, and was subsequently demoted two divisions to the Cheshire County League. We had a new manager as well, Alan Hampson, who had just been sacked by South Liverpool. Alan was very thoughtful, very knowledgeable and he had a great ability to spot a good player, including Jimmy Case who played for him as a 17-year-old in 1971 before eventually moving to Anfield.

Alan wasted no time in making his first signing, bringing Kevin Wainwright, a striker, over from South Liverpool. The new gaffer's first training session in pre-season was lively, he kept encouraging me to get forward into the box and I banged in a few goals. He came up to me afterwards, smiled and put his arm around my shoulder. One more thing was about to change. What Alan said next altered the course of my football career.

"You know something, I think you can play further up the park. Have you ever played as a forward?" he asked me.

"Nope".

Pretty much every game I'd ever played was in central midfield, including the two times Chorley came up against Alan's South Liverpool team in August and September the season before. The new gaffer explained that he was impressed by my performances in those fixtures and thought I had a decent eye for goal.

Looking Forward

"I think you can play up front alongside Kevin Wainwright. He's a traditional number nine and can be the hold-up man. He'll provide the protection so you can do all the stuff around him."

What I didn't know was that Kevin was already aware of the manager's plans. That was part of Alan's pitch to get Kevin to leave South Liverpool and join him at Chorley. As it turned out, Kevin knew I'd be playing up front before I did!

I hit it off with Kev right away and we quickly developed an almost telepathic understanding. We managed to score fifty-two goals between us that season. I got thirty-six, of which several were set up by Kev, and he scored sixteen despite missing several games through injury. He was also a great guy off the pitch and we had many laughs together, including in the changing room after a particularly tough pre-season session. The wage packets used to get left where you sat. There was a ten pound note in each of our envelopes. "All that bloody hard work for just a tenner!" But I suppose it wasn't too bad in those days, considering I was also getting a few quid each week from Metal Box.

Our goalscoring exploits soon attracted the attention of various scouts. I'd heard a whisper that Everton and Preston North End, who'd both watched me prior to the leg break, were once again keeping tabs on my progress. Verdi Godwin was another regular visitor to Victory Park. A lifeguard on Southport Beach, he also scouted players up north for Plymouth. But I didn't find out about that particular interest until I went to visit Kevin in hospital...

We were playing against Witton Albion and Mick Wearmouth, our centre-half, sent a long clearance forward in my direction. I knew I was offside so I just left it, however Kev saw it bounce and thought the ball was there to be won. He got in behind the defender but at the same time the Witton goalkeeper came rushing out of his box. They both went to head the ball, Kev just got there first followed by a mid-air collision with the keeper and a nasty-looking landing. That wasn't the worst of it, though. The goalie then came down on top of poor Kevin with a knee landing on his chest. Jerry Keegan, our trainer, ambled on just after Kev had vomited copious amounts of blood.

"What seems to be the problem?" asked Jerry when he eventually got to the stricken patient. He had a look inside Kev's mouth then proceeded to suggest the only damage was a bitten tongue! Within an hour Kevin was in hospital with a punctured lung and several broken ribs. Needless to say, Jerry never got a job in a medical practice.

I subsequently played up front on my own for a few games – which was a new experience for me – but before doing so I went to Chorley Hospital to see how Mr. Wainwright was feeling.

"The chairman came to see me last night," said Kevin. "And he told me that not only were Plymouth Argyle looking at you, but they were keeping tabs on me as well."

There was a fair bit of speculation about me in the local paper around that time, but this was the first I'd heard of a specific team showing an interest. I had no idea who Verdi Godwin was at that point – I'd never heard of him – but apparently he and the sheepskin hat he always wore had been regular fixtures at our home games at Victory Park. And with Kev in hospital, Verdi would get to see something a little bit different over the next few games – me playing up front on my own.

I actually did alright as a lone striker, continuing to score at a decent clip, and it wasn't long before word got out that

Plymouth was in fact the team with a concrete interest when Argyle manager Tony Waiters made the long trip north to watch me play at the rather sinister sounding Dark Lane ground in the village of Newchurch in Lancashire. We lost 2-1 to Rossendale United that day – I played alone up top again as Kevin was still in recovery after biting his tongue – but I scored our goal and played well.

Watched by Plymouth Argyle manager Tony Waiters on Saturday, Paul Mariner scored Chorley's only goal – but it wasn't enough to secure revenge for the Magpies. The Third Division club manager kept his promise in coming to watch the 19-year-old player perform and Paul must now wait on a decision from the Pilgrims. Paul played well in the game, figuring prominently in the Magpies' attack, but although Chorley played better than the previous week – when they were beaten by Rossendale at Victory Park – they once again couldn't outwit United, whose determination must be rated as one of the best in the Cheshire County League.

Clive Naish's match report, The Chorley Guardian

This was the first time Tony Waiters had seen me play in the flesh following the recommendation from Verdi Godwin. The relationship between those two began in 1959 when Verdi saw Tony play in goal for Macclesfield Town and recommended him to Blackpool, where he'd go on to make more than 250 appearances and also play for England five times in 1964. Many years later the two of them also worked together as part-time lifeguards on the beach at Southport where Tony was from and Verdi lived.

I actually found out how Verdi's interest came about many

years later when I popped in to see him on the way to visit my mum and dad. I always stayed in touch with him, and would try and go to say 'hi' at least once a year when I was up seeing my folks. Verdi told me he first watched me play in 1971, a month or so before I broke my leg against Lancaster City, and it was my warm-up that caught his eye. Some players just loosen up before games, but I was always pretty intense and used to put myself through a proper workout before finishing up with shooting practice. And on this particular occasion, unbeknown to me, I had stood out before the match had even started. Verdi explained that I'd done enough before the injury for him to keep tabs on my situation, and although he continued to go to Victory Park when I was recovering, his visits to watch Chorley became a lot more frequent at the start of the 1972-73 season when I was back in the team. And he told me Alan Hampson was a smart man for playing me up front. The best bit was when Verdi explained that he'd already decided he was going to tell Tony Waiters about me, but made one final trip to Victory Park before making the phone call to the manager of Plymouth Argyle.

"A couple of other scouts soon joined me," Verdi told me "but after you and the Chorley players went back inside I announced to them that I'd seen enough. And I left without seeing any of the action. The only reason I showed up that day was to make sure you still had the same professionalism and enthusiasm pre-match as you'd shown the first time I watched you the previous year!"

I thought I'd played pretty well against Rossendale United in front of the watching Tony Waiters, but didn't hear anything more for a couple of weeks until the club received a letter from Plymouth Argyle. They were inviting me down for a five-day trial at the beginning of May. This was around the time that I was coming to the end of my apprenticeship and I had an offer on the table to become a full-time mechanical engineer. Although appealing, my main aim had always been to become a professional footballer and this trial was an incredible opportunity to impress and perhaps do just that. Ted Facey, my gaffer at Metal Box, was very supportive of the opportunity and gave me the week off work.

After playing what turned out to me my last ever game for Chorley on the Saturday in their final match of the season, I made my way to Wigan railway station the following day ahead of a six-hour journey to Plymouth, via Wolverhampton and Birmingham New Street. I'd not visited Plymouth before but I had been to Devon and Cornwall on holiday, and I just remember how long it took to get there from Lancashire. I had really long hair at that time, it was down my back because I was a massive rocker, and I used to get some weird looks from people on public transport. In fact on the train journey down from Birmingham to Plymouth an older lady got on after about an hour and sat down opposite me. I caught her staring a few times before she proceeded to ask if I was in a band. I told her I wasn't.

"Well, are you famous?"

"I'm not. But I hope to be one day."

* * *

I was very nervous going into a professional environment at Plymouth Argyle but thankfully I was rooming with a great lad, a goalkeeper called Milija Aleksic who went on to play for Tottenham. The following morning he asked what I wanted for breakfast before picking up the phone in the hotel room. "No,

I'm okay," I said, thinking there was no way that I could afford room service. "Don't worry, the club will pay for it. Order what you want." This was already a brand new experience for me. We had a bit of breakfast and hit it off really well.

The plan that Plymouth boss Tony Waiters had put in place for my week's trial was as follows: training on Monday and Tuesday then travel to Cornwall, three friendlies – at Penzance on the Wednesday night, away to Porthleven the following evening and a game at St. Austell on the Friday night – then travel back up north on the Saturday afternoon. Written instructions were left with the coaching staff because Tony was actually away in Scotland with the England youth team and wasn't going to be present for the first game at Penzance, but the manager was back in attendance at Porthleven on the Thursday.

The league season actually ended for Plymouth Argyle on the first day of May, but the first team played Manchester City the following day in a testimonial for Mike Bickle and then Plymouth playing three games in Cornwall was seen as a way to reward the club's Cornish fan base for their loyalty throughout the season. It was also seen by the manager as an ideal opportunity to have a look at me on trial.

It all went pretty well, I have to say. Against Penzance, I scored after twenty-five seconds with my first touch of the game, got the assist for the second goal then scored the third – not a bad way to make a first impression. Against Porthleven, with Tony Waiters in attendance having travelled down from Scotland earlier that day, I scored again in a two-one win at Gala Park. Then, at Poltair Park in St. Austell, venue for the last game of my trial, I played the full game, and scored again, taking my total for the Cornwall trip to five goals in just three hours of football. A smile from Tony and a pat on the back as I left the pitch at the end – "come see me in my office tomorrow morning and we can have a chat."

I had a real spring in my step going in to see him the following day and was properly excited. "We want to sign you but from what I understand Chorley are going to ask for too much money," said Tony after the opening pleasantries and plaudits. "So it doesn't look like we're going to be able to take you." I was stunned. My head was spinning and I didn't even bother asking him any questions, I just thanked the manager and left his office.

I got on the train ahead of the long journey back and immediately burst into tears. It seemed as though everything had gone so well and I could not believe my dream of becoming a professional footballer was about to be shattered. Once my emotions settled down I tried to think of a way to resurrect the move. Having time to think on the journey back was actually a good thing and I came up with one or two ideas of what to say to the Chorley board members. Unfortunately with it being the end of the season a few of them had gone away on holiday and I wasn't able to arrange a meeting with them until Tuesday the twenty-second of May, the day of my twentieth birthday.

The time in between was really tough, especially with speculation continuing in the press that Plymouth were still keen to sign me but the asking price would need to come down. What I didn't know at that stage – and only found out much later – was of a difference of opinion at Plymouth Argyle about the merits of spending several thousand pounds on a non-league striker from the seventh tier of English football after Tony Waiters admitted to the board that he was having second thoughts because of the price.

As it transpired the unlikely hero in all of this was Verdi Godwin. He'd called Tony for an update on my situation and when the manager explained that he wasn't one hundred per cent sure after discussing it with the board, Verdi told Tony if the move wasn't sanctioned then he would resign and Plymouth would have to look for a new northern scout.

The conversation with Verdi, and subsequent ultimatum, prompted Tony to have further discussions with Argyle chairman Robert Daniel. Tony didn't want to lose the services of his good friend and someone who did an excellent job for the football club. Eventually a solution was found. The six members of the board – the chairman, the vice-chairman and four directors – were split three apiece as to whether to continue negotiations with Chorley. So it was decided that Tony and his coaching staff would get the chance to break the deadlock by way of a vote. And, according to Plymouth Argyle secretary Graham Little, they voted in favour by one to proceed with further talks. Who voted for what I do not know, but I was told that the board subsequently agreed to buy Verdi Godwin a brand new colour television to thank him for bringing me to the club's attention!

I spent the Monday night before the Tuesday morning meeting putting the finishing touches to my speech for the Chorley board – including the first planned use of the line about being prepared to walk to Plymouth to play for Tony Waiters – and I was ready to argue my case at the following day's meeting and plead with them to reduce the amount they wanted for me.

I'd barely finished sitting down and saying 'good morning' when the chairman took over. "Look Paul, we had further discussions with the Plymouth board over the weekend and we've agreed to drop the asking price to six-thousand pounds

because they've now included various add-ons. We've negotiated a ten per cent sell-on clause plus two additional payments,
the first when you've played twenty full games for the Plymouth
first team and a further payment if you complete fifty games.
We don't want to stand in the way of such a fantastic opportunity for you, but we just felt you were worth a fair bit more than
what they first offered. And Happy Birthday by the way!"

I couldn't have been happier at hearing those words and
let out a rather loud 'YESSSSSSSSS'. Then I did something
that to this day I don't know where it came from. Chorley had
voluntarily dropped down two divisions the year before because
of issues with finance so they weren't really in a position to play
hard ball with Plymouth, although trying to get as much money
for me as possible was admirable. Sensing an opportunity, I
asked for ten per cent of my transfer fee. There were no agents
back in those days and I never was any good at negotiating
with the managers I played for. But after some to-ing and
fro-ing they agreed to give me six hundred quid once I put pen
to paper with Plymouth Argyle and they received the money
for my transfer. Looking back now, I was probably stupid for
doing that given the potential risks involved, but thankfully I
got away with it. Let's call it birthday money, shall we?

The first thing I did when I got home was give my dad, Jim,
a great big hug and I remember exactly what he said to me.
"That's you properly on the football ladder now, son, and if you
want it then start climbing." Seeing the smiles on the faces of
my parents is something that will stay with me forever. Tuesday
the twenty-second of May, 1973 was also the day I officially
finished my engineering apprenticeship so a triple reason to
celebrate one of the happiest birthdays I've ever had.

The first contact I had with Plymouth Argyle was the

following day when I spoke briefly with Tony Waiters on the phone. He explained there were still one or two things to finalise at their end but it shouldn't be long before I could put pen to paper. I was planning to travel down to London at the end of the week to finish off one or two projects for work and asked Tony if it was still okay to do that – he agreed, then suggested we meet in London on the Monday to complete the paperwork.

With Tony Waiters watching on, I signed my contract with Robert Daniel, the Argyle chairman, and I was officially an employee of Plymouth Argyle Football Club. Talk about an emotional roller-coaster; from Tony watching me at Rossendale to not hearing anything for a while to impressing on trial then thinking the move was going to collapse. But all the frustration was worth it in the end and all I could think about was how happy this had made my parents.

After all the formalities were taken care of, Mr. Daniel shook my hand and told me – with a straight face – that if I could help attract crowds to Home Park like a certain number ten had done a couple of months previously then I'd certainly be worth the transfer fee they'd just paid Chorley.

I asked Robert who he was referring to.

"Pelé," he replied, with a smile.

3

My [League] Cup
Runneth Over

Edson Arantes do Nascimento played on the hallowed turf of Home Park in March 1973 when, along with his Santos teammates, they faced Plymouth Argyle in a glamour friendly. The attendance of 37,639 produced record gate receipts for the club of around twenty thousand pounds, although five thousand of that was due to the Brazilian club as part of the agreement.

I heard all about the game from Plymouth secretary Graham Little – a lovely man – when I set foot inside Home Park for the first time in July 1973. Graham was giving me the tour and when we walked out the tunnel he explained how Pelé – still one of the best players in the world even at the age of 32 – had graced the pitch right in front of us back in March.

"But did you know, Paul, that Pelé and his teammates were told to remain in the dressing room and not play the game?" said Graham. "The match nearly didn't take place."

He went on to tell me that the contract he had personally signed with Santos would pay them a guaranteed two-and-a-half thousand pounds, based on the same agreement the

Brazilians had with Fulham a few days earlier when a crowd of eleven thousand turned up. However, after their President saw how big the attendance was at Home Park a few minutes before kick-off he demanded the same amount again otherwise his players would stay inside and refuse to play, a request that Argyle chairman Robert Daniel was grudgingly forced to accept.

Graham told me the club probably made around twelve thousand pounds from the game after everything was taken into account – expenses, bribes to Santos etc. – and they spent half of that money on me.

"So you've got Pelé to thank for us being able to afford to sign you!"

* * *

It was July 1973 and my first pre-season as a professional footballer was just getting underway. The club had arranged digs for me in Dayton Close in Plymouth and I was staying with Mark Nickeas, a defender from Southport who'd also been scouted by Verdi Godwin. Just like I had done with Milija Aleksic, we hit it off straight away.

Pre-season was decent – the club had recently built a new training ground – and there was a fair bit of integration between the first team and the reserves because Tony Waiters wanted players coming into the first team to be ready if given the chance and not be overawed. I realised early on that I was good enough and belonged at that level. All I wanted to do was play. I might have been a young kid but I said to Tony when I joined that I hadn't come to Plymouth to play reserve team football. The Northern Premier League in my first season at Chorley was a decent standard – it was the highest level you could play without going full-time – and I felt I was ready to play in the Argyle first team from the minute I signed for them.

I was well aware that I would have to start out in the reserves but I was determined not to stay at that level for long. I wanted to get off to a quick start so my first few weeks were spent doing extra training to try and get noticed. Myself and Mark used to take it in turns to try and score past Milija on the grass opposite Home Park, where the Plymouth Life Centre is now located. We'd go over there every day and practise our shooting for an hour or two after training in the morning and, thankfully, it wasn't long before it paid off.

Plymouth was such a friendly place. This was my first time properly away from Mum and Dad but it really was a home away from home. From the lovely older couple whose house I was staying in – just like spending time with my grandparents – to the players at the club making me feel welcome; a great start to my life as a professional footballer.

They were a mixture of Scottish and Lancashire lads at the club, a sprinkling of boys from Devon and Cornwall and a couple of characters from Yorkshire – Jimmy Hinch (who left for Hereford United shortly after) and a brilliant guy from Rotherham called Neil Hague – and the banter was fantastic. But there are three men in particular who I want to single out. The biggest influences on me in my early years as a pro were Jim Furnell, Dave Provan and Bobby Saxton. Jim was a goalkeeper who'd played for Liverpool and Arsenal. Davie was a gentleman and such a big help. He had loads of experience, playing for Glasgow Rangers against Bayern Munich in the 1967 European Cup Winners' Cup final, and was always available for advice or an arm around the shoulder. And Bob was another gem who later went on to manage the football club. I got really friendly with Bob, and his wife June, and I used to babysit their kids. He was even the best man at my first wedding!

I can honestly say I would not have had the career I went on to have without the help and guidance from teammates like Jim, Davie, Neil and Bob. Off the field stuff like getting my pension sorted out, planning for the future, but also tips on what to do and what not to do on the pitch. So why did they take me under their wing? Well they'd all seen and played a lot of football, and no doubt saw that I was a hard-worker and had a fair bit of ability, so they probably thought 'Okay, this kid might have a chance so we'd better look after him and make sure he doesn't end up going down the wrong path.' Up to that point in my life I'd never tried any alcohol, just didn't fancy it. It was always milk or orange juice, so the club didn't have to worry about the social scene getting me into trouble. That came later in my career...

I remember a chat with Jim Furnell after training one day shortly after I'd signed. "Oi, Lenny, I need to have a word with you". Lenny was my nickname at Plymouth because I had long hair. They thought it resembled a big mane so they called me Lenny the Lion. "I'm going to give you a bit of advice that's going to stick with you throughout your time here," said Jim. Expecting either a pearl of wisdom from one of Plymouth Argyle's best ever goalkeepers or a verbal boot up the arse, he said, "buy yourself a fucking good raincoat because it lumps it down all the time in this part of the world." Then he walked off. That was Jim's sense of humour, slightly off-the-cuff but usually pretty amusing. But he was a fantastic mentor. Throughout my early career in football I was fortunate to have so many experienced pros willing to help me get better.

My [League] Cup Runneth Over

* * *

I got off to a flyer for Plymouth Argyle reserves, scoring twice in my opening three games. The same couldn't be said for the first team, however. They drew one-all at home to Chesterfield in their opening league fixture before going down two-nil at Tranmere Rovers, then losing one-nil against Brighton and Hove Albion at Home Park. Just one point and one goal after three matches in Division Three. Manager Tony Waiters decided wholesale changes were required. So he introduced three youngsters with a combined age of just fifty-six for the next home game in midweek...

Tuesday 11th September, 1973
Plymouth Argyle 5-0 Rochdale (Hore, Rogers, Mariner 2, Davey)
On the morning of the match manager Tony Waiters took me aside and told me I'd be playing that night against Rochdale. Wingers Alan Rogers and Brian Johnson – both making their first league starts – were to come in for Harry Burrows and Alan Welsh and I'd be replacing striker Jimmy Hinch, who had failed to score in the first three games. Don't feel sorry for Jimmy by the way. He ended up in America playing for Los Angeles Skyhawks before going on to be a hugely successful estate agent in Los Angeles, and his wife became an immigration lawyer in LA, so they made a lot more money than if they'd stayed on the south coast of England!

One hundred and twelve days after putting pen to paper on a professional contract and here I was, about to make my Plymouth Argyle debut. And I'm not sure it could have gone any better. John Hore opened the scoring and Alan Rogers grabbed his first goal for the club to give us a two-goal lead at half-time. Then, ten minutes into the second half, I decided to gamble and make a run into the box to try and get on the end of a delivery from Stephen Davey. With a nod of the head and a swish of the long locks, Lenny the fucking Lion had delivered a debut goal. Ten minutes from the end I scored my second to make it four-nil before Steve Davey got number five with time running out.

> Mariner, Rogers and the third young newcomer, Brian Johnson, slot into the pattern of first-team football as if they've done it all before... The fans were thrilled with Mariner's contribution and are already predicting a bright future for the Lancashire lad. But his manager is anxious to keep his performance in perspective. "You don't make a reputation on just one game," said Waiters who, although cautious, was the first to agree that he did exceptionally well. "He was perpetual motion and deserves the praise he is getting. He showed a tremendous appetite for the game but he still has a long way to go to make a consistent Football League player"... It could prove the best slice of business Argyle have done for a long, long time.

I can't tell you how many times I've read that piece in Harley Lawer's wonderful book *Argyle Classics: Memorable Moments in Plymouth Argyle's League and Cup History* but it never, ever gets old. A five-nil win against Rochdale – our first of the season in the league – and two goals meant it was the dream debut and, unsurprisingly, I only managed about an hour's sleep that night.

I remember going to the newsagents early the next morning to buy the papers – it must have been around five-thirty – and by six o'clock I was sat at Plymouth Hoe reading the match report over and over again. My mum still has the clippings in a scrapbook. Seeing those headlines inspired me, it gave me so much thirst for more but in my mind I was just getting started. Small steps combined with big ambitions.

It really was a night I'll never forget. Especially the Plymouth fans in the Devonport End. I still have a fantastic relationship with those supporters – they presented me with a trophy at the end of my career which is now in my mum's kitchen in Adlington – and there was nothing better than scoring at that end and hearing them chant my name. But I wasn't daft enough to think it wouldn't have been possible without my teammates. The players you play with help make you the player that you want to be. If I didn't get the service the night before against Rochdale, the crosses into the box, those through balls, the corners, then it wouldn't have been such a successful debut.

I kept my place in the team four days later when, unsurprisingly, Tony Waiters named an unchanged line-up for the trip to Southport at Haig Avenue. I scored again in a one-all draw but our league form over the next few weeks was patchy with just as many draws and defeats as wins – I went four games without a goal before scoring in a two-all draw with Shrewsbury Town. Then came the second round of the League Cup at the start of October, and a big one at home to Portsmouth.

Tuesday 9th October, 1973
Plymouth Argyle 4-0 Portsmouth (Machin, Davey 2, Mariner)

Having already won away at Torquay United in the first round at the end of August prior to me getting in the team, more than thirteen thousand were in attendance as Pompey from the league above came to town in round two. Tony Waiters told us beforehand to have no fear – the bigger they are the harder they fall. We were sensational and I don't think they knew what hit them. Ernie Machin opened the scoring, Steve Davey added two more goals and I got number four as our place in round three was sealed. Our reward? An away tie against top flight Burnley in the third round at the end of the month. 'Oh well, at least the club will get a nice payday' seemed to be the general sentiment in the local media, and who can blame them with Plymouth taking on a team from two divisions above, but that win over Portsmouth gave us so much momentum and I really believed we had a chance of beating Burnley because we had nothing to lose. Youthful exuberance, perhaps, or maybe just a lack of fear because of a lack of previous footballing scars.

Tuesday 30th October, 1973
Burnley 1-2 Plymouth Argyle (Hankin – Waldron OG, Hague)

An 87th minute winner against the team sitting third in Division One, and no-one can say we didn't deserve it. Yes, we rode our luck at times but we were brilliant, a real team effort, and subsequently handed Burnley their first home defeat of the season. To put that into context they'd beaten Chelsea, Manchester City and Queens Park Rangers in the league at Turf Moor and drawn with Coventry City, Tottenham Hotspur, Derby County and Manchester United. Seven games, three wins, four draws and no defeats. Until lowly Plymouth Argyle travelled 250 miles north on a Tuesday night and went home with the win.

Could we dare to dream? Well we were now playing with house money, very much so, and when the draw was made for round four of the League Cup I think every team left in the competition either wanted to face us or Division Four side Exeter City. Their cup run had been just as unlikely as ours, beating Swansea City after a replay then winning away at Rotherham United and West Bromwich Albion, but it was Wolverhampton Wanderers who were pulled out the hat to face Exeter. We were drawn against Queens Park Rangers. Another team from Division One. Another away tie. Another away win?

Tuesday 20th November, 1973
Queens Park Rangers 0-3 Plymouth Argyle (Welsh 2, Davey)

Terry Venables, Frank McLintock, Gerry Francis, Stan Bowles – 'your boys took a hell of a beating'!

Yes it was Norwegian commentator Bjørge Lillelien who first uttered those famous words on radio eight years later in September 1981 when Norway beat a certain England team that I may or may not have been a part of in a World Cup qualifier. And yes he was referring to Lord Nelson, Lord Beaverbrook, Sir Winston Churchill, Sir Anthony Eden, Clement Attlee, Henry Cooper and Lady Diana rather than Terry Venables, Frank McLintock, Gerry Francis and Stan Bowles. But I'm going to have to explain what the fuck happened in Oslo later in this book so please indulge me for a moment as I recall our magnificent League Cup fourth round win at Loftus Road.

Wow, what a result this was against a team containing some of the biggest names in English football. It was a very similar performance to the previous round at Burnley, but this time a much more comfortable scoreline. And it was thoroughly deserved.

Despite the defeat, several of the QPR players came in to the changing room after the match to congratulate us – a touch of class – and once again the journey back to Plymouth was a happy one following an unexpected victory.

Wolverhampton Wanderers, Liverpool, Manchester City, Coventry City, Millwall, Norwich City, Birmingham City and Plymouth Argyle – the eight teams remaining in the 1973-74 League Cup. Six of them from Division One, Millwall from Division Two and the mighty Plymouth Argyle of Division Three. At this point we didn't care who we were drawn against or if the game was home or away. We feared no-one.

LEAGUE CUP QUARTER-FINAL DRAW
Wolverhampton Wanderers versus Liverpool
Coventry City versus Manchester City
Millwall versus Norwich City
Birmingham City versus Plymouth Argyle

Bring it on! Another team from Division One. Another away tie. Another away win? Before the trip to face Birmingham City, however, there was the small matter of two FA Cup ties sandwiched in between. I may only have scored once in the League Cup up to that point but I was on target in the FA Cup first round win over Brentford – as was opposition left-back Stewart Houston with a stunning own goal from twenty-five yards with just three minutes remaining. I also scored the winner against Walsall in round two as we maintained our unlikely cup form that season.

Wednesday 19th December, 1973
Birmingham City 1-2 Plymouth Argyle (Hatton – Welsh, Davey)
By this point things were getting silly. Surely the giant killers

only had so much ammunition? Surely Trevor Francis and the big boys from the top flight would finally end the dream of the plucky team from Division Three? Actually my biggest concern going into this game was the day on which it was played. Every League Cup tie I had been a part of that season took place on a Tuesday night. This was on a Wednesday. No need to worry.

And then there were four.

LEAGUE CUP SEMI-FINAL DRAW
Plymouth Argyle versus Manchester City
Norwich City versus Wolverhampton Wanderers

Finally a home game at Home Park, but only because the semi-finals were played over two legs. Before we talk about the semis there's the small matter of an FA Cup third round tie away to Manchester United. When the draw was made my mind immediately wandered and I had a vision of swapping shirts with George Best at the end of the game. Eight months after working in a factory and studying mechanical engineering and I'd be playing against one of the legends of the game at one of the game's legendary venues, Old Trafford. Well one out of two ain't bad. George Best was dropped by manager Tommy Docherty after failing to turn up for training and actually never played for Manchester United again.

Saturday 5th January, 1974
Manchester United 1-0 Plymouth Argyle (Macari)
The first time I had tasted defeat in a cup competition while playing for Plymouth Argyle. This wasn't a vintage United side, but we weren't at our best either. It might sound like a daft thing to say that we were disappointed at not beating Manchester

United at Old Trafford, but after winning at Burnley, Queens Park Rangers and Birmingham City in the League Cup we honestly believed we had a really good chance of doing something similar in the FA Cup. Tony Waiters told us to play the opponents, not the opponent's reputation, but I think we were a little bit guilty of doing the latter and in the end it cost us. When you look at the bigger picture there's absolutely no shame in a team from Division Three only losing by a single goal at Old Trafford, but we sat in the changing room afterwards thinking it was a missed opportunity. With the first leg of the League Cup semi-final at home to Manchester City just eighteen days away, however, Tony was quick to remind us of that before we got back on the bus for the long trip back to Plymouth.

Wednesday 23rd January, 1974
Plymouth Argyle 1-1 Manchester City (Davey – Booth)
A national power crisis during the Three-Day Week meant a 2pm kick-off for the first leg, but the afternoon start didn't prevent more than thirty thousand fans from turning up at Home Park for the visit of Denis Law, Rodney Marsh, Colin Bell, Franny Lee and co. The pre-match team talk was pretty similar to the games against other Division One sides earlier in the competition – Tony Waiters just telling us to go out and enjoy ourselves and make sure we leave absolutely everything we've got out there. 'Play the opponents, not the opponent's reputation'.

Five minutes before half-time Steve Davey continued his excellent goalscoring form in the competition when he put us ahead, capitalising on a mistake from Willie Donachie, and the huge crowd went nuts. The thing that stays with me all these years later is the noise when the ball hit the back of the net. It was unlike anything I'd heard before. Unfortunately Tommy Booth got his head on a Mike Summerbee corner twenty minutes into the second half to give City an equaliser they probably deserved, but we held on to earn a draw and that was a decent result to take to Maine Road for the second leg seven days later.

Wednesday 30th January, 1974
Manchester City 2-0 Plymouth Argyle (Bell, Lee)
Our three previous visits to Division One teams in this competition resulted in wins at Turf Moor, Loftus Road and St Andrews. And our hopes of making it four out of four were given a boost pre-match with the news that injured pair Denis Law and Rodney Marsh would both miss the second leg. But that's about the only positive because goals from Colin Bell and Franny Lee gave City a deserved two-nil victory and our amazing League Cup journey was finally brought to an end at Maine Road in front of more than forty thousand spectators. Goliath had finally got his own back on David, but only at the fourth attempt.

It was an incredible run and our Cup exploits were certainly a welcome distraction from some indifferent league form. We may have been denied a trip to Wembley for the first time in Plymouth Argyle's history, but the memories made during that League Cup campaign will forever be etched into the minds of those who experienced it.

Although disappointed, I sat in the changing room at Maine Road in my kit for a good fifteen minutes after the game before getting changed. I just wanted to take it all in. Where I was, what we'd done as a team, what was next? So many things to think about. A whirlwind of an adventure in such a short space of time.

Not even a year ago I was playing in the seventh tier of English football at places like Dark Lane in the village of Newchurch in Lancashire. And it was less than three years since we had to get changed upstairs at the Mitre Pub in Chorley before helping carry the goalposts half a mile down the road to play for St Gregory's. I thought about my dad, Jim, and my mum, Peggy. I thought about my uncle and the rest of my family. I thought about Ted Facey at Metal Box. And I thought about Verdi Godwin, and wondered if he'd be watching the highlights from Maine Road on his new colour television.

4

Going Up

Fifty thousand pounds was a lot of money to spend for a club like Plymouth Argyle in 1974, but two important additions – each costing twenty-five thousand – ended up being worth every single penny. Scottish striker Billy Rafferty joined from Blackpool – and we'll get to him shortly – but let's start with the other new arrival. It wasn't another player, though, it was a brand new team bus!

At Tony Waiters' insistence, the club upgraded our preferred mode of transport for away games to ensure we were able to travel far more comfortably. The new bus was equipped with televisions, toilets and card tables, as well as drinks dispensers to help celebrate wins or drown our sorrows if we lost. "It's not a question of pampering the players," Tony explained to the local news channel upon taking delivery of the vehicle, "we're simply trying to prepare our players in the most professional manner possible."

I wouldn't say we were pampered but it did make the long journeys a lot more tolerable. It's funny going online and looking back at Tony's interview now and seeing the bus again brings back so many memories of the hundreds of hours we spent onboard going to away matches. At the time it seemed like a luxury palace on wheels – and the club even let Liverpool borrow it for a few days to try it out – but it was the perfect example of Tony Waiters and his methods being at least one step ahead of everyone else. He knew we probably travelled more miles than any other team in the country and, because of that, wanted us to be as fresh as possible when arriving at grounds after a long trip.

So that was the bus, and the other addition that year was my eventual strike partner, Billy Rafferty. What a boy. He made his debut against Watford in March 1974 because I was out injured and we only managed to start three games together – all in the same week against Halifax Town, Hereford United and Blackburn Rovers – before Billy suffered a recurrence of a knee injury against Blackburn and missed the rest of the season. Neither of us scored in those three matches we played together and I wouldn't say we showed many early signs of developing the partnership which ended up being so successful. Thankfully the issue with Billy's knee wasn't too serious, he was able to get part of his cartilage removed and was ready to go when we returned for pre-season in July.

The team played a lot of friendlies and that certainly helped me build an on-the-field relationship with Billy Rafferty in pre-season. Tony Waiters arranged a couple of games behind closed doors against local clubs Torquay United and Exeter City to begin with, and we beat them both quite convincingly with Billy and myself on target each time. As the new season approached, Billy and I were getting to know each other's game better every single day.

A week and a half before the start of the new season Plymouth played a friendly at Bolton Wanderers. We stayed up in Lancashire for a few days – which gave me the opportunity to spend a fair bit of time with family and friends – and we trained at Burscough FC, a non-league club where the manager had some contacts. Our direct opponents in that Bolton game were Sam Allardyce and Roger Jones, two of the toughest centre halves you could come up against, but Billy and me tore them to shreds and gave them all sorts of problems. We drew the game one-all, but the score didn't reflect our dominance and that was the first time I really thought we were a proper strike partnership. And the thinking was if we could make that pair from the division above look poor then we didn't need to fear any defenders in Division Three.

Two days after the Bolton game we trained at Burscough's ground on the Friday morning, with the plan being to return to Plymouth afterwards. The last thing we worked on was our attacking corners. Wanting to end the session on a high, I tried to score with a diving header but my momentum carried me into the post and I ended up with a deep cut on my forehead which had to be stitched and dressed. Eight days before the opening game of the season at Preston North End and I now faced a race against time to be ready. The mood on the long trip back to Plymouth was pretty sombre and the bus journey seemed to take longer than ever. But I was determined to be available for the game at Deepdale, although the final decision wouldn't be mine to take.

* * *

Tony Waiters decided to change the team around a little bit for 1974/75 after we finished seventeenth the previous season. It was probably an aging squad when I first signed for Plymouth Argyle in May 1973, but Tony managed to freshen it up with the likes of Colin Randell – who had a fantastic range of passing – and John Delve, plus a few others who had played at a higher level. Mike Green joined from Bristol Rovers and was made captain while Bob Saxton was brought back into the team and his experience was vital, as was that of John Hore, who was a super teammate. A local boy from near St. Austell and he could put his foot in. John was well aware of his limitations – he certainly wasn't the most stylish footballer – but you knew exactly what you were going to get when he walked out on to the pitch. And he was strong and skilful when he needed to be.

Hughie McAuley was brought in from Liverpool reserves in October to play out wide, and Brian Johnson usually played on the opposite side. Left-back Phil Burrows came from York City to replace Colin Sullivan, who went on to play at a higher level with Norwich City. We had a well-balanced team with many unsung heroes, including our veteran goalkeeper Jim Furnell who would come for crosses all day and was playing some of the best football of his career in his late thirties.

You knew the wingers were capable of providing service from out wide. You knew that the centre of our defence was going to be resolute and strong and hopefully not give too much away. The full-backs had the ability, closed the ball down and stopped crosses from coming in. And Jim was fantastic between the sticks. So we had a great team spirit and every single one of them brought something to the party. It certainly wasn't a dressing room conducive to shyness, the banter was top drawer and if you stepped out of line then you knew you were getting it. Loads of characters. Some were young like me and enjoyed going out and socialising, while others were married and led more settled lives. But there were so many funny guys in that changing room.

Going Up

* * *

If I had to to pick out five memorable league games from that campaign, I would go for the following...

Saturday 24th August, 1974
Plymouth Argyle 2-1 Grimsby

There wasn't too much that stood out about this one at the time, but it's nice to look back on it as the first time Billy Rafferty and myself were both on target in the same game. Billy scored a screamer from twenty-five yards in the second half after I'd scored a screamer from twenty-five inches in the first half – it's always nice to score from close range from a distance similar to the length of your nose...

This was our first win of the season after an opening day loss at Preston – thankfully I was able to play at Deepdale, despite the wound on my forehead – and a disappointing first-round League Cup exit to Bristol Rovers. Following that loss, we wouldn't lose at home again until the following January.

Tuesday 15th October, 1974
Plymouth Argyle 1-0 Aldershot

The start of a sixteen-game unbeaten run and I set up Billy for the only goal. Following a turnaround in form there's usually some sort of catalyst, and I reckon there were two specific things that happened that helped turn our season around. The first was the arrival of a new chief coach – Alan Brown – whose intense fitness regime for the players really paid off as the season progressed. And the second was the signing that week of winger Hugh McAuley from Liverpool for twelve grand – a brilliant bit of business by Tony Waiters, and Hugh's creativity was a big help for Billy and me. What a shrewd signing he turned out to be. The team scored nineteen goals in the sixteen games before Hughie joined then scored thirty-seven goals in the next sixteen games. That tells you everything you need to know.

Saturday 11th January, 1975
AFC Bournemouth 3-7 Plymouth Argyle

This was the day when everything just clicked. We were playing with such confidence, having not lost for three months, and it was only a matter of time before one of our opponents was on the end of a thumping. It would be Bournemouth. I scored twice, Billy was also on target and I honestly believe there were probably only a handful of teams in the country that could have coped with us that day. The way we played, specifically in that first hour at Dean Court, was never bettered during my time at Plymouth Argyle.

Tuesday 4th February, 1975
Plymouth Argyle 2-1 Blackburn Rovers

Kick-off had to be delayed because of the huge crowd of nearly twenty-nine thousand, apparently the largest for a league game at Home Park since the final match of the 1959/60 season. Tuesday night under the floodlights and a proper noise inside the ground for the match against the league leaders. Billy scored the first then got the assist for the second as we went top of the table for the first time that season – the unbeaten league run stretching to fifteen games. What a brilliant night all round.

Tuesday 15th April, 1975
Plymouth Argyle 1-0 Colchester United

Going into this game on the back of an eight-game unbeaten run and knowing a win would clinch promotion after seven long years in Division Three, the significance of the fixture was not lost on anyone associated with the club. But we had shown previously we could handle pressure in various cup ties and that was part of Tony Waiters' pre-match team talk. Preparation wasn't too different from most other games, in fact there was less time for build-up and hype because we'd drawn at Walsall just three days previously so that probably helped us.

Nerves were on show during the goalless first half, I think that was pretty evident to everyone at Home Park, but thankfully it took only five minutes of the second half before the deadlock was broken. It's the one goal most Plymouth fans remember, and it was one of the easiest I scored in my career. Their goalkeeper, Micky Walker, made a mistake and gifted possession to Billy on the right. My strike partner played it short across the six-yard box, laying it on a plate, and my first-time finish sparked delirium among the crowd of twenty-three and a half thousand.

Considering we were eighteenth at the start of October, this win over Colchester not only secured promotion but also took us top of the table. Quite the run of form, and perfectly timed. Now we had a title to try and win.

A welcome distraction, though, was provided in the form of our FA Cup run. It started in the first round at Dartmouth. We were two-one down with four minutes remaining and on the verge of an embarrassing cup exit to the non-league minnows at tiny Watling Street. Then Alan Rogers sends in a corner two minutes from time and I get my head on it to level things up. Sixty seconds later Rafferty and Randall combine for the winner in the last minute. Phew.

More than seventeen thousand inside Home Park for a second round tie with Crystal Palace. The fans saw Billy score what we thought would be the winner with fifteen minutes remaining. But Palace were awarded a penalty in injury time. Their skipper, Terry Venables, stepped up to take it but our goalkeeper Jim Furnell produced a brilliant save and that proved to be the last touch of the game, sparking a pitch invasion, and Jim needed a police escort to get back up the tunnel! Palace boss Malcolm Allison was all talk in the press in the build-up to the game but I don't recall hearing much from him immediately afterwards…

Next up were Blackpool and Billy scored both goals against his former club to set up a tie at home to Everton. Our biggest game of the season in front of a full house of thirty-eight thousand and I missed out because of a throat infection. How's your luck?! It was kept quiet by Tony Waiters, who didn't tell the local press, and it wasn't until the team was read out on the public address system forty-five minutes before the game when Plymouth supporters first became aware I wasn't playing.

It's just one of those things, but at least my replacement, young Barrie Vassallo, managed to score in his first senior game. That was the only highlight for the Plymouth fans packed into Home Park – the First Division leaders were far too good for us and ran out comfortable 3-1 winners, our first loss since mid-October.

Towards the end of the season Home Park was a proper bear pit, packed to capacity and it was brilliant to play in front of such passionate supporters. People were coming up from the deepest parts of Cornwall and all corners of the south-west to support the football club. We had a great manager, a fantastic coaching staff, the players in the team were outstanding but the fans were the unsung heroes. They'd give the opposition a roasting and it was no surprise that we only lost one of our last eight home games. Sadly, though, that was the day when the BBC Match of the Day cameras came to town. It was rare for them to feature highlights of a game outside the top flight – let alone a fixture in the third tier – but they chose our home game against Wrexham in mid-March when, of course, we laid an egg, losing three-nil.

We were unbeaten in the eight games following the Wrexham loss and that meant we went into the Colchester United match knowing a win would secure promotion to Division Two with three games left to play. It might have been fitting in the eyes of some that Billy and me combined to score the goal that took us up, but it really was a huge team effort to get us over the line. The atmosphere at the final whistle against Colchester was incredible. Joy and relief combined.

Billy was a fantastic teammate. We complemented each other ever so well because we could read each other ever so well. The rest of the boys knew what they were getting from us – our work ethic was good, we liked to defend from the front and we both chased lost causes. And one of us always provided an option or an out ball for our teammates if they were in trouble and needed to play it long. Forty-seven goals between us in 1974/75 – Billy managed twenty-six and I got twenty-one – and at least one of us scored in thirty-two of our fifty-two matches, with both of us scoring in the same game on seven occasions. That's not a bad record!

Defeat at Peterborough United in our final game – when a win would have clinched the title – meant we had to wait a couple of days to find out our fate. Sadly, Blackburn Rovers, needing just a point to become champions, got what they needed in a goalless draw at home to Wrexham forty-eight hours later. While it would have been nice to pick up league winners' medals, promotion was our main aim. Job done. The Plymouth Argyle fans deserved that, they really did.

Something else I'm proud of is both Billy and myself playing in every single league game. He started them all and the only time I didn't was when I came on as a sub at Aldershot. Yes, you need a little bit of good fortune to avoid injury but we had that, and I was so pleased for Billy when he was named Player of the Year in Division Three. So richly deserved.

5

On the Move

Climbing up telegraph poles on the shale field at the back of Home Park. Picking up stones on Dartmoor. Just a couple of the weird and wacky training methods that Plymouth Argyle chief coach Alan Brown had us doing to keep fit. At the time you wonder why the hell you're involved with daft stuff like that, but a lot of the old school methods definitely helped improve our fitness levels. Tony Waiters was well aware that playing in Division Two was a big step up for us, but he was also a fitness freak and knew that being one the fittest teams in the league would give us an advantage over sides of similar ability.

It did, and we finished sixteenth of twenty-two, five points clear of the drop. Tony's target throughout the season was thirty-eight points for safety and we reached the magic number with a goalless draw at Fulham in the penultimate game of the season. We pretty much knew we were safe from relegation three days before after beating Southampton one-nil in front of more than twenty-five thousand, the biggest crowd of the season at Home Park. That result was big for us. It was one of only two wins we managed in our last ten games and ensured we had enough points on the board to avoid being dragged into a relegation dogfight.

There were thirty goals for Mariner and Rafferty in 1975/76 – sixteen for me and fourteen for Billy – and while that may have been seventeen less than we scored the season before, the standard of opponent was a lot higher in Division Two and I think we can be proud of our goalscoring efforts. That partnership I had with Billy was probably the most solid of any I had in my career. We were unselfish. We defended from the front. We worked hard out of possession. We were tough. We always helped each other out. The old Third Division wasn't for the faint of heart, players could handle themselves, but we were brave, we were honest and we did our fair share. And not only did we excel in that league but we were also a constant threat for opposition defences after getting promotion. Billy was a fantastic complement for me and I hope I was a good complement for him.

But the partnership was broken up in April 1976 when Plymouth Argyle accepted a bid of just twenty thousand pounds for Billy from Carlisle United, five thousand less than they paid to get him from Blackpool two years previously. I won't pretend to know much about the terms of the transfer but when I found out how little Carlisle paid for Billy I was very surprised. I would have thought forty goals in 101 games would be worth a lot more than twenty thousand quid. We paid five grand more for our fucking bus and it couldn't hit a cow's arse with a banjo, although it wasn't bad at defending when it was parked...

I'd been aware of the speculation about my own future throughout the season. In fact I'd been reading transfer stories in the newspapers ever since I scored those twenty-one goals in our promotion season. There were reports that various managers and scouts were coming to games to watch me, but none of that affected me and not once did my game improve or suffer because of who was in the stand. No point worrying about something you've got no control over. I just wanted to do my best, and with sixty-one goals in 155 games for Plymouth I think I did that.

I scored in each of Plymouth's first five league games at the start of season 1976/77 and the speculation about my future was intensifying. At that stage I was flying and any striker will tell you when that happens then you're on cloud nine – you think you'll score every time you step on to the pitch. A few of the newspapers were saying that I was on my way to West Ham United. Ron Greenwood, who by that time was general manager having 'moved upstairs' in 1974, had been to watch me on four separate occasions. But I was also going to Ipswich Town, according to reports, because they regularly sent scouts to Home Park to keep tabs on me. Oh, and Johnny Giles, manager of newly-promoted West Bromwich Albion, was supposedly also keen.

When specific stories like that used to appear in the local newspaper there was usually a fair bit of truth in them because the journalist was in and around the club most days and they were usually very well-connected. And that's exactly how it transpired – there was indeed concrete interest from Ron Greenwood at West Ham United, Ipswich Town boss Bobby Robson and Johnny Giles at West Bromwich Albion. In fact, West Brom had a bid rejected at the end of September.

I [eventually] spoke to all three gentlemen (although the chat with Johnny Giles came after the decision had been made). First up was dinner with Bobby and his Ipswich coach Charlie Woods at the old Holiday Inn on the Hoe on the first Saturday

in October. We met just after eight o'clock in the evening –
Bobby had travelled down from Bristol after Ipswich had
beaten Bristol City in the afternoon while Charlie was at Home
Park that day to watch me play against Luton Town. I was
very impressed with what they had to say, Bobby especially,
and following that meeting I was able to dig a little bit deeper
and do some proper research on Ipswich Town. Their reserves
were top of the Central League, they'd won the FA Youth Cup
the previous year in 1975 – ironically thumping West Ham 5-1
in the final – and the first team had finished sixth in the top
flight (the old First Division) the previous season.

West Ham was next, but it wasn't pre-planned like dinner
with Bobby and Charlie had been. And I had no idea it was
going to happen when I woke up on the morning of Saturday
the sixteenth of October 1976. I went through my usual routine
on the day of a home game – a full English breakfast and a nice,
strong cup of tea while reading the newspaper.

Representatives from Ipswich and West Ham will likely be
in attendance at Home Park today to watch Argyle striker
Paul Mariner, with both clubs keen to sign the twenty-three
year old.

Very little fazed me. Not the story, not the opponents that day
– Cardiff City – and certainly not the speculation about my
future. I knew if I kept scoring goals then something was likely
to happen, but at that stage there was no decision for me to
make. I used to like reading the match programme when I got
to the ground, but that day the boys had also left a copy of *The
Pilgrim: Official Club Newspaper of Plymouth Argyle* where I usually
got changed.

On the Move

'MARINER ~ ARGYLE'S BIG DILEMMA' screamed the headline of volume three, number eight of said club newspaper. 'No management in its right mind wants TO SELL A STAR PLAYER. But just how long can you stand in the way of a player who in his heart wants to go to a crack club when the chance presents itself?' it asked.

I read the article in full. The boys teased me a fair bit as I was doing so, pretending to cry and saying they'd never see me again after I moved to bigger and better things. They were half right. I played my last game for Plymouth Argyle that day and scored my last goal for them. The sixth-minute strike against Cardiff City on appearance number 155 was my sixty-first in a Plymouth Argyle jersey. There would be no appearance number 156. Neither would there be goal number sixty-two.

The chat with Ron Greenwood took place in Tony Waiters' office following the two-all draw. Ten minutes or so after the full-time whistle, the club secretary, Graham Little, came in to the changing room and told me to go upstairs and see the chairman after I was showered and changed. I wasn't told what it was about or why I had to go, but I left behind a mixture of wolf whistles and various other comments from the rest of the boys. A couple of them even attempted a duet of Vera Lynn's 'We'll Meet Again [don't know where, don't know when]'.

Ron explained it was the fourth time he had been to see me play and that I had scored on every occasion. He told me how impressed he was with my all-round game and outlined why West Ham were interested in me and where they saw me fitting in to the team. Obviously I was well aware of him from his time in charge of the club previously and his team playing some unbelievable football at times; Trevor Brooking, Bobby Moore, Billy Bonds, absolute legends of the game, fantastic players and a great history of wanting to get the ball down and play football. So a move to West Ham United, the football club, was very attractive to me. However, being a bit of a country bumpkin from Horwich I didn't know whether I'd be able to handle the big city and I was actually afraid of moving to London at that point in my career. It frightened me.

Everything Ron said made sense, he was a very impressive man, and it was a very similar conversation to the one I'd had with Bobby Robson and Charlie Woods. I hit it off with Bobby and Charlie and I hit it off with Ron. Of the two options, though, I was attracted to Ipswich because they were close to the top of the First Division at the time and I liked the idea of living in the countryside. I didn't say a word to Ron about any of that. I just listened to what he said and answered any questions he asked.

After I left the room, Ron continued his chat with Argyle chairman Robert Daniel and, from what I was told at a later date, he left Home Park that night pretty confident a deal would get done and that I would be a West Ham United player within a few days. Unfortunately for Ron, however, Tony Waiters and Ipswich Town boss Bobby Robson had a subsequent conversation that weekend and reached agreement on a transfer fee totalling two hundred thousand pounds – one hundred thousand in cash plus two Ipswich Town players, John Peddelty and Terry Austin moving to Plymouth – plus an extra twenty thousand if I went on to play for England.

Tony phoned me on the Sunday night having spoken to Bobby:

"Where do YOU want to go?" he asked.

"I want to go to Ipswich," I told him.

"Just as well, because that's where you're going. We agreed a deal with them earlier today."

6

Mini Driver

"Any chance I could give training a miss tomorrow, gaffer? I'm getting married at one o'clock and wouldn't mind having an extra couple of hours to get ready." "No chance. See you in the morning." And he hung up the phone.

It was business as usual as far as Tony Waiters was concerned. We were due to travel up to London on the Tuesday to meet Bobby Robson and discuss personal terms with Ipswich Town, but in his eyes I was still a Plymouth Argyle player until the deal was completed. And that meant preparing for the trip to face Bristol Rovers the following weekend.

A few weeks previously, when Alison and I were booking a time and date for our wedding, we thought one o'clock on that particular Monday afternoon would probably be a safe choice. Tony's refusal to give me time off plus a potentially life-changing trip to London less than twenty-four hours later were not part of the initial equation. Monday suddenly became rather manic. I trained in the morning, had a quick shower, went home, put my suit on and then got married in Plymouth in a small ceremony. Argyle teammates Bobby Saxton, Jim Furnell,

Milija Aleksic and Mick Horswill all managed to attend the wedding and I was grateful to them for that.

* * *

Five of us travelled up to London by train on the Tuesday from Plymouth – our chairman, the vice-chairman, manager Tony Waiters, secretary Graham Little and myself. We were due to meet Bobby Robson and the Ipswich secretary at three o'clock at the Great Western Hotel (now the Hilton) next to Paddington station. The transfer fee verbally agreed over the phone on the Sunday was worth two hundred thousand pounds.

It was, by now, common knowledge that West Ham United were out of the picture, but it wasn't until Tony Waiters told me on the train on the way up when I found out that West Bromwich Albion still had an interest in signing me. Tony explained that Johnny Giles, the West Brom manager, and chairman, Bert Millichip, were also travelling to London in a last-ditch attempt to get me to change my mind and persuade me to move to the Midlands rather than East Anglia.

I'd already decided that I was going to sign for Ipswich Town, but I loved watching Johnny play when I was growing up and I wanted to meet him face-to-face to tell him, even if it was just out of courtesy. I had too much respect for him not to do that.

The brief discussion with Johnny Giles and Bert Millichip took place at the Football Association headquarters at Lancaster Gate in London and lasted no more than five minutes. I explained my decision, thanked them for their time and apologised for their wasted journey.

Thankfully the subsequent meeting, with Bobby Robson at the Great Western Hotel, was rather more productive. Personal terms were agreed pretty swiftly after the two clubs signed off on the transfer and Bobby kindly agreed to my request to have a few days back in Plymouth to pack up my stuff and say my goodbyes. The plan he suggested was for me to travel up to Ipswich on the Sunday afternoon then meet the press at Portman Road the following day after training and have the obligatory 'shaking-hands-with-the-new-manager' photograph taken.

A whole new challenge lay ahead. I'd gone from playing for Chorley in the Cheshire County League – the seventh tier of English football – to Division Three with Plymouth, then promoted to Division Two and now I was on the verge of moving to one of the best teams in the top flight. I know a few players have done something similar over the years – a rapid progression through the ranks – and a few of them must have thought, "Holy shit. Can I pull this off?" But the impending transfer to Ipswich excited me, it certainly didn't faze me, and that's what I told Bobby Robson. I wasn't moving to Portman Road to try and play my way into the Ipswich team like I did at Home Park when I first moved to Plymouth. I had full confidence in my own ability and told him I was ready to play right from the start. Someone had to wear the number nine jersey and score goals so why not me?

Having a fair bit of time to think on the train journey back down to the south-west was a good thing after the chaos and commotion of the previous few days.

There were a lot of general thoughts going through my head, but at the forefront of my mind was the speed of which everything had happened over the previous five years and how my life had changed immeasurably in that timeframe. I'd given Plymouth Argyle my all for three years, and loved every minute of my time there, but I was excited about what lay ahead and felt I was ready for the next chapter of my career.

I also thought about my old club Chorley. When they sold me to Plymouth they negotiated a ten per cent sell-on clause as part of the deal, so they were about to receive an extra twenty thousand pounds after I completed my move to Ipswich. They'd already bought a washing machine from the proceeds of my sale three years before. Maybe it was now time for a new tumble dryer?

* * *

This was Bobby Robson's eighth full season in charge of Ipswich Town, having taken over at the start of February 1969 at the age of just thirty-five. His first managerial role was with Fulham – the team he played more games for than any other club during his playing career – but they were relegated and he lasted less than a year. In fact, Bobby discovered he'd been removed from his position while outside Putney station in London and seeing an Evening Standard placard with the headline 'ROBSON SACKED'.

Bobby's start to life with Ipswich was nothing to write home about, finishing eighteenth, nineteenth and thirteenth in his first three seasons. Thankfully his relationship with chairman John Cobbold was strong because these days I doubt many managers would have survived after those first two campaigns. But things really started to pick up in 1972 and over the next three years they finished no lower than fourth and were back playing in Europe for the first time since they won the league in 1962.

I was joining a team that had finished sixth in Division One the previous season, their lowest finish since 1972, and the season I joined was the only one of ten [1973-83] that Ipswich Town weren't playing in European competition. But they were still one of the best sides in England at that point in time. They had started the season well, having won five and drawn three of their opening ten games and were part of a group chasing Liverpool at the top of the table. But Bobby Robson was still keen to sign another goalscorer.

Trevor Whymark was the club's top marksman the previous season with fifteen, but Ipswich had not had a twenty-goal striker since Ray Crawford in Division Two in 1968 when they gained promotion back to the top flight.

I did my homework on the club before signing and put together a list of personal aims and targets – the main one being becoming the first Ipswich player to score twenty or more goals in Division One since Ray scored thirty-three in 1963.

* * *

I'm not sure Mini 850 cars were designed to carry quite as many personal belongings as I managed to cram in for the drive up from Plymouth to the Copdock Hotel in Ipswich. As it turned out they weren't, and I would soon have to use some of my signing bonus on a new motor...

After a good night's sleep it was off to Portman Road to make things official. But not before my first training session. The drive from the hotel on London Road to the ground should normally only take about ten minutes, but something clearly wasn't right with my Mini 850 and I don't think I managed to get above twenty miles per hour at any stage of the journey. Steam started to pour out from the front of the bonnet when I eventually pulled in to the car park. I'd had the car for a while and knew it was probably reaching its limit, but I thought I'd at least be able to make the short journey to the stadium without any issues.

As I got out of the car to check the problem (the head gasket had blown) a Jeep pulled up alongside me with a very inquisitive driver. This larger-than-life character with long flowing blond curly hair rolled down his window and, in a north-of-England accent, said: "Hello, son. How are you doing?" It was Kevin Beattie. "What seems to be the problem?" he said, sarcastically. The new signing from Plymouth was certainly making quite the first impression at his new club...

I introduced myself, explained what I thought was wrong, and his response told me exactly what kind of teammate he was going to be. "Don't worry, come with me and we'll sort it out." So we left the smoking car behind and he took me into the groundsman's shed where I first met one of my other great mentors in football, Northern Ireland international Allan Hunter. He was sat on an oil drum having a cigarette (!!), soon joined by Kevin once he'd moved a couple of lawnmowers out of the way. There I was, standing in a rickety old hut in the company of the two Ipswich Town centre-halves – the bedrock of the team – who were having a smoke before training. 'This is my type of club,' I thought. 'I think I've got a chance here'. Certainly more of a chance than the still-smoking Mini 850 in the car park which Kevin had completely forgotten about.

Next was the dressing room. I couldn't wait to get the gear on but, first things first, I had no idea where to sit. The nerves were making me feel sick. I noticed a gap next to where Clive Woods was sitting so I sat down there and got changed. As I was getting ready, I heard a Scottish voice. "Alright mate, how are you?" My first encounter with Johnny Wark, who to this day remains one of my best friends. He was only nineteen when we met − four years younger than me − but he was already established in the first team that season. Me and Warky hit it off straight away and he really helped me through those first few days. We ended up being roommates for away games until he left for Liverpool in 1984. Warky, Allan and Kevin all took me under their wings at the start of my Ipswich career and I was able to settle in very easily because of them.

Things weren't all cozy with my new teammates that first morning. I was walking out to the training pitch when Brian Talbot − who was an absolute v-12 engine in that Ipswich midfield − enquired, "Who the fucking hell are you?" Rather embarrassed, I responded, "They just signed me from Plymouth." To which he replied: "Plymouth? Where the fucking hell is Plymouth?" I just smiled but I remember thinking 'I'll fucking show you who I am.'

It was actually just what I needed. The nerves were soon replaced by anger because I felt I had a point to prove. I went on to have the training session of my dreams; even Mister Talbot must have been impressed as I was banging them in from all angles. That felt really good, but still not as good as shaking hands with Bobby Robson after training as he officially welcomed me to Ipswich Town.

* * *

There was just something about the football club that made it feel like my home away from home right from the beginning. The banter in the dressing room was decent and the people behind the scenes were like an extended family to me. You could relax around pretty much everyone at the club, and that didn't change from the first day I joined Ipswich to the day I eventually left. The manager had an open door policy and encouraged the players to express ourselves, and there was never any tightening up around the chairman or directors.

That was especially true during my first week at the Copdock Hotel, where I was staying until I found a place of my own. A couple of times after training when I got back to the hotel I was invited to have lunch with John Cobbold, whose family owned Ipswich Town. He'd not long stepped down as club chairman due to ill-health – with his brother Patrick taking over – and 'Mister John' would insist that I joined him and his friends for some food then a game of cards.

The Cobbold family's association can be traced back to the club's origins in 1878, with John's role as chairman lasting from 1957 to 1976. He was quite the character; extremely eccentric, very generous and he was like a father figure to me in those first few weeks. John's knowledge of the game was limited, but he was well aware of that and neither he, nor his brother, ever tried to interfere with events on the playing side. I think one or two in the Cobbold family would themselves admit that football wouldn't have been their chosen specialist subject on 'Mastermind', but that worked to the club's advantage because the Board members just let Bobby Robson get on with it. "Look, you're the manager. Get on with the job. We believe in you." It was a welcome approach that's pretty much unheard of nowadays at clubs with interfering owners.

Bobby used to tell a great story about a game at Leicester in January 1974 when Ipswich got spanked five-nil. John Cobbold approached him afterwards to compliment the side on playing such 'enterprising football' and asked the gaffer if he was doing anything special in training. "Mr Chairman, we lost. Leicester also play in blue so we were playing in our yellow kit today!' But John didn't have a monopoly on the family's eccentricity.

Several years later, after Ipswich had fallen into the relegation zone, his brother, Patrick, was asked by a journalist from a national newspaper if it was time to panic. "We only panic at Ipswich Town when we run out of white wine in the board-room!"

* * *

I knew the day before the game that I'd be playing against Manchester United at Old Trafford. It wasn't something Bobby Robson did very often, but he took me aside after training on the Friday to give me the news that I was starting. Not a bad place to make my debut for Ipswich Town!

After lunch, we got on the team bus to go up to Manchester. Everybody knew the configurations and who sat where. Everyone except me. The card tables were up the back, those who don't play cards were in the middle and the directors plus the manager and his coaching staff sat at the front. It was like Monday morning all over again when I was trying to find a place to sit in the changing room that didn't belong to someone else. I knew not to sit at the front of the bus, a place right at the back usually had to be earned based on prior experiences at Plymouth and the middle seats were already taken. So I sat at the first available card table as near to the middle as possible, kept quiet and didn't look anybody in the eye.

Allan Hunter then got on the bus – a towering figure normally but he appeared Hulk-esque when up close and personal. He stopped right beside where I was sitting, gave me the death stare for what felt like an eternity then looked towards some of the lads up the back. "Big Man, do you want to play cards?" I asked him, sheepishly. "I'll have to have long fucking arms to do that," he barked in his very deep Northern Irish accent. "Why's that, then?" said one of the lads sitting nearby. "Because Mariner's sat in my fucking seat," he bellowed. I almost shit myself. I stood up and vacated the seat immediately. Then, with a massive grin on his face, Allan parked his arse where I'd just been sitting and laughed. "Mariner, sit down here beside me." Initiation test passed, just, but an immediate change of underwear required.

Allan was a massive influence throughout the time we were together at Ipswich. The way he carried himself and went about his business, he was unbelievably professional but he also lived life to the full. He loved a pint and he loved a cigarette, even if it meant sitting on an oil drum in the groundsman's shed to have one! He was also a great family man. A fantastic professional and he taught me a lot.

* * *

Saturday, 30th October, 1976

Another night in a hotel room, but this time when I woke up it was just a few hours until my Ipswich Town debut. And this time I had a roommate. I'd been up since seven-thirty after a sleep that could only be described as regularly interrupted. Not by John Wark, just by nerves and over-thinking. I always tried to appear calm on the outside but a lot of the time before big games the same couldn't be said for my insides!

Warky was still asleep at ten o'clock, by the way, but as I would find out over the years that was his routine every time we had an overnight stay before a game. Very little flustered him and he was actually the perfect roommate to have, especially the night before my debut.

True to his word, Bobby Robson named me in his starting line-up to face Manchester United. Mariner for Bertschin was the only change to the side that had beaten Manchester City the previous week at Portman Road.

Two minutes in at Old Trafford and we were ahead. I was involved in the build-up, picking it up on the right and, under a little bit of pressure from Arthur Albiston, sending it back to George Burley who'd come forward from his position at full-back. He took a touch then played it inside to Clive Woods who was in a bit of space just outside the box. A touch with his right foot to control, time to turn, another touch to set it up then a left foot shot from twenty-two yards. It certainly wasn't the best or hardest shot that Clive had ever taken, but Alex Stepney made an arse of it in the United goal and it was one-nil.

I nearly scored in the second half, Stewart Houston clearing my header off the line, but we ran out pretty comfortable winners in front of the largest crowd I had ever played in front of up to that point – 57,416.

Making my Ipswich debut at Old Trafford and winning one-nil was the perfect start to life at my new club. I regularly had dreams as a kid about becoming a professional footballer, scoring goals and playing at the highest level at places like Wembley, Old Trafford and Anfield. It's rare that dreams come true, but when they do you have to savour every single minute. I took my time coming off the pitch at the end because I wanted to take it all in.

It was a good win for Ipswich – United had only lost once at home in the league the previous season and we were one of only three teams to beat them at Old Trafford in Division One in 1976-77 – but it certainly wasn't the huge shock it would be today if Ipswich won away against Manchester United. The boys were confident of victory before the game and were not overly surprised when we came away with the win. That was the mentality in the dressing room and I bought into it straight away. Respect the opponent but don't fear them. 'Let them fear us' was Bobby Robson's mantra.

Next up was my home debut for Ipswich Town against West Bromwich Albion at Portman Road. It was also an opportunity to see a familiar face, someone I'd met less than three weeks previously at the Football Association headquarters at Lancaster Gate in London. West Brom boss Johnny Giles and I shared a joke before the game and he told me I'd made the wrong decision in not signing for him. When he saw me after the game he just shook his head and smiled!

Carlsberg don't do home debuts, but if they did...

Ipswich Town 7 [seven] -0 West Bromwich Albion – it was one of those results with so many goals for one team that the vidiprinter on Grandstand used to spell out the score in addition to using numbers. The win took us into second place in Division One and, at the time of writing, that scoreline remains the joint-biggest home league win in Ipswich Town history.

I want to rewind things a little bit and tell you about something that happened before the game, just to give you a little insight into how Bobby Robson's mind worked. The boss had a quiet word with me after naming his team. "Look, I'm probably not going to play you for the full ninety minutes. I know you've had a lot on your plate following the move so we'll see how things are going around the sixty or seventy minute mark." Of course I wanted to play every minute of every game but I was the new boy and had no intention of being confrontational, especially towards someone I had so much respect for. "That's fine boss. In fact, I was actually hoping to try and get back to Plymouth tonight after the game to see my wife and pick up more of my gear. Would that be okay?"

This is the kind of manager Bobby was – less than an hour before kick-off and the manager went to check the train times for me. A few minutes later he returned with a glint in his eye: "I've found a train that leaves Ipswich at five o'clock," he said, excitedly. In those days half-time was only ten minutes so it seemed like it might be possible. "Here's what we'll do. I'll take you off before the end, get yourself a quick shower, I'll have a driver waiting for you and you'll still make the train."

Guess what happened? Keith Bertschin replaced me with around twenty minutes remaining and after I got showered and changed there was a vehicle waiting outside the main stand to take me to the railway station.

> The car transporting Paul to the railway station was besieged by hundreds of admirers eager to shake his hand. I should know; I was the anxious driver charged with the task of making sure he didn't miss his train!
>
> **Former Ipswich Town PR officer Mel Henderson,**
> **twtd.co.uk, July 2021**

As for the game itself, I was partnered up front with Trevor Whymark, a silky footballer with a tremendous first touch and unbelievable in the air. Trevor couldn't have been much more than eleven-stone wet, but he had deceptive strength and was a tremendous hold-up man. He was also great at getting down the channels and could finish with both feet. We linked up really well together, and I think our relationship on the pitch helped me get the respect of my teammates a bit quicker because they knew the two of us would score goals when playing together.

West Brom were a very tough team, extremely hard-working, but they had no answer for us that day. Trevor scored four goals, Warky got our second and Kevin Beattie grabbed the third with a thunderbolt, an absolute bullet, and I remember later reading a quote from West Brom goalkeeper John Osborne saying he was actually pleased to not get in the way of the ball because it was the hardest hit shot he had ever seen.

I scored the fifth and it was a peach. Picking the ball up just inside their half after Trevor laid it off, I ran about thirty yards then put it into the top bin from just outside the box. Alistair Robertson and John Wile were the central defenders for West Brom, a tough but very fair defensive partnership, but I didn't fancy taking the ball that much further to allow them to try and stop me so I just pulled the trigger and BANG. My first goal for Ipswich and it was probably one of the best I ever scored. It was right after that when Bobby subbed me.

It was a whirlwind first couple of weeks at my new club and, apart from my probably still-smouldering Mini 850, I don't think it could have gone any better.

7

Growing Pains

I learned to grow a few tomatoes, nothing fancy mind, and I'd struggle to tell you the difference between Sungold, Floridity and Rosada. But it helped me relax and switch off. My wife, Ali, was the one for the gardening whereas I just destroyed most things – she had the green fingers and I had the brown thumbs. I could cut the grass, chop trees and do the weeding, I wasn't entirely useless in the garden, but when it came to creativity and cultivation I just left that to her.

The tiny village of Preston St Mary in Suffolk – population one hundred and seventy-seven – was where we chose to live and we found a beautiful old place to call home, Mortimers Farm, which was constructed way back in 1390. Consisting of ten acres with an attached barn complete with living quarters, it was the essence of country living, perfect for this bumpkin from Lancashire, and situated less than twenty miles from Portman Road in Ipswich.

Wherever I've lived in my life it's always been important for me to feel part of the local community, and moving to Preston St Mary was no different. I was down at the local post office one afternoon and noticed a flyer on the wall: '*The Lavenham,*

Paul Mariner

Preston St Mary & District Gardening Club is looking for new members. Beginners welcome.'

Wanting to learn to grow more than just tomatoes, I started attending the monthly horticultural get-togethers. But things escalated rather quickly after I joined – they had a famous person in their midst – and it wasn't long before the locals realised I could potentially open doors for their club (I still don't know which doors!) so they invited me to become president. I couldn't really say no. But the role, understandably so, came with responsibilities. None more so than arranging the annual fucking outing to the Chelsea Flower Show.

A trip to Stamford Bridge this most certainly was not, but all I had to do to begin with was collect names of those interested in going. Seemed simple enough. Things soon got rather more difficult, though, when it came to sourcing, then booking, a bus to take the members to London. Playing in front of a full house at Portman Road, Old Trafford or Anfield was a doddle compared to organising that bloody day trip!

* * *

Replacing David Johnson at Ipswich Town was never going to be easy. He'd done well at the club in the three and a half years he was there and scored a decent number of goals – thirty-four in 138 league games – before leaving for Liverpool in August 1976.

Bobby Robson's decision to sign Paul Mariner certainly raised a few eyebrows, it really did. Approving the sale of David Johnson – and not just to a random club but to Liverpool, one of our main rivals and possibly a better team than we were – and replacing him with a bloke from Plymouth Argyle?

Growing Pains

I know the supporters couldn't believe what the manager was doing and neither could I. I just thought 'he's got this wrong'. And, of course, the incoming player was not signed from Leeds United or Everton or a similar team from the top flight, he was coming from Plymouth. That had to be a gamble in itself.

I played in Bobby's first game in charge of Ipswich in 1969 and also his last in 1982 and I don't think he signed many more than a dozen players in those thirteen or so years. Looking back now, I can't remember a single signing that he got wrong. But at the time there were serious doubts about this one, there's no question about it. Paul was replacing a really good player in a successful side. Johnno was brilliant in the dressing room and it was a big, big ask for PM to fill his shoes, it really was.

Paul may have been nervous about coming in and felt it was quite a daunting task, but you wouldn't know from his first training session and then his first game at Old Trafford. I was impressed right from the off. And if you can start like he started, and you have the personality that he's got, then there's no point looking backwards, is there?

Mick Mills, Ipswich captain

David Johnson was a tough act to follow. Football supporters have long memories, they appreciate the good times but if things aren't going well they'll let you have it regardless. However, when you're scoring goals against the top teams – and I was fortunate enough to do that in the first few months after joining Ipswich – then you have the chance to cement yourself as a fan favourite. I was a bit of an unknown to many people when I signed so in my mind I was under pressure to do well straight away 'and show them'. Try to make a mark nice and early was the main objective. I was also desperate to bond with my teammates as quickly as possible so that performance and goal on my home debut against West Bromwich Albion – plus two assists for Trevor Whymark – was massive. It really helped me settle.

I was quickly accepted by the dressing room and, thankfully, the fans also took to me immediately. I was well chuffed with their reaction following my debut goal, although me blowing them kisses after scoring and acting like a bit of a dafty was, looking at the footage now, rather cringeworthy. I might've been a bit full of myself, but I'd just got a massive move to the First Division and scored a peach of a goal on my home debut so I think I was entitled to lose my head a little bit, but the goal celebration needed a bit of work. Thankfully I was able to hone that going forward, usually either two hands in the air after scoring or a simple raising of the right arm. That was more than sufficient. So yeah, it sort of went hand in glove. The lads took to me pretty much straight away and I thought 'okay, I've got a chance of doing really well here'. And the relationship I had with the Ipswich fans was fantastic right from the off – they were amazing from day one and that continued all the way through my time there. It was an ideal start for me at Ipswich Town, and, to be honest, I never really looked back.

* * *

Bobby Robson was a huge help in those first couple of months. He knew I was raw but he was also aware that I was talented and every now and then at training he'd offer a few words of advice just to keep me on the right track. One of the first instances of that was when he told me to "hold it up, keep the team playing in the middle third by always providing an out ball, score goals when you get the chance and if a teammate is better placed then make sure to lay it off to give us a better chance to score. It's a team game."

He also said something to me after I'd gone a few matches without a goal, and this stayed with me throughout my career: "Look, son, if you want to have a chance of reaching the very top, of being a proper top class player, then break your performances down into six games. You're going to need to have four decent games – and you might not necessarily score but you'll play your part – one very good game, and one excellent game". Quite simply his advice was aimed at maintaining a consistency of performance. Don't ever let your standards drop. Bobby's man-management was second-to-none. And if you had a poor game? "Then make sure it's in isolation and you bounce back properly next time out".

Bobby bought me for a decent amount – relatively speaking – and was under a bit of pressure for signing a guy from Plymouth Argyle in Division Two to replace a striker who'd just gone to Liverpool. But he knew what it took to be a goalscorer – he scored plenty himself for Fulham and West Brom when he played – and obviously saw something in me that he thought he could develop and improve.

We didn't lose a single game for the rest of the calendar year after I signed and I struck up a really good partnership with Trevor Whymark up front. The pair of us used to try and defend from the front so we were always putting opposition defenders under pressure, which was sort of the hallmark of British strikers in those days. That's the way the teams liked to do it. Basically, we just closed the ball down and that started from the front – I think the hipsters like to call it a high press these days. Trevor and I helped each other on the pitch and we also had a great friendship off the field as well.

One of my favourite goals in that first season came at the start of December against Liverpool at Portman Road and I remember it vividly, like it was yesterday. Going in to the game they were top of the league and we were second. Their team at that time – led by Keegan and Toshack – played some frightening football and it wasn't a surprise when they went on to win the European Cup a few months later against Borussia Monchengladbach in Rome. But on that particular December day we came out on top, and I was delighted with the power I managed to get on my header. You know, I don't think I've ever headed a ball so hard in my life. And for a Lancashire lad to score against Liverpool, that was extra special. They went on to dominate in Europe for many years so that was a big win for us and a huge goal for me. In fact it wasn't until we lost one-nil to Spurs at White Hart Lane towards the end of January that I experienced defeat while wearing an Ipswich Town shirt.

The second half of the season, on the whole, was decent as well – I scored in a four-one victory at Arsenal and managed to get my first hat-trick for Ipswich against West Ham United in a four-one win at Portman Road in March. And I received my first England call-up on the back of those three goals against the team that wanted to sign me just a few months earlier.

* * *

Wednesday, 30th March, 1977

I had never even been to Wembley before, let alone played there, so to be on that England bus driving up to the Twin Towers, then go inside the ground and out on to the turf before the game gave me goosebumps. The old Wembley Stadium is my favourite ground of all time, but prior to the World Cup qualifier against Luxembourg in March 1977 I had only ever seen it on television.

I suppose you need three things to be a successful footballer: 1. ability, 2. timing, and 3. a bit of good fortune. The first is a must for everyone who hopes to make it, but if you also have number two and number three then the likelihood is you'll do pretty well in the game. I had ability, but without timing and a bit of good fortune I doubt I would have been called up by Don Revie to that particular England squad to face Luxembourg.

I had only scored once in seven league games prior to facing West Ham, not exactly form that would have the England boss beating a path to Portman Road to watch me play. But a hat-trick against the Hammers in the final game before the international break ensured my timing was decent, and the bit of good fortune came when a member of Don's coaching staff was at the West Ham game and saw me score three.

England: 1. Ray Clemence, 2. John Gidman, 3. Trevor Cherry, 4. Ray Kennedy, 5. David Watson, 6. Emlyn Hughes, 7. Kevin Keegan (c), 8. Mick Channon, 9. Joe Royle, 10. Trevor Francis, 11. Gordon Hill

I was named among the substitutes, having been given the number sixteen jersey, and Aston Villa's John Gidman made his debut at right-back (the only cap he ever won for England). Kevin Keegan scored after just ten minutes but that was the only goal in the first half against a side we were expected to beat fairly comfortably, which led to quite a few in the crowd of 81,718 showing their displeasure as the players went back to the dressing room at half-time.

As they were going off, Les Cocker, who was Don Revie's assistant, turned to me and said, "Come on, Paul, let's get you warmed up". I was thinking 'great, I'll get a chance to go on to the pitch at Wembley in front of all these fans and smash balls into an empty net'. Now in addition to the West Ham hat-trick, I also scored three goals in a practice match at training the day before the Luxembourg game. My confidence at that point was sky high and during the interval I was banging them in left, right and centre from various crosses on either side, each one accompanied by an 'olé' from the England supporters when it hit the back of the net, their attention having shifted from the brass band playing in the centre circle.

The players were coming back out so I weaved my way through the last remaining remnants of trombones, horns and tubas and walked over to the bench before starting to put my tracksuit back on. "What the fuck are you doing?" said Les. "I'm getting ready to watch the second half, cheer on the lads," I replied. "Get your fucking gear off. You're going on." My legs turned completely to jelly. Within sixty seconds or so I was standing on the halfway line waiting to come on to play alongside Kevin Keegan and Mick Channon, two of the biggest names in English football at that time. I couldn't believe it. A dream come true.

Five and a half years previously I'd just signed for Chorley and was playing a reserve game against Everton in the Lancashire League. In their team that day was Joe Royle, the striker was coming back from injury and needed a run-out. Fast forward to the Empire Stadium, Wembley and Joe was the player I was now replacing to make my England debut. It's funny how things work in football sometimes.

Just five months after joining Ipswich Town, and at the age of twenty-three years, ten months and eight days, I became the 928th player to represent England. I'll be honest, my memories of the evening once I crossed the white line just before the start of the second half are incredibly vague. I remember getting the ball at the edge of the box, turning and firing off a shot and their goalkeeper making a great save. But that's about it. I couldn't tell you anything about the other four goals we scored, resulting in a five-nil victory, without going online and checking. All I know is that the second half seemed to go by in a flash.

The whole thing is a process, you know? You play football and you do your best for your club. You score goals and you hope that's enough to get recognition from your national team, but that call never comes for most players. I was fortunate to get the call. Running on to the pitch at Wembley at the start of the second half against Luxembourg and the whistle of Polish referee Paul Bonett signalling the start of an international career which lasted more than eight years: representing my country for the very first time was the proudest moment of my career. I got thirty-five caps more than I ever thought I would get and I'm very, very honoured to be able to say I've played for England.

* * *

Liverpool hard man Tommy Smith didn't play at Portman Road when we beat them one-nil earlier in the season, so the return fixture at the end of April was the first time I'd ever played against him. The build-up to that game was pretty intense. They were the defending league champions, unbeaten at home for thirty-five games and favourites to win another title. We were seen as unlikely contenders, looking for only our second ever championship, and our first for fifteen years.

It was the first time I had ever played at Anfield, I wanted to make an impression, and within the first ten minutes I went careering into Tommy Smith as he played a ball up the line. I certainly didn't mean to cause him any harm – I suppose you could call it a striker's challenge – but I absolutely smashed him and he hit the deck straight away. While Tommy was on the ground receiving treatment John Wark came over to me: "Shit Marrers, you shouldn't have done that!" I started laughing, giving it, "Nah, no problem. Not a problem, don't you worry about it Johnny Boy." Warky then told me I was the one who should be worrying!

Within a few minutes Tommy saw an opportunity for revenge. Paul Cooper sent a long clearance towards me and, with the ball in the air, Tommy came charging in and head-butted the back of my noggin while his knee paid a visit to the bottom of my spine.

Tommy was smart, though, claiming he got some of the ball in the 'challenge' and both him and I needed our head wounds checked by the physios. I certainly came off worse but thankfully I was able to resume after a fair bit of treatment. And no, I don't recall attempting any other tussles with Mister Smith that day, or in the future!

Liverpool beat us two-one at Anfield and went on to win the title again. Ipswich Town finished third and I scored ten goals in twenty-eight appearances in my first season at Portman Road – I would definitely have signed up for that when I first joined the football club.

Paul Mariner was a wonderful addition to our dressing room. Again it comes back to his personality, you know, he was just such a funny guy, he really was. He used to say some crazy things, and a lot of them were very crude, including if he needed to go to the toilet PM had this saying: 'gotta go now boys, I've got one in the channel'. And if he was even

An early picture with Dad. When he took me to see Tottenham at Burnden Park in 1963, it was a day I will never forget

With mum in recent years. An incredible woman who took pride in seeing my football career take off

Family always comes first. Bath time with my sons Dan, Joe and George

(Below) An early newspaper picture of
Lenny The Lion, aka yours truly

Image courtesy Greens On Screen

presents the Division Two Charity Cup to Bill Darlington, the St...
ford Sports captain, at Kimberley Stadium, Saltash.

WEYMOUTH STA[R]
ON TRIAL
WITH ARGYLE

By Graham Hambly

TWO TRIALISTS are included in a squad of 18 players
for Plymouth Argyle's three-match tour of Cornwall,
starting with tomorrow's visit to Penzance. They are Rodney
Adams from Weymouth and Paul Mariner, who has played
in the Cheshire County
League.

YOUNG LISKEARD
PIPPED BY
BAXTER GOAL

A YOUTHFUL Liskeard side
fully extended high-riding St.
Austell in the South-Western.

Adams, who previously had
three seasons with Bournemouth,
has been with Southern League
side Weymouth for the past four
seasons. During the past campaign he has made 63
appearances and has been
closely watched by Argyle
manager Tony Walters and chief
scout Ellis Stuttard.

A clerk with a brewery firm,
Adams has impressed with his
fine attacking midfield perfor-

(Above) a press clipping about my
Plymouth trial. I scored after 25 seconds
against Penzance – not a bad start!

In action against Bury for Plymouth Argyle. My dream move from Chorley nearly didn't happen

Marrying Alison in October 1976. I thought Monday would be a quiet day for the wedding and the boss would let me off training! Plymouth team-mates Bobby Saxton, Jim Furnell, Milija Aleksic and Mick Horswill joined the celebrations before I travelled to London the next morning

'Can I make the big step up?' I was excited by the challenge of joining First Division Ipswich

Playing against the likes of Newcastle United (left) created a real impression and, in 1978, I was named the Roy of the Rovers Centre Forward of the Year – it doesn't get much better than that!

In the rough and tumble world of Division One football, I showed I could mix silk with steel, as I challenge West Brom goalkeeper Tony Godden here in front of a sea of faces

Good performances in domestic football inevitably led to international recognition and I made my England debut in 1977. Here I am after scoring against Wales (above) in the British Home Championship, and in action in the same competition against Scotland at Hampden Park (below)

We thought it might not be our day but we got the goal in the end. Winning the 1978 FA Cup final for Ipswich against Arsenal at Wembley was like an out-of-body experience

Once the hard work was done on the pitch and the trophy was collected, the celebrations continued in the dressing room with Alan Hunter, manager Bobby Robson and Kevin Beattie

Mixing it with the best, taking on Liverpool at Anfield in 1980, and (below) in front of the Ipswich Town team bus – under Bobby we were enjoying some journey

more desperate for the loo we'd hear 'touching cloth now, son, touching cloth'. His humour was quirky and unusual, probably typical North-West, but he was very funny and so easy to get on with, as well as being terrific company.

Never mind me being his captain and helping him, he was actually a big help to me at times as well. On several occasions Paul took over responsibility for the front section of the team because he wasn't a shy boy. Trevor Whymark, his strike partner, was very laid back – he would arrive early for games, get changed then find a spot in the corner of the dressing room, put his feet up on the bench, and read the programme from cover to cover.

However, you could never ask Trevor to lead the line because he didn't have the personality to do it. He was a decent player, a good goalscorer and he had great technique which helped bring others in to the game. But we needed somebody like Paul, the opposite of Trevor Whymark, who was happy to carry the weight of the team on his own shoulders if required.

Mick Mills, Ipswich captain

I don't remember ever thinking we were going to win the league – Bobby never talked about that specifically – but we weren't too far away. The defeat to Liverpool at Anfield in April was a defining result and we ended up finishing five points behind them. It was a decent marker to lay down, though. We had a talented squad, including some of the boys who'd won the FA Youth Cup in 1975, and the depth of talent at the club was very strong.

Maybe we could have added a couple more players to the squad, but in those days you only had one sub and there was no rotation system in place so it was tough to do that and keep everyone happy. But with players coming through the ranks, allied to the talent we already had in the first team squad, the future most definitely looked bright.

8

Wem-ber-lee

When I was twenty-five I was at my worst. I didn't like myself back then or who I'd become. I just didn't know it at the time. Believing you belong is one thing, behaving like an entitled jerk is something else entirely. I got a little bit carried away with myself early on at Ipswich because things were going so well. 'A bloody brat' and 'a bit arrogant' were just two of the comments made by members of the media. I can't disagree with either of them. In fact that's pretty tame compared to what they could have said.

I started to believe my own press, which is one of the worst things you can do as a footballer. They build you up to knock you down in England and I was in the process of being built up and built up. But I loved that and embraced all of it. I had no interest or intention of acknowledging the consequences of what goes up must also come down. I was young and I had an opinion. At that age you think you know everything about the game, and about life, but actually you know very little.

Ever since the day I signed for Plymouth Argyle in 1973, most of what I experienced in football was positive. I'd been riding a wave of euphoria and, I'll be honest, I just got caught up in everything. Gone was the wide-eyed, grateful and inno-cent young kid who'd just turned twenty. Within five years he'd been replaced by an obnoxious self-centred prick who thought he was the centre of the universe and the world revolved around him. Far too many narcissistic tendencies and nowhere near enough humility.

Thankfully one or two more sensible teammates, senior players, had a word with me. They just said you've got to give and take a little bit better. But that only came about after my enhanced self-importance reached its peak in 1978 following the adulation that came with Ipswich Town winning the FA Cup for the first time in the club's history.

* * *

The summer of 1977 and my first full pre-season as an Ipswich Town player. Four. Long. Weeks. Tournaments over in the Netherlands, a couple of warm-up games at home plus some very hard mornings and afternoons on the training ground. A lot of running, we didn't see much of the ball initially, and it was just laps to begin with. At least we weren't climbing up telegraph poles in Plymouth or picking up stones on Dartmoor.

I used to dread the beginning of pre-season training because you knew it was going to be tough right from the start, and you'd be as stiff as a post getting out of bed because there were no specialist fitness programmes to follow to keep yourself ticking over. When the season was done, bang, that was it, and apart from eating and drinking to excess most players didn't do a thing for six weeks or so until pre-season training started, unless they were representing their country at either the World Cup or the European Championship. It's a lot more scientific these days but back then you just had to get through it.

Pre-season was the bedrock of your fitness. The ball would gradually be introduced after a week or so, we'd play small-sided games then the squad would usually travel abroad. Bobby Robson always loved going to Holland. We used the Papendal training centre near Arnhem a couple of times – a fantastic facility which is now the National Sports Centre for the whole of the Netherlands – as well as locations in Amsterdam, Zeist and Rotterdam.

"I believe the pieces are in place for us to have a good season, boys". I remember Bobby gathering the squad together and giving a rousing speech shortly before we left to come home in the summer of 1977. He was half right. We certainly did well in the FA Cup, but I've got no idea what happened to our league form that season. We finished eighteenth, winning only once away from home.

* * *

One defeat in our first eleven games in all competitions – a two-one loss at Leeds United – ensured a pretty good start to the season, which also included my European debut, playing seventy-eight minutes in Sweden against Landskrona BoIS in the UEFA Cup. I scored my first goal in Europe in the return leg when we beat the Swedes five-nil then my first ever goal for England, away to Luxembourg, two weeks later. Two more goals against UD Las Palmas in Spain in the UEFA Cup helped secure a four-three aggregate win and set up a third round clash with Barcelona.

The first leg in front of a packed house at Portman Road was memorable and we won three-nil. Roger Osborne was brilliant in midfield and completely nullified Johan Cruyff, a huge help to us that their best player had such little impact. I played really well in that game without scoring: my header was saved and Trevor Whymark knocked home the rebound to make it two-nil then Brian Talbot just beat me to a header to make it three. Unfortunately the second leg at the Nou Camp wasn't quite so memorable. We lost three-nil and, with no further scoring in extra-time, the tie would be decided by penalties. Rexach, Asensi and Amarillo all scored for Barcelona and Brian Talbot, Colin Viljoen and Clive Woods all missed for us. I believe I was due to take our fifth penalty but I never got the opportunity to do so.

Apparently there was a bit of speculation in the Spanish press the week after the second leg suggesting Barcelona were keen to sign me, and one or two English papers subsequently picked up the story. I asked Bobby the following day after training if it was true. He told me Barcelona had indeed made an enquiry, they wanted to sign me and asked how much I would cost, but Ipswich told them I was not for sale and that was the end of the matter.

If things had happened differently and Ipswich had accepted a bid from Barcelona, instead of telling them I wasn't for sale, would I have gone? One hundred per cent. Getting to play with Cruyff and Neeskens – yes please. But I had no problem with Ipswich saying I wasn't for sale, I was their player and that's their prerogative. And it's not as if I was desperate to leave the club – I was loving life at Portman Road. But the interest from Barcelona did inflate my already-enlarged ego even further, meaning those sensible teammates who latterly persuaded me that the world did not actually revolve around Paul Mariner would just have to reach up a little bit higher to get me down from my perch of self-importance.

Wem-ber-lee

* * *

When I was doing well at Ipswich I used to love the adulation – scoring goals and the crowd chanting my name – and of course I milked it, but I reckon a lot of people thought I was a cocky bastard. There were those who wanted to be like me and, I'm sure, plenty others who disliked me. But during those times when I wasn't doing so well I wanted to display a strength of character that would allow me to keep going, whether it followed a missed chance or a poor performance. I developed a thick skin, an ability to block out unwanted noise and [wrongly] had the mentality that I was always right in everything I did.

I made a lot of mistakes when I was younger, one of which was thinking I needed to have the same mentality off the field as I had on the pitch. This happened for a short period of time in my first couple of years at Ipswich but thankfully didn't last too long. It wasn't intentional arrogance but I can see now why people would have thought it was. For whatever reason there was a point in my life when I felt I had to portray supreme confidence externally to help mask nerves or internal doubt; 'holy shit, this is a massive game today'. I wasn't frightened of much – I've always loved a challenge – but there's a fine line between confidence and arrogance. I thought you had to have supreme confidence in your own ability when reaching a certain level, but I soon became aware that could easily spill over, allowing people to perceive me as being ultra-cocky, a brat, big-headed, you know, all those terms. And I was probably guilty of every single one at various times. I'm not proud of that by any stretch of the imagination.

Separating athletic arrogance from off-the-field confidence is easier if you have a split personality. There's the on-field persona, an off-the-field persona and now, with the advent of social media and an ever-seeing eye, there needs to be additional personas that players need to portray depending on situations. When playing at the top level back in the day there was Paul Mariner when I was on the pitch, Paul Mariner when I was out with my teammates and also Paul Mariner away from football altogether. Three different versions. And not all of them were nice.

While a lot of what was written about me in my early days at Ipswich Town was true, I did take umbrage when one newspaper writer said that making money was the only reason I played football. I don't think anybody plays the game not wanting to make money, but it certainly wasn't the main reason why for me. When I joined Plymouth Argyle at the age of twenty I had no idea how far my talents would take me – the dream growing up was simply to become a successful professional footballer but I never really got much further than that, I hadn't really contemplated the 'What Happens Next?' round.

I was relatively late getting into the sport and, coming from a family who brought me up well and taught me the importance of making a little go a long way, might not have been as naïve as younger players trying to make a name for themselves. I set up a pension plan really early, not long after I joined Ipswich. I loaded up the pension to begin with and while that meant I sort of went without for a little bit, it certainly helped when the final whistle sounded on my playing career. You've got to remember that most footballers don't come from much, and I was no different. Everybody wants to improve themselves and we all have different ways of doing that. A win bonus back when I played was a significant percentage of your weekly wage – not like today when the base salary of a Premier League player is massive – so I would go above and beyond to try and get extra cash from a win bonus or a goal bonus, leaving everything out there in every match, and so would the other players. I was no different to anybody else.

* * *

The FA Cup was a bit of an escape from our league campaign. We had a decent squad at Ipswich that season but showed very little consistency on the park. We were at the wrong end of the table, injuries were piling up and we just couldn't get a fine balance. Thankfully the FA Cup was our salvation. Our path to the quarter-finals was relatively straightforward to begin with, but our form ahead of the third round tie at Cardiff City wasn't great, leading Bobby Robson to declare that it was "the most important match the club is going to play this season." There were one or two moments of anxiety but I scored twice and we ran out pretty comfortable two-nil winners in Wales.

Next up, a home tie in round four against Hartlepool United from Division Four. We took the lead inside ten minutes, although the penalty award was a bit dubious to say the least. I had possession inside the box and Derrick Downing stole the ball off me fair and square. But the referee pointed to the spot and Colin Viljoen made no mistake. Look, there were plenty of times during my career when I thought I should have had a penalty and nothing was given so maybe these kind of decisions do even up over time, but it was certainly a soft award – although I wasn't complaining. I volleyed home our second just before the half hour but Derrick Downing pulled one back for them shortly before half-time and it was game on. Paul Cooper had to produce a really good save right at the start of the second half, but further goals from Brian Talbot and Colin Viljoen, his second of the game, helped us win by four goals to one. Credit to Hartlepool, though, because for a team three divisions below us they certainly put up a fight and I had a proper battle throughout with Billy Ayre, United's tough old-school centre-back from the North East.

The fifth round tie against Bristol Rovers from Division Two in mid-February was much trickier than it should have been. We were drawn away from home and the pitch was frozen, the entire surface was covered in snow with the exception of the lines, which the referee insisted were cleared or the game wouldn't go ahead. Visible lines or not, the game should never have gone ahead! It was bloody freezing and underfoot conditions were treacherous – like trying to skate on ice while wearing slippers – but Robin Turner's first goal for Ipswich ensured a half-time lead. They scored twice, however, both from corners, and we were in trouble. Thankfully Robin got his second four minutes from time after I'd taken the orange ball on a mazy dribble down the left before cutting it back inside for him to do the rest and we escaped Eastville with a two-all draw. I say 'escaped' because Rovers player-coach Bobby Gould scored a perfectly good goal just before the end which would have been the winner, but it was ruled out because the linesman flagged for offside. I can say this now; it was one of the worst decisions I've ever seen during my time in football. Peter Aitken put pressure on Allan Hunter, who tried to play it back to Paul Cooper in goal. But Allan under hit the pass and it went straight to Bobby who rounded Coop and slotted home. Gouldy went off to celebrate, but the linesman had already raised his flag thinking Peter Aitken, not Allan Hunter, had played the pass to Bobby. A huge let-off. The replay at Portman Road ten days later, thankfully, was a lot more straightforward. We won three-nil – goals from Mills, Mariner and a cracker from Clive Woods – to set up a quarter-final tie at Millwall.

* * *

Saturday 11th March, 1978
FA Cup quarter-final
Millwall 1-6 Ipswich Town

Into the Lions' Den, quite literally, and what a day this turned out to be. Sadly, not for the right reasons. Getting the chance to play in an FA Cup final at Wembley was getting closer and I don't think I was the only Ipswich player with slightly more pre-match nerves than normal. In fact I was rooming with Warky and he must have gone to the bathroom for a shit about six times. It was rare for Johnny Boy to have more than a couple of dumps in the hotel.

Millwall fans were renowned for being partisan and they had some proper rascals among their support. Some of them featured on the BBC current affairs programme 'Panorama' in November 1977 - *'F Troop, Treatment and the Half-way Line'* – which got up close and personal with notorious hooligans like Harry the Dog, Bobby the Wolf and Mad Pat. Unfortunately there was a nasty undercurrent surrounding our quarter-final. Stones and bricks had been thrown at coaches full of Ipswich fans before the match, and when we got back to our bus afterwards there wasn't a window left that hadn't been smashed. It was very scary.

As for the game itself, George Burley fired home a screamer from way out after ten minutes to put us ahead and that just seemed to annoy the lunatic minority among the home support even more, with several scuffles breaking out on the terracing and in the stand. A short time later some of them invaded the pitch and play had to be stopped. The referee took the play-ers off the field and we were in the dressing room for nearly twenty minutes as a large police presence tried to restore some semblance of order outside. Being on the pitch when all hell broke loose was frightening but once we got inside I didn't feel we were ever in too much danger. However, a few of the boys had friends and family in the stands and not knowing if they were okay was definitely a worry.

When we came back out for the restart I ended up scoring a hat-trick – pouring additional fuel on an inferno – and we thumped Millwall by six goals to one. I felt for our supporters who travelled down to London and got caught up in all the mayhem. It was unsavoury to say the least. You're in a cocoon as a player, and sort of protected from everything, but it couldn't have been much fun being an Ipswich fan at that game. It would have been nice to get the hell out of dodge straight after the match and get back up the road as quickly as possible, but with all the windows having been smashed on our team bus it took additional time to locate a replacement to take the players back to Ipswich.

The result was great, and we were through to the semi-fi-nals of the FA Cup, but it was a bad day overall and Bobby Robson didn't hold back when he spoke to the press afterwards: "To think we fought the war so that hooligans like these could survive. These people are not human and have no place in society." A further comment from Bobby: "They [the police] should turn the flamethrowers on them" also made headlines, but that quote came from a private conversation with friends after the game and was only made public later that evening on *Match of the Day* by host Jimmy Hill, a close friend of the gaffer. Bobby wasn't happy it got out, and sought to clarify his feelings a couple of days later once he'd calmed down. "When people go to games with the sole intention of inflicting damage on human bodies, the only answer is not to play football in that part of the world." And that's exactly what happened; the Den was closed for two weeks after the crowd trouble and Millwall was banned from staging FA Cup ties at home for the following two seasons. A rather lenient punishment if you ask me.

* * *

Saturday 8th April, 1978
FA Cup semi-final (at Highbury)
Ipswich Town 3-1 West Bromwich Albion

West Brom had already beaten us at their place in the league and got a draw at Portman Road so we knew this was going to be tough – under new boss Ron Atkinson they were a much improved side from the one we put seven past on my home debut the previous season. Albion were always somewhat uncompromising, but they had some fantastic individual players, were very dangerous going forward and extremely tough defensively.

Two goals in the first twenty minutes, though, and we were off to the perfect start at Highbury. Brian Talbot was as brave as a lion to get his head on the end of a brilliant cross from Mick Mills, splitting his head open in the process after colliding with John Wile and that was the end of his afternoon. Millsy himself got the second from close range. I remember thinking 'okay, we're all right' and the two-nil lead lasted until ten minutes from time when Allan Hunter decided to make the game interesting and inexplicably handle the ball in the box for no apparent reason. Tony Brown scored the resultant penalty to make it two-one and things got a little bit more chaotic than we would have liked.

The boys held firm, though, and managed to score a third in the ninetieth minute. The goal might have looked pre-prepared from the training ground, but it was actually just something we concocted ourselves prior to the corner kick. I turned to Warky and said, "Johnny, you make the run near post, I'll block your man and hopefully you'll get a free header." "Aye, nae bother big man," came the rather unassuming reply. Clive Woods delivered it perfectly, I did what I said I'd do and Warky was left in acres of space on the penalty spot. He didn't even need to move that much. Bang. Three-one. Game over.

We were in the FA Cup final, our fans were going crazy and it was next stop Wembley. There's a lovely photograph of me, Allan Hunter, Kevin Beattie and Bobby Robson in the Highbury dressing room after the game. Big Allan's on the brandy, Bobby's on the whisky, Kev's got a small can of pale ale and I'm holding a polystyrene cup full of tea! The gaffer had the biggest smile on his face. With all due respect to the 1973 Texaco Cup, this was the first major final he'd been in as a manager and it didn't take him long to tell us that we weren't going to Wembley just to make up the numbers. "Boys, we're going there to bring that famous old trophy back to Ipswich for the first time."

* * *

Bobby Robson made a few changes for the league game at Aston Villa the weekend before the FA Cup final. Trevor Whymark played instead of me, Paul Overton replaced Paul Cooper between the sticks and Colin Viljoen took the place of Roger Osborne. Me and the goalie were rested, but it was the decision to drop Roger that left the squad confused. There was a suggestion that Bobby thought Colin would be better suited to the wide open spaces of Wembley than Roger, but the gaffer wanted to test Viljoen's fitness levels because he hadn't played much that season. Villa thumped us six-one.

Roger was a very popular member of the squad and we all wanted him to play in the cup final. I think the result at Villa Park kind of forced Bobby's hand to recall him, but that didn't stop Millsy, as club captain, going to see the gaffer to convey our feelings. We were a close-knit squad and this wasn't something that happened very often. To be fair to Bobby, he was always very approachable. Whether he would actually listen to you, I don't know, but he was an expert at sincerity and giving the impression that he was taking on board everything that was said. Now he might have thought it was the biggest load of shit he'd ever heard in his life, but he never let on and he always made you feel important. As it transpired, Roger was indeed recalled to the starting line-up for the FA Cup final. Would that have happened if the boys got a good result at Villa instead of losing by six goals to one? We'll never know.

* * *

I did a Q&A with a newspaper leading up to the 1978 FA Cup final and one of the questions asked what my favourite musical instrument was. I said piano. I have no idea why I said piano. I vaguely remember sitting down at one for a photoshoot, but the best you'd get out of me is a one-fingered rendition of Do Re Mi. In the summer of 1978 I received a letter from a parent saying how pleased they were that I played the piano because they'd been able to persuade their youngest child to do likewise – 'look, your favourite Ipswich player plays the piano and now you can do likewise...' Pleasure to be of service!

* * *

Sopwell House, a luxury Georgian country house hotel nestled among twelve acres of Hertfordshire countryside in St. Albans, contains sixteen suites and one hundred and twenty-eight rooms. In one of the suites, three nights before the 1978 FA Cup final, Bobby Robson devised a game plan to beat Arsenal at Wembley. Our accommodation was first class – providing the players with everything we could possibly need to prepare for the biggest game of our lives – but the same couldn't be said about our training facilities nearby because of heavy overnight rain. With those pitches unplayable, Bobby found a local high school playing field for the Thursday session. With more mud than grass, Wembley it most certainly was not but at least we had somewhere to work on Bobby's master plan.

Spirits were high all week ahead of the final, and even another torrential downpour as we walked to the training pitch/swamp didn't dampen our spirits. "I'm changing the system," said the gaffer after gathering us together in a circle. That got our attention! It was also when we found out the cup final team. I would be up front on my own with Clive Woods and David Geddis on either side of me. Brian Talbot, John Wark and Roger Osborne were the three in midfield. George Burley and Mick Mills the full-backs with Allan Hunter and Kevin Beattie in central defence in front of Paul Cooper.

One of the young boys with us played the role of Liam Brady, he was to be Roger Osborne's man – "shut Liam down and we shut Arsenal down – even if he goes for a shit then you go with him." Talbot and Wark – "you two take care of Alan Hudson and David Price". Woods and Geddis – "when Arsenal have the ball at the back you pair need to get right on top of their full-backs – Rice and Nelson – and stop them playing out from there". Bobby's plan was to stop the supply to Frank Stapleton, Malcolm Macdonald and Alan Sunderland. It was a 4-3-3 when we had the ball which became a 4-5-1 out of possession, rather different from our usual 4-4-2 formation. Oh, and Mariner – "make sure you give Willie Young and David O'Leary plenty to think about." We worked on this for about forty-five minutes or so, first of all just walking through it then putting it into practice in a little ten versus ten game with the reserves playing the role of the Arsenal players. And that was about it. Bobby knew we'd be fired up for the game and didn't want us overdoing things in training, so forty-five minutes working on shape was enough on that particular day.

The cup final tactics proved that Bobby could think outside the box. I'm not saying it was all the gaffer; it was Cyril Lea, it was Charlie Woods, it was Bobby Ferguson and the backroom staff; I'm sure they all chipped in with ideas. It was a really solid game-plan; target their main strength – have Roger look after Liam Brady, their supplier and a top player – then stop the supply lines from the full-backs. It's a pretty simple plan really. But when you've got no time to work on it, and it's just been thrown together a few nights before the cup final, a lot relies on the game intelligence of the players, which in those days was remarkable, and it looked as though we'd been playing that system all our lives.

There was a doubt over Kevin Beattie's fitness until pretty late on, but three cortisone injections did the trick and he was available to take his usual spot alongside Allan Hunter in central defence. Trevor Whymark, sadly, didn't make it. He'd been struggling for a few months with a knee problem and had only been able to play in some games. Unfortunately this was not one of them.

* * *

From the Bolton Evening News, Friday 5th May, 1978

The FA Cup final on Saturday may be an all-Southern affair, but for two local families and a Horwich school it's the most important date of the year. Hoping to continue his goal-grabbing escapades for Ipswich will be Bolton-born Paul Mariner. His parents, Jim and Margaret (Peggy), live in Castle Drive, Adlington. Paul's grandfather Tom Turnbull, of Whitwell Gardens, Horwich, will also be at the match along with other relatives from Bolton. Paul learned his early football from sports master Mr Alan Smalley, at Horwich Secondary School, now Rivington and Blackrod High School.

* * *

Saturday 6th May, 1978
FA Cup final
Arsenal 0-1 Ipswich Town

"Fuck's sake lads, the bookies are offering odds of 5-2 for us to beat Arsenal this afternoon."

Reading the morning papers at breakfast, Mick Lambert couldn't believe the generosity of the local turf accountants. Confidence levels among the squad ahead of the game were through the roof, despite a below-par league campaign, and there were more than a few takers at the price as various denominations of bank notes were thrust in Mick's direction. You wouldn't get away with it now, but there were no rules or regulations preventing that kind of thing happening back in the day.

On paper we had a very good team with Coop between the pipes and Burley, Hunter, Beattie and Mills at the back. Mick Mills, our captain and leader, was a fantastic player for both club and country. Further forward the likes of Osborne, Wark and Talbot, that's a really solid midfield unit, then the pace and trickery of David Geddis and Clive Woods providing me with service. There's no way we should have been a 5-2 shot.

When you look back now at footage from Wembley you'll see what looks like a bright, sunny day. That's what most people remember. But it doesn't tell the full story, far from it, and it wasn't until we got to the stadium that we found out the game was actually in doubt. Heavy rain a couple of hours before kick-off had left a fair bit of surface water on the pitch and we were told that match referee Derek Nippard might call the game off. As it turns out, he only agreed to give the go-ahead after ground staff assured him they would remove the excess water.

I was towards the rear of the group, just behind Warky, as we lined up in the tunnel at Wembley. The Arsenal players were standing to our right, less that a yard away. Shortly before walking out, their centre-forward, Malcolm Macdonald, who was such a nice guy, turned to Big Allan Hunter, a ferocious Ulsterman, and said politely, "Allan, the very best of luck to you this afternoon". The big man gave him a stare that nobody would ever want to receive, then yelled in Malcolm's face: "I'M GOING TO BREAK YOUR FUCKING LEGS". I thought 'oooo, game on, here we go!' That set the scene for what was to follow.

Looking down the tunnel all I could see from there was Arsenal fans in the stands at the far end of the stadium, just a sea of red and white. I'd paid very little attention to the build-up that week – I couldn't tell you what was on television or in the newspapers – so I had no idea how the one hundred thousand tickets had been distributed. I just thought because we were the so-called lesser team that they would probably have a lot more supporters than us. How wrong I was. Emerging into the sunlight we were hit by a wall of noise from that same end of the stadium, and if you look at the footage you can actually see a lot of our boys turn round and just marvel at just how many Ipswich Town fans were there. The hairs on the back of my neck stood up and even now I'm getting tingles just thinking about it. Standing side-by-side on the pitch and having a little bit of time to take a proper look around, that's when we saw that the vast majority of Wembley was blue. It was a phenomenal life experience, hearing one hundred thousand people going absolutely crazy, and I just wish time could have stood still for even just a minute. All my mates kept reminding me in the week leading up to the game to 'make sure you take everything in, Mariner' because 'you might never get another chance to play in an FA Cup final'. I never did.

Cup final day means regimental precision in the build-up where timings are concerned, and the search for a glimpse of family and friends in the stand was soon replaced by cordiality when presented to Princess Alexandra from the Royal Family. I don't mind a bit of pomp and ceremony – listening to the FA Cup final hymn, Abide with Me, being sung was a particular favourite moment – but there soon comes a time where you just want to get on with the game. I've watched the tape back so many times and I always have a chuckle when I see myself looking over at our fans just before kick-off – I still couldn't believe the noise they were making. Now it was up to us to give them even more to cheer about...

* * *

11th minute – Arsenal 0-0 Ipswich Town

11th minute – Arsenal 0-0 Ipswich Town

It was a very humid day and the pitch was quite heavy but it was still playing pretty fast. Clive Woods played it across goal from the right hand side of the penalty box, Roger Osborne slid in and tried to direct it towards goal and I remember it coming to me really quickly. It fell nicely but I just couldn't keep it down and I hit the bar with Pat Jennings beaten. I really should have done a lot better with the shot, absolutely. I should have reacted quicker. You know, now I'm a bit longer in the tooth, I'm always harping on at young players, strikers, and telling them to expect to receive the ball in the box regardless of circumstance, be ready for it, don't wait for things to happen, and even if you're off-balance, find a way to somehow get your shot on target. Well, in that instance, I should have done all of those things. Instead, I didn't do any of them.

Half-time – Arsenal 0-0 Ipswich Town

No goals, but Bobby was happy with our first-half performance because we'd followed instructions and played exactly the way he wanted with the system he'd designed. Ipswich were the better side and if the big dumpling up front had kept his shot down, instead of hitting the bar, then we'd be in front. David Geddis also had a couple of half chances, Pat Jennings tipped Kevin Beattie's header over and Brian Talbot fired wide. At the other end we'd managed to nullify their big guns – Roger Osborne did a hell of a job on Liam Brady, who was one of the best midfield players in the country – and Hunter and Beattie combined to keep Stapleton and Macdonald quiet, which wasn't an easy task. Alan Hudson was probably Arsenal's best player up to that point, creating opportunities for David O'Leary and Alan Sunderland, but it was goalless at the break.

52ⁿᵈ minute – Arsenal 0-0 Ipswich Town

So close to the opening goal again, this time John Wark hit the post. I was able to control a long ball and lay it off to Warky, he struck the shot as sweet as you like from the edge of the box but it hit the woodwork. The rebound came at me very quickly and I tried to place it but got my timing horribly wrong. Another instance where I should have done better. We were creating chances. We just weren't taking them.

65ᵗʰ minute – Arsenal 0-0 Ipswich Town

Liam Brady was replaced by Graham Rix. He was injured, but hadn't had much of an impact anyway.

72ⁿᵈ minute – Arsenal 0-0 Ipswich Town

I thought the third time was meant to be a charm?! Practically a carbon copy of Warky's earlier attempt – this time just a yard or two further out – and exactly the same outcome, pretty much striking the same area of the same post he'd hit twenty minutes previously. The only difference being this time I wasn't there to fuck up the rebound! When you're dominating a football match and you hit the woodwork three times then you start to think that maybe it's not going to be your day.

74ᵗʰ minute – Arsenal 0-0 Ipswich Town

Pat Jennings to the rescue again! Clive Woods, who'd been a constant thorn in Arsenal's side, hung up a deep cross from out wide on the left and George Burley's excellent header was brilliantly saved by the Northern Irishman.

77ᵗʰ minute – Arsenal 0-1 Ipswich Town

"Geddis... taking on the defender and winning.... Osborne... one-nil!" - *David Coleman on BBC.*

At last!! A little change of pace from David Geddis down

the right and he did brilliantly to get the better of Sammy Nelson before drilling a low cross into the six-yard box. I was loitering at the back post, not involved directly in the move but Pat Rice knew he had to keep tabs on me so that took him out of the equation. David's cross wasn't dealt with properly by Willie Young and his poor clearance went straight to Roger who, unmarked, made no mistake from about ten yards out. Ozzy had put so much into the game and had very little left in the tank when he scored so that goal celebration turned out to be the final straw for him, and he promptly fainted when turning round and attempting to go back into his own half for the restart. Thankfully Roger was being revived by some smelling salts but it was the first time I'd seen that happen to a player on a football pitch!

84ᵗʰ minute – Arsenal 0-1 Ipswich Town

Arsenal shots on target were few and far between and the late effort from Malcolm Macdonald, which was comfortably saved by Paul Cooper, would prove to be their final attempt on our goal. It was also the first time Malcolm had threatened our goal in the whole game. Maybe Allan Hunter's pre-match pep talk was more effective than we thought!

Full-time – Arsenal 0-1 Ipswich Town

Euphoric is probably the best word to describe the feeling when referee Derek Nippard blew his whistle for full-time. Embrace the nearest teammate, then the next one and so on but in truth it's like an out-of-body experience and you've got no idea what you're actually meant to be doing. You're just looking around for somebody to hug. Anybody who's won something as part of a team will know it wouldn't be possible without the help of your colleagues and your pals. The ones you're in the trenches with day in, day out, week in, week out and it's a very special moment when you win something. We were the best of mates, that's what got us through. The team spirit in that Ipswich Town team was phenomenal.

Then I spotted Arsenal defender David O'Leary slumped on the turf so I went over to him. It was part of the culture under Bobby Robson at Ipswich Town. He drummed it into us: you win with class and you lose with class. So that's the way we tried to go about our business on the pitch. David was just a young lad and I wanted to check if he was okay after a nasty head knock near the end. Clive Woods swung in a corner from the left and it was meant for me to flick on, but it went over my head. David went to head the ball clear but Mick Lambert, who'd come on as the sub for Roger Osborne, came thundering in at the same time to try and get a header on goal. Mick, who was built like a tank, was a split second too late in getting to the ball and David got whacked instead. He was in a lot of pain and probably should have gone off but Arsenal had already brought on Graham Rix for Liam Brady. Thankfully David was fine and I told him he would probably play many more times at Wembley. As it turns out I was right, because Arsenal won the FA Cup the following year and David O'Leary was part of the team that beat Manchester United.

Winning the FA Cup at Wembley just meant so much. The white horse final of 1923. The performance of Stanley Matthews for Blackpool in 1953, even though his teammate Stan Mortensen scored a hat-trick against Bolton Wanderers. Goalkeeper Jim Montgomery's heroics for Sunderland in 1973. All that history. Then adding the name of Ipswich Town to the trophy in 1978. It's just something that you dream of as a kid without ever thinking your dreams will become reality. Walking up those Wembley steps, seeing the captain lift the trophy, getting the chance to do so yourself. What a day.

Back down on to the pitch to begin the celebrations in earnest, trying to spot family and friends in the stand, collecting the knitted woolen scarves and homemade rosettes that had been thrown from the terracing, drinking milk from glass bottles during post-game interviews, Millsy wearing that stupid hat for the lap of honour that he's regretted ever since, seeing the massive smile on Bobby Robson's face. So many things going on. Such a brilliant day. Glorious. Every single second of it.

Officially there were forty thousand Ipswich Town fans at Wembley but I'm convinced there were even more than that because a lot of the neutrals seemed to support Ipswich as well and it looked like three quarters of the stadium were celebrating with us. And what a noise they made.

I love looking back at the footage of that game, seeing all the different outfits the Ipswich supporters were wearing and trying to read all the homemade signs that people must have spent hours putting together. You don't see those kind of things at cup finals anywhere near as much these days and that's a shame.

I'm lucky enough to have an FA Cup winner's medal, and how many players have got one of those? There's probably less than two thousand medals in the whole world, even to this day. Winning my first trophy with Ipswich – the first time the club had won the FA Cup – with those players, that tight-knit squad with that wonderful manager, the man who bought me and gave me a chance, it's one of the greatest feelings in my life.

With success comes celebrations and it was on to the Royal Garden Hotel in Kensington for the club's official banquet followed by a night out afterwards, although the details of that are being preserved for any sequel to this book...!

I reckon I got about an hour's sleep before it was time to get back on the bus for the trip back to Ipswich on the Sunday morning, and I was as rough as a badger's arse. First stop, the Army & Navy pub in Chelmsford – well known to the boys as a halfway house on the way back from games in London or the south-west. The last time we'd been there was after the semi-final win against West Brom at Highbury and the landlord asked Bobby to make a promise that we would stop in again after the final if Ipswich won the cup, which the gaffer agreed to do. Getting us in to the pub was easy, getting us back out was rather more difficult!

A good time was had by all, and Warky had us in stitches when he told us the story about his family being miserable after the game – 'Twenty of them – brothers, sisters, aunts, uncles, third cousins twice-removed – had come down to Wembley on a minibus from Glasgow and I couldn't wait to show them my medal. But when I eventually caught up with them, the first thing my sister did was complain that I'd hit the post twice. It turns out they all had a fiver on me to score the first goal at twenty to one and she claimed I owed them a hundred quid!'

With celebrations planned in Ipswich later that day, Bobby was keen to get us back on the bus and back up the road, although that was easier said than done. 'Just one more gaffer, please, just one more.' It's roughly forty miles from Chelmsford to Ipswich along the A12, and pretty much every mile of that road was covered in scarves, flags, you name it, and there were fans everywhere by the side of the road. Of course the journey back took a lot longer than normal, given the circumstances, and it got especially slow as we approached Ipswich.

Wem-ber-lee

As we reached the town centre you couldn't even see the road in front because of the number of supporters that had gathered to get a glimpse of their homecoming heroes. Thankfully I was able to savour every single minute of that bus ride, and what a fantastic memory to look back on. Then the celebrations that followed. Wow. They estimated more than one hundred thousand people – which is most of the town's population – saw the open top bus parade and us showing off the trophy at the Cornhill before the team went on to attend a private civic reception. The whole weekend was a remarkable experience and one that none of the Ipswich players will ever forget.

9

Bobby

Winning the FA Cup was huge for Ipswich Town, but it was also very important for Bobby Robson. It confirmed his status as a top football manager and it marked his arrival as a boss who could win things as well. Bobby had first dibs on the trophy, rightly so, and took it home on the Sunday night – complete with police escort – and slept with it under his bed. No such shenanigans for me, I was happy to put my 1977-78 Top Scorer award on the mantlepiece.

Twenty-two league goals in my first full season with Ipswich was decent, and I certainly would have signed up for that at the start of the campaign.

The Daily Express newspaper was offering a prize of ten thousand pounds to the first player who managed to score thirty goals in Division One – I had enough to be top scorer at the club but still finished eight short of Everton striker Bob Latchford, who won the ten grand.

• • • • • • • • •

Terry Austin, David Barnes, Rod Belfitt, Frank Clarke, Ian Collard, Paul Cooper, Bryan Hamilton, Mick Hill, Allan Hunter, John Jackson,

Bobby

David Johnson, Tony Kinsella, Paul Mariner, Arnold Mühren, Kevin O'Callaghan, Jimmy Robertson, Pat Sharkey, Frans Thijssen.

It's incredible to think I was one of only eighteen signings Bobby Robson made as manager of Ipswich Town between 1969 and 1982. He came in for a bit of flak in October 1976 when he spent a fair bit of cash on a young, unproven striker from the second tier of English football; criticism of Bobby was dangerous because of his track record and he usually proved people wrong. When I signed for Ipswich, one of the first things he told me was that he believed in me and to forget about any outside noise. The only person I had to impress was him. He promised to help me improve and he promised to give me an opportunity. There were only two things he wanted me to guarantee him in return; effort and honesty.

* * *

The two most important men in my life are my dad, Jim, and Bobby Robson. Sadly both of them have now passed, but my dad was my hero and Bobby was both a father figure to me and a life coach. I wouldn't be half the person I am today without the guidance of those two wonderful men.

My dad will always be with me, wherever I go and whatever I do, and I still think about Bobby every single day. The things he would say to us, the little adages he would use, lots of comical moments, lots of great coaching moments, lots of poignant footballing moments, but the compassionate side of Bobby Robson was up there with the best people in life. He was very similar to Sir Alex Ferguson and that was why he was so great; he knew the history of every single player in his squad, he knew all the wives and names of any kids and he was a man of fine detail. Not only was he manager of Ipswich Town but he was in charge of the whole club, even down to making sure the toilet rolls never ran out, he was that involved. His attention to detail was incredible. He tried to make life as easy as possible for all the staff, not just the players.

Bobby knew everybody at the club, and more importantly always made time for them, whoever it was, whatever they did, he would always ask how they were. And it was sincere. Always a kind word as he passed by. He'd make you feel special. He'd make you feel like the most important person in the world. That's something you can't teach. You've either got it or you don't, but when you do it is such a special trait and helps create that team spirit, that family atmosphere and everyone loves coming to their work each day. Liverpool had it in the 70s and 80s – Stevie Nicol never stops talking about it – and I'm sure Manchester United had it under Fergie. The great teams, it's a trait they all have. The way the players are together, the relationship they have with the coaches, the relationship they have with the rest of the staff – that's what we had at Ipswich and it was all because of the gaffer.

Even the little things were not forgotten about. When we used to play away from home, if the games were in the north-west Bobby would ask how many tickets I needed for my family, then he would sort out seats in the director's box for my mum, dad and grandfather. For a lad that came from Lancashire, knowing my mother and father were sitting in the plush seats watching their boy play at Old Trafford and at Anfield and at Goodison; that really was something. You can't put a value on that. Here was one of the best managers in the country taking time to think outside the football box, so to speak, and make sure my family was looked after and enjoyed their day.

It was also very smart, very clever on his part because he

probably got another five, ten per cent out of me in those games because my family was there watching and I was desperate to impress them. Imagine the conversation if your mum or dad met up with their friends and said they'd spent the afternoon in the director's box at Old Trafford or Anfield or Goodison watching their son play against Manchester United, Liverpool or Everton – their pals wouldn't get a word in all evening!

Bobby didn't have to do things like that but he did and it was a massive thing for a player. He was also very sympathetic. If you lived many miles from home, or far away from where other members of your family lived, he would always try and give you time off to go and see your parents or close relatives. The gaffer never stopped thinking about other people.

* * *

I always tried to play the game with a smile on my face, and that was down to Bobby. His message was simple; don't get too high when you win and, likewise, when you lose, don't get too down in the dumps – always try and keep a level head. When the game was over that was it, learn from it then time to move on to the next challenge. Bobby wasn't just manager of Ipswich Town, he loved being an educator and always made sure the lines of communication were open, often asking for the opinions of his players. You always knew where you stood with him. He wasn't really a manager who read the riot act too often, but when he did you knew you were in trouble. And with me that was usually related to off-the-field activities, a lot of the time nocturnal and pretty much always involving alcohol. But I was relatively well-behaved in the Ipswich dressing room and if we had any clashes in there over the years they weren't sufficient enough that I can recall any major fall-outs.

The one thing I remember vividly was Bobby's team talks. Fuck me, they went on far too long. And it became a bit of a running joke among the lads, so much so that we used to bet every week on how long Bobby would speak to the boys for, and it was rarely less than half an hour.

We drew up a sheet, starting at thirty minutes and with subsequent blocks of two minutes. Let's say I had thirty to thirty-two and Brazil had thirty-two to thirty-four; if Bobby was about to finish around the thirty-one minute mark then Big Al would ask another question so the speech went on a little bit longer. But Warky might have had thirty-four to thirty-six minutes so he'd ask Bobby to explain the answer he'd just given to Big Al! Chaos, but so much fun.

It was rare for Bobby's team talks to go beyond forty minutes, which was important because we always tried to be in the players' lounge before the first race came on television as most of the lads in that team liked a bet. The game was kicking off in about an hour but it was an afterthought around two o'clock every home game – at that particular point it was all about being in front of the TV before the horses came under starter's orders.

When I was working in the States later in life I used to call Bobby once a month. His nickname for me was Nipper. He'd say, "How you doing Nipper, you alright?" I'd say, "Yeah, yeah, I'm fine." "You alright for money, is everything alright? Is your family alright?" I'd say, "Yeah, everything's great, Boss." It was the same beginning to the conversation every single time. But that was just him, and I know he also kept in touch with all the other lads that played for him.

Do I resent Bobby for blocking a potential move to Barcelona? Not really, but I must admit there was a wry smile on my face when he went there as manager in 1996. Once he'd settled in Spain I called him and offered the services of a forty-three-year-old with more than a few miles on the clock but still capable of playing the last few minutes off the bench if required. A football equivalent of *break glass in case of emergency*. And I wouldn't be hard to deal with.

"You've now got the chance to make it up to me, gaffer, after what you did in 1977 when you told Barcelona I wasn't for sale."

"Nice try, Nipper!"

Selective memory is helpful in sport, never mind just in football, and the ability to quickly put a negative behind you or erase it completely from your mind can be a huge asset. Think of tennis – missing an easy shot – or golf – failing to hole a short putt – and it's exactly the same in football after fluffing a chance.

Of course you can use negatives or bad memories to inspire you, but on other occasions it is best just to park certain things in a small corner of your mind and not bother revisiting them. That's what I did with the interest from Barcelona. It was nice to feel wanted but whether or not I got the chance to speak to them was out of my control.

That's the thing with football, you don't know which twists and turns are just around the corner. You think about managers that have gone on to do great things – Bobby Robson is a perfect example – or players getting a move to great teams. Then there are managers or players who probably deserved the chance to go on and do great things or get a move to a great team and it didn't happen for whatever reason. You just don't know. I was an Ipswich Town player and Bobby told Barcelona I was not for sale and that was that. End of story.

Paul Mariner

I remember a particular training session at the start of the 1978-79 season which was taken by first team coach Bobby Ferguson. Aware that Arnold Mühren had fallen out with FC Twente, Bobby Robson had flown over to the player's home in Volendam to try and persuade Arnold to move to England and join Ipswich Town. The following morning the pair of them flew to Suffolk in a private plane as Bobby stepped up the charm offensive and as the plane flew overhead Bobby Ferguson stopped training, explained what was happening then made us all wave furiously up at the sky!

The gaffer not only had a love affair with football but he especially loved certain types of football, and was greatly influenced by them, and the way the Dutch played the game was high up on that list. His preference was for a possession-based style, but Bobby knew that was only possible with the right players playing in the correct system. That's why the signings of Arnold Mühren in August 1978 and Frans Thijssen in February 1979 – both from FC Twente – were so important to the way he wanted us to play. Bobby was very fond of the Dutch way of playing – getting it down and funneling possession of the ball from the back through the midfield – and he thought that would marry well with the defenders we already had. In my time at the club there were always two good centre backs who could mix it up with the best of them, whether it was Hunter, Beattie, Osman or Butcher – all international footballers – but they could play a fair bit as well and had tremendous football brains.

Bobby always tried to pick the best system for the players he had available, rather than some managers who shoehorn their guys into a pre-determined formation, and he was able to develop a bespoke system for Ipswich Town following the arrival of the two Dutchmen. Arnold and Frans weren't the final two pieces of the jigsaw but they were both vital parts of the puzzle and, with them, the manager was closer to having a squad that was capable of competing every year for the main prizes. There's an old saying in football about knowing your players, and we knew each other's game inside out. We knew if Frans Thijssen was being closely marked that he'd still want the ball, but it would have to be played quickly in to his feet. The same for Gatesy, and Alan Brazil too. We knew what everyone else in the team was capable of and what they wanted. We knew their strengths and how to get the best out of each other.

I would always be the hold-up man. I would show for the ball in the middle third, try and keep the team playing, be an out ball for defenders if they were under pressure while others would run the channels. I think Bobby realised that he probably couldn't play Eric Gates as an out-and-out forward, and Eric wasn't really suited to playing out wide, so he found a role for him off the front two. And it worked with the personnel Bobby put together, it just clicked. I know it wasn't, but it felt like the system was tailored for me − I just felt so comfortable. The players we had were technically fantastic. They could put the ball wherever they wanted it to go and were happy to have possession anywhere across the back or in midfield. And if the forwards made the run then you knew you were likely to get the ball. I had different partnerships during my time at Ipswich but it didn't matter whether I was alongside or just ahead of Trevor, Big Al or Eric, I loved playing with them all. They all helped me and I think I helped them.

* * *

1978 and 1981 – two different Ipswich teams put together by Bobby Robson with two different styles. The '78 team was a bit more industrious while the '81 side was built on star power, but players in both teams got on unbelievably well on and off the field. If you ask any coaches or managers or players who've been in successful teams they'll likely tell you the same – good camaraderie and spirit in the squad is one of the main reasons why success is possible. And I don't believe that's only in football. I think it's the same in all team sports. It's also not just in sport by the way. Every successful company usually has a fantastic team spirit among the staff because you're all fighting for the one goal, and that's the success of the company or, in our case, the team.

The reason I think the '81 effort stood out was because we had a really good chance to win the treble. We lost to Manchester City in the semi-final of the FA Cup when we really should have won. We also threw away the league from a really strong position, winning only two of our last eight games. That meant having to play AZ in the first leg of the UEFA Cup final only four days after Aston Villa clinched the title, but we managed to put all that behind us and were back to our best in a three-nil win at Portman Road. Two weeks later we went to Amsterdam for the return leg and got the job done, so I think the '81 team winning the UEFA Cup on the back of two separate domestic disappointments was quite the achievement.

A few of the lads took cortisone injections before games towards the end of that season and most of us were playing on fumes. It's still a case of what-might-have-been, though, and it's easy to forget how close we came to winning the league.

We beat Aston Villa home and away that season, and in the FA Cup, and we thought we were a better team than them. But they picked us off right at the end. Fair play to them for doing that, but we really threw it away that year. We were cruising to the title, at least it looked that way, then for some reason just hit the skids. But even with two games to go we still had a great chance. I'd scored in the first half to give us a one-nil lead up at Middlesbrough in our penultimate game while Villa were losing two-nil at Arsenal, and that was their final match of the season. We just needed to hold on against Boro then beat Southampton in our rearranged, and final, league game to win the league on goal difference. However Bosko Jankovic scored twice for Middlesbrough in the second half at Ayresome Park and they beat us by two goals to one, gifting the title to Villa.

Ultimately we were the victims of our own success. Competing on three fronts – the league, the FA Cup and the UEFA Cup – pretty much right to the end meant we played a total of sixty-six games during season 1980-81. Aston Villa played twenty games fewer than us. Their players would have been a lot fresher and I think they only used fourteen players throughout that entire campaign. I read a piece online in the East Anglian Daily Times from 2013 with the headline 'Did Paul Mariner's goal cost Blues the league title?' – at first I was confused but the writer went on to explain that things may have been different that season if I hadn't scored the winner against Villa in round three of the FA Cup. If they'd beaten us instead then that would have meant six fewer games for us in an already crowded season. Ifs, buts and maybes, but at least we ended the season with the UEFA Cup and didn't walk away with nothing.

We were two players short of a championship-winning side and if I got an injury I couldn't put in a big-name player, I had to look at a youngster. In that respect, we did phenomenally well. It was a brilliant side, the best I ever created or worked with. I had a great team at PSV that won their league, I had fantastic players at Barcelona like Figo, Ronaldo, Luis Enrique, but that Ipswich team was phenomenal. The likes of Gates, Brazil, the two Dutchmen, they were brilliant. It was a perfect system and one we created to suit the players we had. With Wark in the middle, Gates could push on, but if there was a problem, one whistle from the dug-out and Gates was back alongside Warky, the Dutchmen would go wide and it was a straightforward 4-4-2.

Bobby Robson, January 2003

Our squad wasn't the biggest but under the guidance of Bobby Robson there was a definite bond throughout the whole club. The youths and reserves and the first team all trained on the same field together. The first team squad used the home dressing room and the more experienced players in the reserves were in the away dressing room. The youth team and the younger reserve team players were in the reserve team dressing room. We were always at close quarters so we appreciated what everybody else was trying to do. And we took an interest in what the youth team were doing and went to see them play from time to time, and likewise the reserves, and because of that we were never taken by surprise if one of them was promoted to the first team because we knew their game having seen them play.

* * *

What, if anything, did Paul Mariner have to his game that Ronaldo doesn't?

Heading ability. The one thing that immediately springs to mind is that if Ronaldo has one weakness it's his aerial ability. It's amazing because he's not a small man, he has a wonderful physique and in training on free technical headers he was great, but put him under pressure with a defender and he couldn't do it. Mariner on the other hand was a fantastic target man and brilliant in the air. He could win it, he could flick it on, he could pull to the back post, decide whether to go for goal or knock it back. Mariner had what I call vision in the air. That would be the significant difference between the two.

Four Four Two – February 2003 – Bobby Robson:
One on One

If only I had Brazilian Ronaldo's bank balance!

* * *

When I read Bobby's autobiography *'Farewell but not Goodbye'* in 2005 I must admit I was surprised when he included me along with Gary Lineker, Romario, Ronaldo, Ruud van Nistelrooy, Alan Shearer and Luis Figo on his list of great strikers he's worked with. That's a huge compliment coming from such a great man. We had great respect for each other. I suppose if you're the manager and you buy a player for what was in those days a lot of money, and it works out, then there's a good chance you'll have a strong affinity with that player. Ipswich played some great football under Bobby's stewardship. Yes, we were hard and we were tough, but we could also play a bit. I think Ipswich Town's name is pretty inoffensive in English football – unless you're in Norwich – and it seemed that we were probably everybody's second team when we were playing in Europe.

And that stems from Bobby. In fact, from the chairman to the board to Bobby to Mick Mills, the captain, and the rest of the players, we all pushed in the same direction and were rewarded with winning the FA Cup in 1978 and the UEFA Cup three years later. It really was a team effort.

Sadly we weren't able to follow up the UEFA Cup win in 1981 with success in the same competition the following season, but that was down to a certain Alex Ferguson and his Aberdeen team who beat us in the first round. The Dons were a bit of an unknown quantity to us, but when you look at some of the players they had – Alex McLeish and Willie Miller in the heart of the defence, Gordon Strachan in midfield and Mark McGhee up front – it was a pretty formidable line-up and it's no surprise they went on to have so much success, going on to beat Real Madrid to win the European Cup Winners' Cup less than two years later.

Mid-October 1981 at Portman Road was the first time Bobby Robson and Alex Ferguson appeared in opposite dugouts. It was also the beginning of what would ultimately lead to a very special friendship between the two men. It's fascinating how two great foes in the managerial sphere – both crazy about football and driven by success – became such great friends. But when you delve a little deeper it's not too difficult to see a lot of similarities. Hard task-masters, an insatiable hunger for winning and both of them very protective of their players. Aberdeen and, subsequently, Manchester United players would have run through brick walls for Fergie and we would have done exactly the same for Bobby. Ipswich Town might have been a small-town club but we had big time players and a manager who was one of the best. A great coach, a great tactician, a great man-manager but most important of all, a great man.

10

My Ipswich Teammates

There was something special about playing for a club like Ipswich Town. They were big enough to be successful but just not quite big enough to have a nationwide fan base, and that meant we could go out drinking without attracting too much attention or have outsiders bothering us. Me and Warky would often go for a pint or two in one of the local pubs after home games. If we told the landlord in advance that we were coming he would reserve the big table for us right beside the bar, and we were usually in there by five-thirty. 'Oi, how did you two get in here so fast – we've just been watching you play!' the punters would say, their mood dependent on the result that day.

That sort of thing happened on a regular basis. Football was a way of life in the town and we were able to mingle freely with the locals, win or lose, without any hassle. We had a decent team and were doing well, so that obviously helped, but the players never felt as though we couldn't go out after a defeat for fear of repercussions. We were part of a community that we could trust.

There was a great camaraderie among the squad – we

worked hard and we played harder – and you don't win an FA Cup and a UEFA Cup, and nearly win the league twice, without having good teammates. I've mentioned a few elsewhere in the book, and will do so more in-depth with others in this chapter, and I reckon there were forty-three other players who I shared the field with at least once in Division One while playing for Ipswich Town between October 1976 and February 1984.

Paul Cooper, John Jackson, Paul Overton, Laurie Sivell

David Barnes, Kevin Beattie, Terry Butcher, George Burley, Ian Cranson, Irvin Gernon, Allan Hunter, Mick Mills, Russell Osman, Dale Roberts, Kevin Steggles, John Stirk, Les Tibbott, Frank Yallop

Mark Brennan, David Geddis, Steve McCall, Arnold Mühren, Roger Osborne, Tommy Parkin, Noel Parkinson, Trevor Putney, Pat Sharkey, Brian Talbot, Frans Thijssen, Colin Viljoen, John Wark, Clive Woods, Romeo Zondervan

Keith Bertschin, Alan Brazil, Mich d'Avray, Eric Gates, Anthony Kinsella, Mick Lambert, John Linford, Kevin O'Callaghan, Robin Turner, Trevor Whymark

Apologies if I've missed anyone out – and I'm sure I played with one or two others in various cup ties or friendlies – but everyone played their part, even the reserves who didn't manage to make a first team appearance, yet still helped us prepare for the FA Cup final in 1978 by taking on the role of the Arsenal players we'd be coming up against at Wembley.

* * *

My Ipswich Teammates

Meet my team-mates...

JOHN WARK

Warky was the perfect roommate. There were never any scraps or fall-outs, other than the odd disagreement about what show to watch on the telly. He was non-confrontational, which is just what you want when you're stuck together for long periods of time either on a pre-season trip or an away game in Europe. You need to be compatible, we were, and we're still really close mates. Football is a game where you can develop strong relationships with teammates then all of the sudden one of you gets transferred and it's hard to maintain that bond. Not with John. We went our separate ways in 1984 – him to Liverpool and me to Arsenal – but we always kept in touch. Like all good pals, even if you go months without speaking to each other, the first time you do it's as though you've never been apart. We're like brothers. Johnny's not a high end guy. He's from a tough part of Glasgow and is a staunch Rangers fan. He used to teach me about the history of Rangers and Celtic and how much they hate each other. When Alan Brazil became part of the first team squad at Ipswich there were constant battles because Al loves Celtic, but Warky wouldn't hear a bad word said about his team.

Here's my favourite story about me and Johnny, and it's to do with the PFA Player of the Year Awards that took place at the Park Lane Hilton in London at the end of season 1980-81. Three Ipswich players were on the shortlist of six nominees for the main award – John Wark, Frans Thijssen and myself – and I know how proud Bobby Robson was of that. Word had actually leaked out the day before that one of us had won, we just didn't know who, but we did know that somebody from Ipswich would be celebrating and that meant all of us would be celebrating. The club booked several rooms at the Hilton for the squad, for Bobby Robson and his coaching staff plus a few members of the Cobbold family, the owners. The event was due to start at seven. We got there at noon, just in time…

A decent drinking session on the way down was followed by a decent drinking session in London in the afternoon. I was sharing a room with Warky, of course, so we got the tin flutes on and helped each other with the dickie-bows before going downstairs and taking our seats for the awards ceremony. Dickie Davies from 'World of Sport' on ITV was the host, and when it was time for the main award he read out the shortlist containing six nominees:

Steve Archibald (Tottenham)
Kenny Dalglish (Liverpool)
Paul Mariner (Ipswich)
Dennis Mortimer (Aston Villa)
Frans Thijssen (Ipswich)
John Wark (Ipswich)

He continued: "…and it is the first time that three players from one club have finished in the top three places, so Bobby Robson can be glowing with pride when I tell him that Frans Thijssen, Paul Mariner and John Wark are all in the frame for the Player's Player of the Year Award."

I was lucky enough to win, but the thing that struck me right after Sir Stanley Rous read out my name was Paul's reaction. I honestly don't know if he could have been more excited if HE had won. Marrers – who was sitting next to me – got to his feet straight away, yelled 'GET IN THERE' and clapped and clenched his fists above his head. It meant the world to him to see me get the award. That tells you everything you need to know about Paul Mariner, one of the most selfless individuals I've ever met.

John Wark

Warky was like my brother, my closest friend and I couldn't have been more thrilled for him. The awards ceremony wrapped up shortly after but none of us fancied going outside to search for a pub or club to continue the celebrations, so we just went to the hotel bar where several players from other teams were having a drink. We found a few who we knew pretty well, either from playing with them for our countries or playing against them for Ipswich, and once the bar closed Warky suggested we all go upstairs to our room. So we invited about sixteen guys and the lot of us were drinking and ordering room service until at least four o'clock in the morning, or so I was told!

Breakfast was at eight and the bloody room looked like a war zone. We tried in vain to tidy some of it up before giving up and going downstairs for food. "We need to sort this bill out" I said to Marrers after breakfast. "What fucking bill?" He appeared to have very little recollection of a large portion of the night before. I asked him how much money he had on him. "A tenner." Fuck. I had a fiver. And neither of us had a credit card. "I think we may just be struggling a bit here," he added, helpfully.

So I went to reception and asked for the bill for room 324. Six hundred and fifty fucking pounds!! Thankfully, and with perfect timing, John Cobbold came striding by and saw me in a bit of a panic. "Johnny, have you got a problem?" he enquired in his extra posh voice. "A problem?? The hotel bill is six hundred and fifty quid and Mariner and me have the grand total of fifteen quid between us," I replied in my less-than-posh Glaswegian accent. "Leave it with me, son," and he settled the bill on our behalf before winking at me and uttering the line "…that must have been one hell of a night!"

John Wark

It certainly was, well, what I remember of it! When we got back to Ipswich later in the day I drove Warky around the town centre with his trophy sticking up through the sunroof while I kept honking the car horn and waving to some rather confused passers-by. But we were loving life. Absolutely fantastic times. John Wark, Warky, Johnny Boy – a brilliant player but an even better friend.

MICK MILLS

The combination at Ipswich of Mick Mills as captain and Bobby Robson in charge was absolutely ideal. Mick went on to captain England, so that tells you what a steady influence he was – a real leader for club and country and he was Bobby's eyes and ears on the pitch. Lieutenant Mills at your service. Some people might think he's a bit stoic, but Mick has a wicked sense of humor. It took me a while to get to know him but as soon as he knew he could trust you, that you were with him so to speak, then you had a friend for life. A tremendous footballer, two great feet and just as comfortable playing right back or left back. Brave as a lion, tackled for fun but technically terrific and positionally outstanding.

When I was younger he used to get in my ear and offer advice if he felt I needed it, the important thing at that age was to take it the right way, because the truth can hurt, especially when you're just a kid. Mick was a manager's dream because you knew exactly what you were going to get from August all the way through until May. He was a leader on the field, he could organise tactically and was very aware of what's going on. And he had a great relationship with the gaffer – he played in Bobby's first game in charge of Ipswich in 1969 and he was also in the team for his last game in charge in 1982. Even when some fans were baying for blood in the early days Mick stood with Bobby throughout. Our leader, and a top lad.

KEVIN BEATTIE

Kevin could have been one of the greats. People even spoke about him in the same breath as Duncan Edwards as far as potential was concerned. He made his debut for Ipswich against Manchester United at eighteen, his England debut at twenty-one, he was a central defender for club and a full-back for country. Unbelievable pace, I'd never seen anything like it, and his recovery speed was amazing. And for someone standing only five foot ten tall his aerial ability was incredible. Strong as an ox, a larger-than-life character with flowing blond curly locks, a dream of a left foot and built like a brick shit house with legs made of granite. Sadly the cartilage in his knees weren't made of the same. We didn't realise at first just how bad his knees were. I remember he went in for surgery not long after a routine check-up. Cartilage damage back then meant you were out for quite a while, but he was back in the team after three weeks. I think that sort of threw his body off, he started having back problems and issues with his hamstrings, although he was still the quickest in the club! I think if you point to one injury above others it would be his knee and I think he came back too quickly. Kevin's nickname was The Beast or The Monster; and for someone as tough as him, he was also very fair. But not many players can keep going after five operations in four years and, sadly, Kevin had to retire from football in December 1981.

TERRY BUTCHER

Big Lofty. What a guy. One of my favourites. When he was coming through the ranks at Ipswich you could see he had ability and an unbelievable left foot, but he was really tall – six foot four – and maybe didn't yet have enough pace at that stage of his career. When Bobby first gave him a chance in the first team I thought it was an interesting decision because Terry wasn't the quickest. Slowly but surely the ugly duckling turned into a swan, though, and what a player he went on to be for Ipswich Town, Rangers and England. A real leader, my heavy metal concert buddy and a great pal.

What a career Big Lofty had at Ipswich but after the team was relegated in 1986 he had the opportunity to move to pastures new. I still had the house in Preston St Mary and it was only a few days after the end of the season when the big man came round with Rita, his missus. We were sitting in the garden enjoying the sunshine and having a beer or two, talking about the forthcoming World Cup in Mexico, when he told me Graeme Souness wanted to sign him for Rangers. I didn't hesitate with my reply, "Terry, get your arse up there. They'll love the way you play and you'll be an absolute legend in Glasgow." He did. And he was.

That famous photograph of Lofty in the World Cup qualifier in Sweden in September 1989 is him to a tee – with his head covered in blood and the soaked bandages doing absolutely nothing to stem the red flow. He would run through a brick wall for his teammates and his manager, for his club and his country.

Terry might not have been the fastest physically, but he was probably one of the quickest players mentally that I ever came across. He used to read things so well on the pitch and was brilliant at anticipating danger, nobody ever really got in behind him. I can't remember anybody ever stitching him up, well apart from the England doctor in Stockholm after that clash of heads with Swedish striker Johnny Ekstrom!

To say Terry is a character is to do him an injustice. He lives life to the full. I think a lot of great players have a split personality; off the field the nicest person you'll ever meet, usually a family guy, but on the pitch an absolute maniac, and Terry gave the impression he'd literally mutilate people if it meant getting a win for his team. Quick-witted, very intelligent, great to be around and just a tremendous bloke. One of the best.

RUSSELL OSMAN

Russ was very much underappreciated for what he did at Ipswich. A rugby union star when he was a teenager, he could have gone on and done great things in that sport but decided to choose football instead, and thankfully he did. He carved out a fantastic relationship with Terry at the back, they were great friends off the field and tremendous central defensive partners on it. Russell had two tremendous feet and was as brave as a lion. His aerial ability was underrated and he always seemed to have a knack for timing tackles perfectly. Became part of our gang when we went to gigs and was tremendous company. A great guy.

GEORGE BURLEY

George was a super player with a great engine and technically fantastic. Not the biggest, but very quick and an extremely smart player with an excellent football brain. Like a will-o'-the-wisp, a quick thinker, very fast over the ground and great at closing down opponents. A real old-school defender who rarely allowed crosses to come in, just a tremendous full-back. And he was a great training partner. We used to go out twenty minutes before the start of a session, never usually breaking a sweat, and just ping balls at each other. He'd help me by drilling all sorts of crosses, or chipping them onto my chest or thigh or in to feet. And I think fans saw the benefit of that on the pitch. I always did my best to make sure I was an out ball for him and gave him an option, and most of the time he'd find me.

ALAN BRAZIL

The word 'personality' is not big enough for him. He's absolutely larger than life. Big Al was great in the dressing room and you always knew when he was around, usually hearing him before seeing him. An incredible finisher, great left foot, pace, strength and balance – we didn't really use him as a hold-up man but he could hold it up very well and we had a great understanding on the pitch. He would run at people, could be an explosive dribbler, get in behind defenders and his finishing was different class.

A tremendous character, Alan's always had a sparkle in his eye and has never been short of an opinion or something to say. It doesn't surprise me he's been doing the breakfast show on talkSport for so long, and it also doesn't surprise me that he's been late for work on several occasions because he's always enjoyed life to the full, whether it was playing football, a day at the races or several beers down the pub. Usually the life and soul of the party, he used to have tremendous battles in training with John Wark, both of them coming from opposite sides of the Rangers-Celtic divide. The English lads didn't really understand what they were on about most of the time.

I remember playing up front with Alan during our successful run in Europe and sometimes we would play against teams who deployed two markers and a sweeper. But that just gave us carte blanche to run riot; we couldn't understand why teams played that system, purely and simply because we had so much movement. We just created havoc by switching the play and isolating defenders one against one.

Some of the best times with the big man took place at Newmarket races. We never took things to crazy levels gambling-wise, that wasn't our scene. We just loved to be around the horses. The most fun I had, apart from the races, was going to the gallops because we had some great friends there – Henry Cecil, Sir Michael Stoute, Clive Brittain, Barry Hills, a lot of the great trainers. We got to know them and some of them would come to watch us play at Portman Road from time-to-time and we would go to the gallops, a great way to relax. In fact I ended up being given a horse! 'Mighty Mariner' was gifted to me by Greek shipping magnate Captain Marcos Lemos, and he paid for all the training fees and the likes at Clive Brittain's yard. I've still got a photograph of me with Mighty Mariner at my mum's house. The most beautiful chestnut horse with a gorgeous white face. Sadly he fell in his first race and had to be put down.

ARNOLD MÜHREN/FRANS THIJSSEN

Different players to a certain degree but out of the same mould and both technically incredible. Arnold's storied left foot was like a magic wand, a joy to witness in training and in games, and he was our Player of the Year in 1979. He wasn't the type who would go crunching into tackles, he was more of an intelligent player who would position himself in the right place to nullify attacks then start one of his own. And most of the time if a run was made he'd put the ball right onto your foot. It was a privilege for Alan Brazil and myself to play with him. Arnold had a great career in Holland before he joined Ipswich, then went on to do well with Manchester United and, of course, he won the European Championship in 1988 with Holland. He always kept himself fit so it was no surprise when he played against the Soviet Union in the final of Euro 88 at thirty-seven.

Frans was unbelievable at keeping the ball. He could have an opposition player on either side of him but he'd still call for it, still manage to somehow get free and still retain possession. That was key in those days, ball retention, because you could stretch the field whenever you had possession of the ball. So when the Dutch boys had the ball we knew we could make runs and drag opponents out of position. Frans was more of a dribbler, Arnold was the passer, but both of them had an incredible work ethic to go with fantastic talent.

Bobby signed some pretty talented footballers in his managerial career and I think those two must be in his top three. Arnold didn't really put his foot in, but he didn't have to put his foot in. Frans loved the tackle, he excelled in the physical side of the game, but he could also dribble and was great at getting balls in to the front men.

After the Dutch boys came to Ipswich I think we, as a team, kept the ball better. We were pretty good at doing that before, but they just made us better. We weren't afraid to keep it at the back, we knew we could roll it into midfield and retain it, and we had pace and power in the final third – all the ingredients of a decent side. And they allowed us to play a different brand of football: Bobby's 4-3-1-2 formation with Eric Gates playing behind Alan and myself.

They talk about Ossie Ardiles and Ricky Villa making a massive impact in British football during their time at Spurs – and they did – but Frans Thijssen and Arnold Mühren also made a tremendous impact after moving to Ipswich Town. I think Ossie lasted a little bit longer in England than the Dutch lads but there was no doubting they all had quality and were an asset to the British game.

PAUL COOPER

Coop was one of the quickest players in the team even though he was a goalkeeper. He fancied himself as an outfielder but most keepers do, don't they? Paul had a tremendous spring, was very good technically and had great feet. Very underrated. Made his name as a penalty expert, he used to save loads of them, and Coop had this tremendous technique where he'd lean to one side and try to second guess what the penalty taker was going to do. I remember him doing exactly that against Derby County in March 1980 and he saved two of their spot-kicks.

ROGER OSBORNE

A shy, archetypal guy from Suffolk with a dry sense of humour who didn't get too down when things were going badly and didn't get too excited when things were going well. Roger had an unbelievable engine and would run for fun as part of that 1978 team that Bobby put together. Probably worth checking his pockets because Liam Brady might still be in there. A great teammate.

KEVIN O'CALLAGHAN/STEVE McCALL

Kevin and Steve were both fringe players, but they each played very important roles. Any time they came in to the side the team rarely missed a beat. These types of players – who don't play that often yet still come in and do a specific job – are worth their weight in gold.

* * *

I attended Kevin Beattie's tribute night in Clacton in February 2019 and it was great to catch up with so many former teammates, despite the sad circumstances. The storytelling would have gone on for days if we'd had the time!

I remember a supporter coming up to me at the bar before we got started and I was asked, "How do you think Bobby Robson's best Ipswich team would do against the big boys nowadays?"

"I think we'd do alright on a level playing field, but if our boys were each averaging between twenty-five and thirty pints a week then I might just have to concede favouritism…"

11

Three Lions

Ron Greenwood put his arm around me before my first training session: "There's one reason you're here and it's because of what you've done at your club. Just do the same and you'll be fine." Joining up with the England squad in March 1977 for the World Cup qualifier against Luxembourg at Wembley was nerve-racking, so many things are going through your mind and you're desperate to do well and not let anybody down, but that simple piece of advice helped me settle. In fact, when I got into coaching later in life I would say something similar to every young player making their debut to try and make them feel at ease – 'just do what you're good at'.

I can't really speak for anybody else but I'm pretty sure most people play football wanting to leave some sort of legacy. To do that you have to work hard and you have to train hard, but you've got to want to do both. Strive to become a pro, get in the reserves, score goals, get promoted to the first team, become the leading scorer, get a move, then rinse and repeat and try to play at the highest level you can. I always liked to have a personal goal to try and aim for. If I achieved that goal then I would immediately set another one. I was always aiming higher.

Paul Mariner

Everybody wants to play for England but only a select few make it. I was the 928th player to do so when I made my debut in 1977. Only 927 people had ever experienced what I experienced; it was a pretty exclusive club to be part of. Everybody also wants to win trophies but there's only a handful lucky enough to do so. A God-given talent is one thing, but you also need drive, perseverance and, of course, a fair bit of luck along the way to achieve great things in the game. How different would my career have been if I'd gone to West Ham or West Brom instead? Who knows, but I don't think I would have enjoyed the same success that I did with Ipswich, success which helped get me into that squad to face Luxembourg and, ultimately, on the plane to Italy for the European Championship in 1980 and to Spain for the World Cup in 1982.

* * *

When I first became part of the England setup in 1977 my roommate was Manchester United winger Gordon Hill. When you played with him you knew the crosses were coming in, perfect for a centre forward, but that was a short-lived relationship. My debut for my country – on at half-time against Luxembourg at Wembley – was one of only three occasions we were in the same squad together, the final time being in Luxembourg later that year when I scored my first England goal and he won his last England cap.

Next to experience Mariner's notorious nocturnal snoring (copyright: John Wark) on international duty was my new roommate for the 1978 Home Championship, Joe Corrigan, the experienced Manchester City goalkeeper. I never did find out from Ron Greenwood or the coaching staff how the roommate system worked – who chose who to go in with who – but on this occasion it may well just have been geographical. Two northern boys together, Joe from Manchester and me from fifteen miles away in Horwich, so no translator was required. Of course with three goalkeepers normally in an England squad one of them would have to room with an outfield player, and if Ray Clemence and Peter Shilton were together, which they usually were, then Joe would draw the short straw.

I first met the big man in the players' lounge at Maine Road when we were enjoying a beer, him more than me, after Ipswich lost two-one at Manchester City in April 1977, then again later that year in November. The second time I had the bragging rights after scoring the only goal of the game past him at Portman Road. It's difficult to get to know someone when you've only spent a short time in their company, but I enjoyed our brief chats so to find out I'd be rooming with Joe was a pleasant surprise. I'd got myself a good one.

Paul was a brilliant roommate and his snoring wasn't actually that loud. Honestly I can't say a bad word about him. He's just a lovely, lovely person. We enjoyed each other's company and we always will. I remember the first England get-together after we knocked them out of the FA Cup in 1981. Paul told me the story of Bobby Robson in the dressing room at Villa Park before the semi-final going through all the Manchester City players one-by-one: "Joe Corrigan – don't worry about him, he's old and past his best. Can hardly move. We'll win this game comfortably if he's in goals." Except they didn't. I kept a clean sheet, we beat Ipswich one-nil that day and went on to face Spurs in the final.

Joe Corrigan

* * *

I didn't feature in any of the eight European Championship qualifiers between September 1978 and February 1980, despite finishing as Ipswich top scorer in each of the two seasons. That was mainly due to the form of Everton striker Bob Latchford, who scored four goals in his first three qualifiers and was also doing well for his club at the time. With a number of more experienced players pretty much guaranteed a place in those squads there wasn't much room available for fringe players, and Bob got the nod, meaning I was the one to miss out.

I was stuck on five caps and one England goal for two years – since the one-nil win over Scotland at Hampden in May 1978 – but a decent bit of form for Ipswich at the end of 1979-80, coupled with Everton having a poor season and Bob struggling in front of goal, meant a recall for the 1980 Home Championship. Talk about timing, the European Championship was taking place the following month.

Not only back in the squad but back in the team for the opening Home Championship fixture against Wales in Wrexham and I was lucky enough to open the scoring. But that was as good as it got. England were thumped by four goals to one and Ron Greenwood made ten changes for the next game three days later against Northern Ireland at Wembley. I came on for Kevin Reeves with twenty minutes to go, meaning only me and Trevor Cherry played some part in both games.

The final fixture was against Scotland at Hampden (by the way I played against the Jocks three times in my career but never at Wembley, they were all in Glasgow) and I was back in the starting line-up. Although I didn't score, I'd featured in all three Home Championship games and was feeling pretty optimistic on the journey back down south that I'd done enough to get a place in Ron Greenwood's England squad for the forth-coming European Championship in Italy. When the call came a couple of days later there was a feeling of immense pride. My first major tournament and the chance to represent my country. The first thing I did after speaking to Ron was phone my mum and dad and the three of us dissolved into tears.

I was one of twenty players who knew we'd definitely be part of the England squad, but for a few others they had to play the waiting game. That's because Ron also named an additional shortlist containing five names – Glenn Hoddle, Bryan Robson, Peter Barnes, Laurie Cunningham and Garry Birtles – with only two of those five going to Italy along with the other twenty. The official squad selection had to be submitted to UEFA by the third of June.

There was one last international friendly for England before the tournament in Italy, that's why Ron hadn't yet named his full squad, and it took place on the final day in May... IN AUSTRALIA. The scheduling was chaotic; depart on the Wednesday for Sydney and return to London the following Monday. Travelling halfway around the world FOR FIVE FUCKING DAYS.

Ron Greenwood's eclectic gang of sixteen was a combina-tion of 'A' and 'B' players with only a handful of members of the Euros squad chosen to go, including Glenn Hoddle and Bryan Robson from the shortlist. Peter Barnes and Laurie Cunningham weren't in the travelling party while Garry Birtles also missed the trip to Sydney – he was busy leading the line for Nottingham Forest in the European Cup final against Hamburg in Madrid. Glenn and Bryan didn't mind making the trip down under – it gave them an opportunity to stake a claim for a place in the main squad – but Joe Corrigan, Trevor

Cherry and me knew we were going to Italy regardless, unless we got hurt down under, so to speak. A fucking inconvenience for want of a better phrase.

It was at Ron's insistence that the game against Australia was classed as a full international. Initially it was just going to be a 'B' fixture as part of the Australian FA's centenary celebrations, but Ron told the Football Association he wasn't taking the boys all that way unless there were caps awarded for his players. The most pleasing part of the trip for me was full England debuts for my two big pals, Terry Butcher and Russell Osman, so it wasn't a complete waste of time. It was also nice for Bobby Robson, who was part of Ron's coaching staff, to take charge of the team in Sydney. That allowed the national team manager to come with us but concentrate more on preparations for the Euros.

I roomed with Joe Corrigan before we flew out to Sydney and the boys had a proper session that night, resulting in a bumper bar bill. The following morning as we were leaving the room I asked Joe if he could take care of check-out and I would settle up with him on the bus. While he was at the hotel reception I tried to persuade Bobby Robson to tell the driver to move the bus round the corner so that Joe would think we'd left without him. His look said it all. It's never good when someone raises one eyebrow higher than the other one in response to a suggestion.

Speaking of Bobby, he was clearly trying to curry favour with members of the Football Association, doing everything by the book, although the players weren't happy when he tried to put a block on us having a drink on the plane. Ron Greenwood pulled him to one side and he said, "Listen, these boys are having to fly to Australia and we're only going to be there for four or five days, they're all professionals so don't stop them from having a good time."

I took 'having a good time' a bit too literally...

* * *

To get to Sydney we had to fly via Dehli. And that's when Paul went missing. Not at the airport before we boarded the plane, but during the bloody flight itself. Disappeared. Gone. We checked everywhere but he was nowhere to be seen. Honestly, we thought he'd miraculously managed to get off the plane. So I went to speak to one of the stewardesses and she said 'just follow me, Mr. Corrigan.' She took me to the back of the plane and it was one of the old jumbo jets that had six of seven toilets together. I'd already knocked on the doors of most of them but to no avail. There was one door that was shut and had a 'no entry' sign on it. Of course I didn't knock on that door. But she did. Still nothing. 'Hold on,' she said, before disappearing for a couple of minutes. She then came back with a pouch containing a little screwdriver. She knocked on the door again – no response – so she slid the screwdriver into the latch on the door and managed to open it. And there was Paul sat with his trousers and his pants down by his ankles. He didn't know what day of the week it was – absolutely gone with the wind. I just wish camera phones had been around in those days because what a picture that would have been! The girl turned to me, put her finger to her lips, told me not to say anything, shut the door, locked it again and put a sign on the outside: 'TOILET OUT OF USE – PLEASE DO NOT ENTER'. Shortly before we landed in Delhi a rather dishevelled Paul came stumbling back down the aisle, didn't have a clue what had happened during the flight and couldn't remember any of the drama. He even tried to order another beverage. Thankfully the drinks service had been shut off.

Joe Corrigan

* * *

The Australia 'tour' itinerary was nuts. We flew out on the Wednesday, arrived in Sydney on the Friday morning, went sightseeing in the afternoon, trained on the Saturday, played on the Sunday and flew back on the Monday. Frightening. Our body clocks were all over the place and we were walking around like zombies most of the time. We were not helped by flying economy class while, of course, the blazers from the Football Association were up the front of the plane in business class. That was always the case when we went abroad.

In fact, not long before we went to Australia, myself and Joe were part of a 'B' squad that travelled to Kuala Lumpur for a fixture, then on to New Zealand where we played another five games, and on the way back we stopped off in Singapore. Again, the players travelled economy class while the suits were wined and dined up front. So me, Joe and a couple of other senior members of that squad had a meeting with the FA in a bid to persuade them to let the players fly business class, especially for long flights. Our pleas fell on deaf ears. There was more chance of me remembering everything that happened on that bloody flight to Delhi than them changing their mind!

The game itself against Australia was rather chaotic. We played at the Sydney Cricket Ground, Glenn Hoddle and me each scored in the first half in a two-one win but the pitch was a disgrace. The turf had been freshly laid, but the grass above the square on the cricket pitch underneath was still about six inches higher than the rest of the surface because the square was baked hard. The grass also cut up like hell and when I went out to inspect the surface pre-match with Big Lofty the conversation was only about one thing – footwear...

> Should we wear moulded boots with rubber soles that we'd normally use if pitches were rock hard or just regular boots with normal studs? I wore small studs and Marrers went with the mouldies. The pair of us often found ourselves on that bloody square in each half, it was like trying to walk on glass and sounded like someone was prancing on a catwalk wearing stiletto heels! One minute you're teetering on this rock-hard surface then all of a sudden you're back on the slippery grass.
>
> **Terry Butcher**

The last half hour of that game was probably the worst I've ever felt on a football pitch because most of us were running on fumes while also suffering from jetlag. And for some obscure reason the three England substitutions were not made until the last five minutes of the game. We were all just glad to get the hell out of there and fly home. Even Bobby Robson described the flight back from Australia as "perhaps the worst journey I've ever had".

> To be honest, take the bit about my England debut out and the trip was a complete pain in the ass. It was right at the end of the season, we were already knackered and then had to spend the best part of forty-eight hours on a bloody plane to get there and back, all within the space of five days. A quick boat trip around Sydney Harbour shortly after we arrived

with Marrers as the impromptu tour guide, a training session on the Saturday, the game on the Sunday then a flight back the very next day. It was ridiculous. I appreciate I've just come across as a miserable, ungrateful git with that opening diatribe – I'm not really – but the thing that sticks out for me from that trip was actually Paul's constant moaning within an hour of arriving in Sydney. Now if Joe Corrigan wants to use the whole of the wardrobe, Joe Corrigan is going to use the whole of the wardrobe. So when I saw Paul in the bar shortly after we checked in to the hotel I asked him how he was getting on with Big Joe. He shook his head. 'Oh HE'S great', said Marrers, '...because all HIS fucking clothes are immaculately hung up and he's used every inch of the wardrobe. My gear is also unpacked... it's piled on the chair in the corner of the room.'

Russell Osman

* * *

The final two names to complete the 22-man England squad were announced shortly after we got back from Australia. Glenn Hoddle and Garry Birtles were the chosen ones, which meant disappointment for Laurie Cunningham, Peter Barnes and a young Bryan Robson. If you look at the players selected for that tournament by Ron Greenwood it really was a golden era in English football, the group boasting a staggering nineteen European Cup winning medals and one Lancashire County Youth Cup medal between us. The biggest issue, however, would be a lack of tournament experience. Only Emlyn Hughes, an unused member of Alf Ramsey's World Cup squad in Mexico in 1970, had been to a major tournament before.

Our final few days before we flew out to Italy were spent at the squad hotel in Hertfordshire. I might have been one of the louder guys in the Ipswich Town dressing room but I considered myself somewhat of a newbie in the national team squad so I toned down my behaviour a fair bit. Some of the boys spent time in Dave Watson and Steve Coppell's room listening to the latest Gerry Rafferty album on Dave's ridiculously large hi-fi, but that wasn't my kind of music. I was into Iron Maiden, AC/DC and Deep Purple – Baker Street didn't really do it for me.

As for some of the others; Mick Mills, Emlyn Hughes and Phil Thompson decided to hire a helicopter to fly them to Epsom to watch the Derby. Mick knew his horses and fancied Henbit to win, which it did indeed at seven-to-one, and with the other two also getting involved the winnings paid for their extravagant mode of transport.

Then came a cocktail party at Number 10 Downing Street hosted by Prime Minister Margaret Thatcher.

> She seemed to take a liking to me for some reason, and came over and took hold of my hand. Suddenly we were off on this excursion. She showed me these paintings of the ex-Prime Ministers that were hanging on the walls and gave me their history. It was very enjoyable – we didn't talk football at all.
> **Dave Watson – Four Four Two magazine, June 2004**

Maybe if I owned a massive portable hi-fi that was eighteen inches long and six inches wide then the Iron Lady might have taken me on a private tour as well!

It was certainly a privilege to be invited to Downing Street, but I'm not overly political and in all honesty I just wanted to get on that flight to Italy.

Paul Mariner

* * *

The one-all draw against Belgium in our opening group game of the 1980 European Championship was a big disappointment. We were expected to win and we thought we would win. We were wrong. And that meant the pressure on England increased substantially ahead of the second game. I was an unused sub in the opener − I certainly didn't expect to start − but with the side needing a win on matchday two I felt I had a good chance of being involved from the beginning against Italy in Turin. But Ron Greenwood picked Garry Birtles ahead of me, having been impressed by the Nottingham Forest striker's performance against man-marking tactics by Hamburg defenders in the European Cup final victory over the Germans. When asked, Ron explained that he thought the Italians would deploy similar tactics so that's why he selected the Forest striker. I did come on for Garry with fifteen minutes remaining, a very proud moment making my tournament debut, but the Italians scored the only goal of the game soon after and I hardly got a sniff up the other end. And that result meant we were eliminated with one match left.

The manager made six changes for the final game, the dead rubber against Spain. I got my hopes up. Surely this time I'd get a start. He's changed more than half the team! Nope. Hopes dashed. Well at least my roommate had a smile on his face after hearing Ron say, "I'm going to put Joe in..." I looked at my big pal, smiled and gave him a wink. But Ron hadn't finished his sentence: "...as the substitute goalkeeper." The big man was as frustrated as me. We went on to beat the Spaniards by two goals to one; once again I came on for the last quarter of an hour, this time for Glenn Hoddle, but it wasn't the overall experience I was hoping for as we failed to get out of the group and I played a total of half an hour in two substitute appearances. Nineteen of Ron Greenwood's squad of twenty-two played at least some part of the three games but we still failed to reach the knockout stages of Euro '80.

"If I've failed, I've failed. I'm certainly not making excuses for the team selection. We did our best, but it just wasn't good enough."

The knives were out for the manager ahead of World Cup qualifying. I just wondered if I had done enough to be kept on if he was kept on.

12

Me and Gillan

Music and football, my two favourite things, and natural bedfellows in the entertainment industry as far as I'm concerned. I wouldn't be surprised if a lot of football players have dreams about being the lead singer in a band – I certainly did – and I'm sure a lot of musicians would also love to be footballers. We look up to them and they look up to us. Ultimately we're both very fortunate to be in positions of privilege. The closest I ever got to being both at the same time was at the Hammersmith Apollo in London after being invited to play the bongos on stage with the frontman of Deep Purple. That'll be Ian Gillan, my dear, dear friend. I'll never forget that eye-bulging look on his face before he burst out laughing when the heavily tattooed rockers in the crowd that night, wondering what the hell this idiot footballer was doing up there, shouted at me to 'GET OFF THE FUCKING STAGE, DICKHEAD'. I smiled and waved back at them. I'm not sure they appreciated that.

Tuesday 21st November, 1981
Gaumont Theatre, Ipswich

Me and Gillan

This wasn't the first time I'd been to see Gillan, the band, play live. I'd also gone to their gig at the Gaumont in Ipswich in October 1980 after reading an article in the Ipswich Evening Star the night before in which Ian Gillan mentioned that Deep Purple, one of my favourite bands growing up, would probably never be getting back together following his decision to quit the band in 1973. If I couldn't go and see Deep Purple again then at least I had the chance to see their former lead singer perform...

"I think [Deep] Purple has become more of a legend than anything else," said Gillan, "and it is best left that way. We're all different people now to what we were ten years ago."

Ian casually told me that he is now 35, and as he spoke from his Pangbourne home, near Reading, his collection of budgies twittered wildly in the background – all of which led me on to ask just how much longer he intends to be a rock singer.

"I personally will carry on singing, although when I'm approaching 50 I don't think I'll be jumping around, to the embarrassment of everybody else. You've got to remember that there will be an awful lot of ageing rock musicians around then. I'd like to get back to something more blues based, but I can imagine huge bands of ageing musicians doing the rounds!"

From the Ipswich Evening Star – Monday 20th October, 1980 – written by Steve Painter

Two things struck me from that article: first of all, thank God Deep Purple are back together again, especially with that lead singer of theirs who's now in his mid-Seventies, and, secondly, the things you say when you're young! The Ipswich boys were regular attendees at the Gaumont Theatre and most of us knew the venue manager, who was delighted when we used to show up.

On this particular Tuesday night I got there early to have a few drinks before the gig and that's when I saw the manager, who I took aside to inquire about the prospects of getting backstage. A few minutes later I found myself inside the dressing room staring at Ian Gillan, who was slouched on a couch with a glass of whisky in hand and flanked by a border collie on one side and his then-girlfriend on the other. He sat bolt upright. "Bloody 'ell, Paul bloody Mariner, I'm so pleased to meet you!" Later that evening I was on stage with Gillan playing those bongos, but this time, the first time, I was able to do so without comment from down the front. A month later Ian invited me to the Hammersmith Odeon in London to see the band and, once more, I was on stage whacking some bongo drums. That was when my friends in the audience passed on such kind advice.

From those first two encounters a close friendship grew and grew over the years and any time Ian was gigging in Ipswich he would come over and stay at my house in Preston St Mary. He'd let me know well in advance if he was going to be in town; I remember buying three bottles of Johnnie Walker ahead of his first 'sleepover', thinking that would be enough for his stay, but they were demolished within hours on the first night. I don't even drink the bloody stuff. Ian and I had a similar outlook on life; neither of us took ourselves too seriously and we're both slightly larger-than-life, although he would always be the one to take things that one step further, and it was usually a step too far! He's an unbelievable character and what a phenomenal talent. He means the world to me.

Me and Gillan

We used to go to a local pub called the Ipswich Arms after home games on a Saturday. About seven or eight of the lads – me, Marrers, Warky, Russell and a few others – would have a couple of pints before going home for dinner around half past seven. Never any hassle from the fans, who were brilliant, and usually around six-fifteen one of them would deliver a recently arrived copy of the Green'Un newspaper to our table. If we'd won that afternoon there was usually a scramble to pick it up first and read the match report but, really, we'd be checking our individual marks out of ten to see who at the table got the bragging rights. If we'd lost that day then not so much. One particular evening we'd been joined by Ian Gillan, who had a gig in town that night, and it was my turn to order a round of drinks at the bar. I took the paper with me to read while waiting to be served but I didn't realise Marrers was already up there chatting to someone, so when I got to the bar I just put the Green'Un under my arm and joined the conversation. Next thing I know I could smell smoke, then I realised my bloody paper was on fire. Gillan had snuck behind me, taken out his lighter and lit the fucking newspaper! I rushed behind the bar and hastily threw the now-burning tabloid in the sink and doused it with water. Ian was absolutely crazy, didn't give a fuck, but he was also one of the boys. A really decent guy, very down to earth and you would never guess he was musical royalty, a millionaire rock star in one of the most popular bands in the world.

Terry Butcher

Ah yes. I've actually got a name for that little party trick. I call it the 'afterburn'. And that tomfoolery at the Ipswich Arms is just one of several methods of implementation. I've

actually done it quite a lot, and the first time I tried it was
with Rik Mayall and Stephen Fry and a couple of other guys.
It was closing time at a posh function we'd been invited to and
all the lights came on. I said, "Oh, what's that, last orders?"
And one of the members replied, "Oh, no, no. No last orders
here. That just means drink up and go." I told him I was
really thirsty. "Don't even try." I turned to Rik and Stephen,
"I think I've got a way of getting another drink." So I took
a copy of the Daily Telegraph from a nearby table, rolled it
up and twisted each end, then I unfastened my belt buckle
and dropped my trousers. Rik asked me what the hell I was
going to do. "Well, I'm going to stick this end up my bum
and I'll set fire to the other end and see how many laps of
the bar I can do before I singe my arse." The barman came
over rather quickly; "Would you like one more drink, sir?
Provided, of course, you pull your trousers up!" We all got
another drink and the 'afterburn' was born. I was renowned
for it in later years and I actually taught my daughter to do
the same thing. We had many a year of good fun late in the
evening while in some rather strange places.

Ian Gillan

* * *

"Fancy joining me at Knebworth?"

Deep Purple was the headline act in 1985, they'd just got
back together after more than a decade apart and were playing
a gig for the first time in eleven years. And Gillan was calling
to invite me. "Oh, and bring two or three of the boys if you
want – full hospitality backstage."

When the package arrived in the post it contained three
'Access All Areas' passes, one ticket and various coloured

wristbands. I was playing for Arsenal at the time but I knew immediately who I wanted to invite – two of my close pals from Ipswich, Terry Butcher and Russell Osman, who both loved their heavy rock. I gave the normal ticket, without additional perks or privileges, to the son of one of my neighbours, who was as big a fan of Ian Gillan as I was, and invited him to join us in the chauffeur-driven limousine taking us to the venue.

There was quite the buzz about Knebworth that year with Deep Purple finally back together and performing again, and the seventy-five thousand tickets had been snapped up quickly. Unfortunately the weather didn't play its part and it rained all day – it's subsequently been called one of the muddiest concerts of all time. Thankfully the band's marquee was quite something and the plentiful liquid available inside made us forget all about the plentiful other liquid outside, although I did sneak out to watch part of Meat Loaf's set.

We managed to spend ten minutes or so with Ian before he and the rest of the boys went to get ready before going on stage. I'd been to many of his gigs, and hung out backstage on many occasions, but this was the most excited I'd ever seen him. As previously mentioned, he'd pretty much confirmed that Deep Purple was never getting back together so for this concert to actually be happening was massive. He wasn't the only one with ridiculous levels of excitement.

With a few minutes to go until the boys were due on stage, me, Terry and Russell finished our umpteenth glass of Bell's whisky – if I didn't know better I'd think they were the official sponsors of Ian Gillan – and vacated the marquee to go and watch the eagerly-awaited concert. I led the way and found a decent spot at the side of the stage down near the front beside an eight-foot black container. But Lofty and Osman thought they could do better and proceeded to climb up said eight-foot black container – despite plentiful yellow and black tape warning them not to – and they perched themselves on top. "What a fucking view, Marrers!"

> We thought we'd found a very nice quiet area at the side of the stage to watch the concert, it seemed like a fantastic spot. Plenty of room for me and Terry to stretch out and enjoy ourselves…
>
> **Russell Osman**

The daft bastards were only sitting on top of the fireworks display for the end of the concert, with ten thousand pounds worth of explosives beneath them! Security were quickly on the scene telling them to 'get the fuck down immediately' and the pair of them sheepishly came and stood beside me.

* * *

Knebworth in Eighty-Five? What a day that was. I remember it well. I took a helicopter from Cranfield. It was just within the limits of being able to fly because the cloud was so low and it was absolutely pelting down, you could hear the rain on the roof of the helicopter. We flew over the massive crowd, and you could actually hear them cheering the chopper overhead, before it dropped us off in a field right behind the stage.

I had two locations backstage; a double-wide caravan as a dressing room and I'd also ordered a marquee which was stocked with a full bar and crates of champagne for my friends. Of course I was excited to be back together with all the boys, and playing such an iconic venue, but I was just as pleased to share the experience with my closest friends. I hadn't seen much of Marrers before Knebworth, it had been a good couple of years, and to catch up again was fantastic even though it was only for ten minutes or so before the show. I also used to love hanging out with Terry Butcher and Russell Osman – the three of them were quite the squad. It's so nice to have the guys around and I value their company a lot, you know, because we don't see a lot of each other being professionals in different lines of work. I'm around the world most of the time and they're on the road every second week playing football, but every now and again the opportunity arises to get together and you quickly pick up as smoothly as you left off. I love having my buddies at my shows, and I want them to have a great time, so it's important to make life as easy as possible for them when they get there. They should want for nothing. When you get invited to a show, and you get your tickets and turn up and nothing is done for you, then it's really just a corporate thing. And you might want to watch the show, that's great, you enjoy it, but if you're also going to see a mate then it's nice to be in the dressing room and have a drink and whatever after the show. These days I don't drink at all when I'm on the road. But that's just because I can't hack it anymore. All my energy is dissipated with a drink now which is why I do most of it lying down in advance!

I had no idea of that story about Butcher and Osman sitting on top of the fireworks, by the way, but that's brilliant! These things happen, you see. You can quickly become detached from reality – especially after a free bar in a backstage marquee – and you just move in this little bubble of happiness. I'm just surprised Mariner wasn't sat up there with them!

Ian Gillan

The concert was fantastic, despite the shitty weather, and Ian was absolutely amazing. I was twenty years old and had just signed for Plymouth Argyle when he left Deep Purple in 1973 and I'd never seen them live in concert. And I didn't think I ever would. So to get the chance to see them in person for the first time and watch one of my idols, now one of my best friends, perform once again in the group I grew up worshipping? Pretty much a perfect day. But not quite…

When we eventually traipsed through the mud and got back to the limousine around two o'clock in the morning – all of us well-oiled and covered in mud – we realised there were only three of us. And we came down with four. We were one short.

We'd lost the young lad, the son of one of Paul's neighbours. Easy done, innit?! We searched the VIP car park and, thankfully, Marrers soon spotted him. He'd fallen asleep beside a similar-looking limousine a few cars down, soaking wet and covered in mud with a pint glass sticking out of his pocket. We threw him in the back of our car, took him to mine and my wife put his jacket in the washing machine to get all the mud out of it. Unfortunately it was a brand new Barbour wax jacket and I think she washed all the waterproofing out of it. And parts of the now-smashed pint glass went in the machine as well which shredded part of his jacket. But it would take a hell of a lot more than that to spoil our Knebworth experience. What a day!

Russell Osman

* * *

Me and Gillan

The Rime of the Ancient Mariner is a poem in seven parts by Samuel Taylor Coleridge. This is Tales of the Ancient Mariner, also in seven parts, told by Ian Gillan, Micky Quinn and me. Enjoy...

Part I

It was near the end of Paul's first season at Portsmouth when he asked me after training one day if I wanted to go with him to London that night to see Ian Gillan record a special one-off show. A chauffeur-driven Rolls Royce and free drink there and back. I've made a lot of tough decisions in my life – this was not one of them.
Micky Quinn

Part II

Roger Glover and I were the presenters of the first ever pre-recorded MTV Europe programme, filmed in early 1987 and broadcast later that year as part of the channel's launch. The producers told us money was no object and we could have whatever we want; we can design the set, we can choose where to record the show, we can have as much alcohol as we want; in return they just wanted us to 'make it lively' and invite loads of friends to make up the audience. Do they have to be from the world of music, I asked. Nope, get who you want. So we hired De Lane Lea studios in Wembley – where Queen recorded demos in 1971 – and Paul was the first person I wanted on my guest list, which also included Adrian Edmondson, Rik Mayall, Kirsty MacColl and several other well-known celebrities.
Ian Gillan

Part III

We were in the green room beforehand with Kirsty and the drinks were flowing. Me and Quinny must have had at least two bottles of red wine each on top of what we'd had in the Rolls Royce on the way up. The instructions were pretty

clear; when Ian and Roger were on stage all we had to do was prop ourselves up on the nearby grand piano and look pretty. Surely we couldn't fuck that up?
Paul Mariner

Part IV

We set up a bar on set and put a few stools in front of the bar. Paul, unsurprisingly, was one of the first at the bar so I poured him a drink and we had a screaming contest. Don't be alarmed, that was a regular thing we did. During the recording, as well as hosting, Roger and I were also bartenders for our guests in the audience, serving drinks, real drinks, with real alcohol. And needless to say the show just deteriorated, or in my opinion improved, as it went along.
Ian Gillan

Part V

At the end of the recording Roger and Ian went over to mingle with a few other guests, so Marrers and me left our post at the grand piano and sat down at the makeshift bar and poured ourselves a couple of drinks. Next thing all hell broke loose.
Micky Quinn

Part VI

Rik Mayall and Adrian Edmondson — in character as Rick and Vyvyan from The Young Ones — decided to start throwing pot plants in our direction. Fuck that for a laugh. The pair of us — both three sheets to the wind after our earlier exploits — swiftly launched a few of the now-broken pot plants back to where they came from. No time to separate the aloe plants from the azaleas.
Paul Mariner

Part VII

I looked up to see what all the commotion was about and by this time

Me and Gillan

Rik and Ade had made their way over to the grand piano, a Bösendorfer probably worth about a quarter of a million, and they started playing some improvised song before totally losing their minds; the pair of them climbed on top of the piano and jumped up and down on it, smashing keys and causing untold damage before being chased out the building by security as they ran for their lives, all of this being filmed by the cameras which were still rolling even though the recording had finished. I mean, it was a brilliant show. A little anarchic, I would say, but I don't think anyone who was there that night will forget about it in a hurry.

Ian Gillan

I know the layout and rhyming of this particular attempt at poetry could do with a bit of work, but I don't think it's too bad for our first collective effort. By the way, me and Quinny eventually got back to Portsmouth about half past two in the morning. Not ideal when we had to be at training less than seven hours later, but we arrived back on the south coast with quite the story to tell the boys. The only problem being that none of them were likely to believe it!

* * *

"Two pints, please, love." Gillan was up to his old tricks and the poor waitress had no idea what to make of him. We were sitting beside each other in a hall during a meeting of the Ipswich Greyhounds Regiment – of which we were both members – and when the waitress delivered the drinks to our table she put one in front of me and the other in front of Ian. He waited until she was making her way back to the bar before proceeding to pour his beer over his head. The girl hadn't been gone more than five seconds when he shouted over to her for another pint. She looked at his empty glass then looked at him, soaked, her, bewildered, and made her way back to the bar, baffled. Gillan then grabbed the pint meant for me and poured that over his head as well. "Excuse me, love. Can my friend have another pint as well?" That prank happened quite a lot, usually when it was warm because it was a quick way for Ian to cool down. Maybe he just couldn't afford to buy a small portable fan??!

* * *

I grew my hair longer when I was younger in the vague hope that one day I'd be the lead singer of a heavy metal band, you know, just in case things didn't work out with the football. That would be the ideal excuse, but the main reason for growing it was simple – I've got a big nose and my ears are like the handles of the FA Cup so I tend to think I look a bit better with long hair, it's easier to try and hide things behind! I used to get ribbed all the time by my kids – they called it 'The Mullet' – but I tried to make the best of what I've got and that's what I thought suited me best at the time.

As well as Ian Gillan and Deep Purple, my two other favourite bands are AC/DC and Iron Maiden and I'm lucky enough to know some of the boys – Brian Johnson from AC/DC and Steve Harris and Nicko McBrain from Iron Maiden. I've lost count of the number of times I've seen both bands live. I do remember going to Italy in May 1998 with the promoter of Iron Maiden's *Virtual XI* album and watching the band play a couple of gigs over there. Then, a couple of months later, being given VIP access to Iron Maiden's concert in Phoenix, Arizona, and just sitting at the back of the Celebrity Theater on my own listening to Steve on bass guitar and Nicko on drums during their sound check before the doors opened to the general public. If you're a normal punter you very rarely get the chance to do things like that – to get in to places you wouldn't normally get in to. I knew how lucky I was and never took anything for granted.

* * *

One of the last ever games I played on British soil before heading over to live and work in America was a charity match in Plymouth. It was the only time I took to the football pitch while drunk-ish. "Marrers, it's Gillan. If I arrange for a private plane to take you to Plymouth City Airport would you come down and play in a charity match with me? I'm captaining one of the teams. Oh, and George Best will be on the aircraft with you."

I used to play pool quite regularly with George Best in the afternoons at a club called Rags in London; just the two of us in a small room set off the main bar. A pound a game was the usual bet with the idea that the winner would buy the drinks – a concept that did very little to improve the standard of play. George was very keen on 'double or quits' – an unnerving principal that can easily accelerate your losses at an exponential rate commensurate with your skills, or lack thereof. Our private game was soon discovered however and it was not unusual, by four-thirty, to see an architrave of members clinging to the roped and curtained entrance to our hideaway. On one particular day I won the first two games and George said, 'double or quits then, that'll be four', which meant a stake of four pounds for the third frame. Chinese whispers got the better of us though when the barman served us another round of drinks and delivered the gossip. Someone in the doorway had said, "They're playing for four grand!" Well that was it, George was cracking up and we decided to play along; so after three more losses George was standing to lose thirty-two grand – according to the congregation. There were oohs and aaahs with each missed pot. Every now and then we'd pause for a chat; the tension in the audience was unbearable. George won that game and so the score was quits, at which point we tossed a coin to see who'd be paying for the drinks, only to find that our modest tab had been settled by a member; thrilled by the excitement and impressed by the nonchalant way the players had competed for such high stakes.

Ian Gillan

I don't remember much about the flight down but I do remember the amount of alcohol available would probably trigger an excess baggage charge. The weight of those bottles was substantially less when we arrived at our destination. I was past my prime and George was well past his but anytime I had the chance to kick a ball about was a good day, especially with legendary figures from the sport and entertainment industry like George Best and Ian Gillan.

Marrers had played on my stage as my erstwhile bongos enthusiast and it was great to get the opportunity to (dis) grace his stage. We had a mixture of legendary footballers who all used to turn up just to kick a ball around, enjoy each other's company and raise lots of money for charity. Conviviality – that's what it was all about. That afternoon was one of many wonderful experiences I had away from the stage when crossing over into the world of football, and Paul was a constant in all of them.

Me and Gillan

I just want to tell you about my favourite football memory, if you'd kindly indulge me. It was in Plymouth, at Home Park, but I can't remember exactly if it was that particular day because Marrers and me played a few games there raising money for charity. A Sunday afternoon and a rare day off with my new wife and my drummer for company before I was supposed to be somewhere in Kent on the Monday. I had a couple of broken ribs following an incident in a cricket game the week before, and I also hurt my foot the night before in a drunk toe-wrestling competition following a gig in St. Austell, but it would take more than that to prevent me from playing. Except I hadn't told my wife about the game. She thought we were having a nice relaxing cross-country drive and maybe enjoying a traditional Sunday lunch in some quaint little pub in some quaint little village. "We're just going to stop off in Plymouth, I've got a football game to play and some friends to see," I told her. "You're not playing football, you've just busted two ribs!" I pretended to cave in and told her I wouldn't be taking part, I'd just sit in the stand and watch the game, but I had my boots in a plastic carrier bag in the boot of the car.

Once inside Home Park: "I'm just going down to the dressing room to see the boys." I'd managed to escape, and the plastic bag containing the boots was still tucked inside my jacket. Success! Normally I would play in goal but because of the broken ribs Marrers told me to play on the wing, "You'll be fine there, well out of the way." So I did. And I had the most wonderful memory because of that. I received the ball from the goalkeeper's throw and scampered along to the halfway line, at which point David Webb, ex-QPR and ex-Chelsea, attempted to violently assault me. But, having stood on the terracing enough watching his legendary sliding tackle back in the day, I somehow managed to flick the ball past him and hopped over his legs, continuing my scamper on up the line. "Pass the fucking ball!" Mariner had an idea this run wasn't going to last much longer. He was right. Another lunge in my direction attempting to 1) maim then 2) obtain possession and I'd had enough, so in sheer panic I got rid of the ball and kicked it as hard as I could aiming for somewhere near goal where Paul and a few other teammates were loitering. The cross turned into a shot and went over everyone's head into the far corner of the net. The celebrations were up there with Ipswich Town in 1978 after winning the FA Cup final. It was absolutely fantastic. The joy of sharing all that with people I respected and loved so much was my finest footballing memory. Paul came over to me just before the restart and, rather than congratulating me on the goal, complained that my cross was shit. "What the fuck was that? I was in acres of space in the box and you didn't even look for me!" he said, before breaking out that famous toothy grin of his and giving me another hug. There's no messing with Paul Mariner; he says what he thinks and he never thinks before he speaks. And that's what I love about him.

Ian Gillan

I'm so lucky to have such a fantastic bond with that man. Such a selfless soul. They don't make them like him anymore. I saw Ian in concert on many, many occasions and have so many wonderful memories; I could easily list my very own Top 40 but I'll settle for my top three…

3. Singing the chorus to 'Smoke on the Water' with Ian and

the Gillan band on stage at the Gaumont Theatre in Ipswich in 1982.

2. Being at the O2 in London in 2017 and Ian dedicating 'Smoke on the Water' to me as I watched from the side of the stage. That was unbelievable.

1. One of the best moments of my life was being at the side of the stage when Deep Purple came to the Pavilion in Boston in July 2007 and they dedicated 'Smoke on the Water' to me. When the boys started to play the famous opening riff, they all turned to the side, smiled and Ian gave me a thumbs up. I'll never forget that. A dream come true.

13

Kings Of Europe

"Oi, you two, fancy coming to see Madness tonight?" Butcher wanted some company at the gig so, reluctantly, me and Warky agreed to join him. Not my favourite kind of music but I loved spending time with the big man so I thought 'why not?' The place was packed and when they started to play Baggy Trousers, Terry told me to hold on to his waist because he was going to start a conga, "and Johnny, you hold on to Marrers". Within seconds Lofty was weaving in and out of people and the conga line got longer and longer. Imagine something like that happened these days – the footage would go viral before Suggs had even finished the bloody song. Afterwards Terry wanted a souvenir of the gig so he bought a Madness t-shirt with 'FUCK ART LET'S DANCE' emblazoned across the front. We were playing away in Europe a few days later and Terry thought it would be a good idea to wear the t-shirt under his tracksuit on the way to the airport. But he forgot to zip up the tracksuit top and took two or three steps onto the team bus before Bobby Robson went absolutely mental. "What the hell is THAT you're wearing?! Get back inside and get changed NOW or you're getting left behind."

Kings Of Europe

* * *

The seeds for European success at the start of the Eighties were sewn at the end of the Seventies. The addition of Arnold Mühren in August 1978 and Frans Thijssen in February 1979 allowed the gaffer to play a more possession-based style and it really suited my game. Injury meant I didn't get another chance to impress Barcelona again when we faced them over two legs in the European Cup Winners' Cup – they beat us on away goals and went on to win the trophy – but we ended the season well, winning ten of sixteen league games following the arrival of Frans in February and losing only once. I didn't play much during the last couple of months but still managed to end the campaign as the club's top scorer for the second year in a row.

You've heard of a game of two halves, well 1979-80 was a season of two halves for Ipswich Town. We were one of the favourites to challenge for the title before the campaign got underway – there weren't many better midfields in the league than Mühren, Thijssen and Wark – but eight defeats in our first twelve league games and a League Cup exit to Coventry City saw any hopes of challenging extinguished early doors.

I've looked back at our results from that season and I still don't think there was a specific turning point. For some reason things just took time to click, but once they did – we only lost two of our last thirty in the top flight – the momentum carried us to a third place finish, only seven points behind champions Liverpool. It's easy to look at specifics and say if we'd won four of the games that we lost at the beginning of the season then we would have won the league by one point, but it doesn't work like that. If your auntie had... you know the rest.

The bottom line is we proved we were one of the best teams in the country and it was up to us to take the momentum we'd built up from that fantastic run of results into the new season.

There's one specific match that season that I remember more fondly than any other, a certain six-nil victory against Manchester United at Portman Road at the beginning of March 1980. Confidence was high ahead of the game; we'd played ten times since the turn of the year and won nine of them, and had just drawn one-all away to champions-elect Liverpool the previous week for our fifteenth game without defeat, a club record. Okay, we might have been fortunate to escape from Anfield with a point after Coop saved Terry McDermott's late penalty (Frans Thijssen chucking mud at the penalty spot just as Terry was running up to take it was rather amusing), but the spot-kick should never have been awarded in the first place because Big Lofty was being fouled by Kenny Dalglish and not the other way round.

Then Manchester United came to town. They'd already beaten us at Old Trafford earlier in the season but that was when we were in a slump. Things were different now. Our good form had moved us up to third, just five points behind United in second who only trailed Liverpool on goal difference, and the television cameras were at Portman Road for the game of the weekend.

Sadly, John Wark's dad died that week so Warky was missing from the line-up. Kevin Beattie came in at left-back and Mick Mills pushed further forward into midfield. The day before the game we worked a bit in training on me dropping a little bit deeper, Bobby Robson's plan was that sometimes I'd play right up alongside Alan Brazil and other times I'd drop in beside Eric Gates to exploit the space – the gaffer felt that was the best way to stretch the United defence and pull them out of position.

Within two minutes we were ahead. Millsy picked up the

loose ball in midfield, his first time pass found Al in acres of space and the big man did the rest. The perfect start. There was something special about the atmosphere inside Portman Road that day; the crowd could smell blood and so could we. With the United defence all over the place we continued to pile forward looking for more goals. I had a couple of chances, Kevin Beattie headed just over from a corner and Big Al was also not far away from scoring.

Then came the second goal after twenty-four minutes. Beatts sent a long free-kick in my direction, I climbed above Stewart Houston and nodded it down to Al inside the box, he returned the favour and I scored from about ten yards. It wasn't the sweetest shot I'd ever hit but it had enough to beat Gary Bailey and the scoreline was a fairer reflection of our early dominance.

Three minutes later it was three. George Burley played the ball down the line for Eric Gates, he cut it back from the byline and after the ball wasn't properly cleared I smashed it into the roof of the net from about a yard out.

No more scoring in the first half, although we did somehow manage to miss three penalties! Gary Bailey saved the first one from Frans Thijssen after Arnold had been fouled. Then, after Jimmy Nicholl's attempted assault on me led to a stonewall spot-kick, Kevin Beattie's penalty was saved by the legs of Bailey. But the referee ordered a retake after noticing that the goalkeeper had moved too early. So Beatts stepped up again, and this time Gary Bailey held on to the ball!

That could easily have given United a shot in the arm, but Bobby told us at half-time to keep getting after them and putting pressure on their defence. 'Don't hold back, get in about them again straight from the whistle'. The gaffer also gave an impromptu live interview to ITV commentator Gerry Harrison at the beginning of the second half…

Gerry: *Bobby, did you reprimand them for missing the penalties or congratulate them on the way they're playing?*

Bobby: *No, we mustn't let the penalty situation upset us, Gerry. We would be very unprofessional if we did that. We've played absolutely splendidly, I'm delighted with the performance. We've disturbed their back four, Buchan has now come out of it and he's trying to mark Gates in midfield and, as a result, Mariner and Brazil have got all the space in the world in which to play. As long as we command the ball, as long as we make those runs in those front positions and as long as we ping the ball in for Brazil and Mariner and we support the ball we should see the game through. The penalty incident is one for the press, it's not for us.*

We picked up where we left off and within eight minutes of the second half Big Al had scored his second of the game. Frans played me in and when my shot was parried by Gary Bailey, Al was in the right place to follow up and make it four-nil.

With just under ten minutes remaining Frans made it five, capitalising on yet more ragged defending from United, then I wrapped up my hat-trick with time running out. A shocker of a pass from Steve Coppell went straight to Eric down the right. He beat his man then had the choice of shooting or squaring it across goal where myself and Big Al – both of us on a hat-trick – were lurking. As unselfish as ever, Gatesy played it over and I got there ahead of Al, sliding in for a simple tap-in with my right boot. My third hat-trick for Ipswich Town – West Ham in the league and Millwall in the FA Cup being the other two – and it would also be the last time I ever scored three in one game for The Blues.

* * *

Finishing third in 1979-80 meant another European campaign for Ipswich Town, our eighth in nine years and our sixth in the UEFA Cup since the club returned to Europe in 1973. Twice we'd reached the quarter-finals of a European competition – in the UEFA Cup in 1973-74 when we lost on penalties to Lokomotive Leipzig and in the Cup Winners' Cup in 1978-79 when Barcelona beat us on away goals – and there was a genuine feeling around the club that we could go even further this time because of the quality of players we had.

1st round – beat Aris Thessaloniki (Greece) 6-4 on aggregate (5-1 at home and 1-3 away)

Warky scored four of our five goals at Portman Road! Granted three of them were from the spot – the Greeks also scored a penalty – but Johnny took each one of them perfectly. I scored a nice volley to make it four-one, making amends after chipping over the bar from an easier chance just a few minutes earlier.

Bobby Robson had so many quality attributes that made him one of the best British managers this game has ever seen, and one of them was leaving no stone unturned. His attention to detail was second-to-none and Bobby is the most thorough coach I've ever worked for.

A perfect example of that was his preparation ahead of the second leg in Greece. The first leg was easy, we scored five and they lost their discipline, playing nearly an hour of the game with ten men. But he warned us ahead of the second leg that we were going in to the lion's den and to prepare for certain types of skullduggery that we might not have seen before. The gaffer knew it would be tough against the Greeks in their backyard and he named an unchanged line-up from the first leg. Bobby's message to us was simple – do not be complacent or take them for granted, even though we had a five-one lead from the game at Portman Road...

> I think anything can happen. They'll try to turn a game of football into a war with their tackling and intimidation and the way they can bring a football match down. I can't control what they can do, but I can control our attitude and the way we will behave and how we will play our game. Strict discipline is required, walking away from scenes, not getting involved in punches and reckless tackling which obviously will go on in the match over there. If we play a good, open, sporting but tough British game we'll get out of it alright and we should see them out of the competition.
>
> **Bobby Robson – courtesy of Aris History Channel on YouTube**

And Bobby was spot on to be cautious because we found ourselves three goals down with just over an hour of the second leg played, knowing if we conceded one more without scoring ourselves then we would have blown a five-one lead from the first leg and would be out of the UEFA Cup. Thankfully, Gatesy scored from the edge of the box with fifteen minutes remaining to calm our nerves, but that game in the Kleanthis Vikelidis Stadium in Thessaloniki served up a good lesson – very few two-legged ties in Europe are done and dusted after the first leg, especially when the return game is away from home.

2nd round – beat Bohemians Prague (Czechoslovakia) 3-2 on aggregate (3-0 at home and 0-2 away)
I played in the first leg at Portman Road but injury kept me out of the return leg in Czechoslovakia. Paul Cooper and Frans

Thijssen were also absent for the game over there. Warky was at it again in the home tie, scoring two more in the competition to take his tally to six goals in just three games. But the icing on the cake was provided by Kevin Beattie, who scored a proper arsehole-winder from a free-kick twenty yards out with five minutes to go. Thank fuck the net was there because that could have caused some serious damage to somebody watching behind the goal due to the speed the ball was travelling. I'd love to tell you about the return leg but I didn't even see the highlights from the game over there on television, in fact I'm not even sure if the game was televised. Based on the first leg, they were a reasonable enough side with one or two decent players – including Antonín Panenka of the famed penalty kick style – and while they were better than Aris, our opponents in the first round, they weren't up to our level.

3rd round – beat Widzew Łódź (Poland) 5-1 on aggregate (5-0 at home and 0-1 away)

For the third round in a row we played the first leg at home and for the third round in a row we recorded a comfortable victory at Portman Road. They travelled over along with a fair bit of hype, having already beaten Manchester United in the first round and Juventus in round two, and were captained by their star player, Zbigniew Boniek. From their pre-match comments the day before the game it seemed like they thought they could take a result with them back to Poland. Johnny Wark thought otherwise. Three more goals for one of Glasgow's finest – nine and counting – one from Big Al and Mariner scoring a diving header that Roy Race would have been proud of.

Once again Bobby Robson treated the return leg with full respect, as if the tie was still in the balance, and George

Burley in for the injured Mick Mills was the only change to the starting line-up from the first leg. The game over in Poland was a bit of a non-event, with the snow-covered brick-hard surface providing a challenge to stay upright, and they knew the tie was over after the first leg, choosing to rest Boniek rather than risk their star man in those dangerous conditions.

Quarter-final – beat Saint-Étienne 7-2 on aggregate (4-1 away and 3-1 at home)

The first time in the competition that season that we played away from home first. This was our biggest test so far, a proper test at Stade Geoffroy-Guichard, because they were quite the team with Michel Platini in midfield, Johnny Rep up front and Patrick Battiston in defence. We'll get to the first leg in a minute but not before a quick recap of what happened the day before the game and how some of the boys prepared for our biggest match of the season so far. This is one of Warky's favourite tales to tell on the after-dinner circuit, although I will say that we did go into one shop first, but only because we knew there were newspaper photographers waiting to get some pictures...

> After a light training session on the Tuesday morning Bobby Ferguson said to us, "Right lads, that's us done for the day. You can go and do some shopping if you want." Shopping?! Aye, whatever. The usual suspects – me, Mariner, Brazil, Cooper, Butcher, Osman and Kevin O'Callaghan – decided to find a little boozer instead and spent about four hours there. This was the day before the game remember. We got back to the hotel at teatime and the gaffer could smell the booze. "The seven of you are all fined a week's wages."
>
> **John Wark**

Kings Of Europe

When we rolled up to the stadium in the bus the place was absolutely packed and I wondered if we were late for kick-off! They hadn't lost there for ages and the gaffer decided to play Terry Butcher at left-back, Beattie and Osman in the middle, with specific instructions for Russell to keep tabs on Michel Platini. It wasn't quite a man-to-man marking job, because Platini loved to come short and Bobby didn't want Russell drawn out of position, but any time he came into our box Russell did a great job shadowing him and if he dropped deeper then Johnny Wark took care of him.

We went a goal down inside twenty minutes to Johnny Rep, who headed home, but what happened next was beyond our wildest dreams. I scored twice – a decent header to make it one-all and a tap-in for three-one – Arnold Mühren got the second, a peach from long range, and Warky scored the fourth with a header. We absolutely destroyed them, and seeing Big Butch bombing down that left flank remains one of my favourite football memories!

What a win, and the dressing room was buzzing after the game. Bobby sat us all down: "Right you seven I'll forget about the fine, but don't you dare go out drinking the day before a game ever again." And that was the first time the rest of our teammates found out we'd been out on the piss the day before!

Taking a four-one lead into the second leg at Portman Road, the message from the gaffer was exactly the same as taking a five-one lead to Greece, a three-nil lead to Czechoslovakia and a five-nil lead to Poland: reset the scoreboard and pretend the tie is level. With the talent they had at their disposal we knew they were capable of mounting a comeback, so Bobby didn't have to worry about complacency in this one.

After a cagey and goalless first half, Big Lofty lived up to his nickname two minutes into the second half, climbing high above one of their defenders and heading in the opener. They equalised ten minutes from time but we were never really in any danger and Warky soon restored our lead on the night from the penalty spot – eleven and counting – before I scored our third a minute from time. A shot from our flying left winger in the first leg, Terry Butcher, was saved by their keeper and I had the easiest of tasks to tap home from close range for my eleventh goal in twenty-one European matches for Ipswich. Not a bad return. And a bloody good result, beating them seven-two on aggregate and knocking out a side who would go on to win the French title a couple of months later was a real feather in our caps. But we decided against asking Bobby if we could go out for some beers the day before the away leg of the semi-final…

Semi-final – beat Cologne 2-0 on aggregate (1-0 at home and 1-0 away)

Cologne in the semi-finals was a great experience and they were a quality team. My England colleague, and good friend, Tony Woodcock played for them, they had a super young winger by the name of Pierre Littbarski and Harald Schumacher was their goalkeeper. It's ironic that we knocked out Patrick Battiston in the previous round because Schumacher would knock out Battiston the following year at the World Cup in Spain!

There was a nasty little undercurrent to this tie, not surprising I suppose given what was at stake, and things kicked off in the tunnel before the game at Portman Road. We were lined up side-by-side and a few of the Germans were having a go; a bit mouthy, 'we'll do this and we'll do that'. But we were also well fired up and I turned to Gerd Strack, a mountain of a man but also one of the mouthy ones, and said to him "You, five minutes, off"', then Butcher waded in and one or two scuffles broke out before things calmed down.

Within the first couple of minutes a cross was hung up to the far post and Strack was underneath it so I took my chance and went hurtling in. BANG. Down he went. I made sure to keep my eye on the ball throughout the challenge but I knew exactly what I was doing and the Germans were not happy. I may also have accidentally stood on the inside of his right knee as I came back down. No foul was given, a corner was awarded, but it wasn't taken until after Strack received some lengthy treatment. He eventually got back to his feet but, limping heavily, was soon replaced by Thomas Kroth, ironically after five minutes, just like I'd promised him. With ten minutes of the first half remaining Johnny Wark scored what turned out to be the only goal of the game and we had a lead to take to Germany for the second leg.

It was around this time when things were getting tough, trying to compete in three separate competitions – the league, the FA Cup and the UEFA Cup – and our squad simply wasn't big enough. Following the win over Cologne at Portman Road in the first leg we then lost three out of four games before going to Germany, including an FA Cup exit three days later at the hands of Manchester City in a game we were expected to win but Kevin Beattie broke his arm and, sadly, never played for the club again. We managed to beat title rivals Aston Villa two-one at their place but any good work done with that result was quickly undone by losing to Arsenal at home and then, two days later, suffering a shocker of a defeat at Norwich in the local derby. Not exactly ideal preparation from the second leg in Cologne, our third game in five days, and we travelled over without injured pair George Burley and Eric Gates. The squad was stretched really thin. And now we were taking on a team who'd beaten Barcelona four-nil at the Nou Camp earlier in the competition...

Fifty-five thousand people were crammed inside the Müngersdorfer Stadion for the return leg, the biggest crowd we'd played in front of in the UEFA Cup that season. Cologne had the better of the first half – Dieter Muller and Bernhard Cullmann, especially, should have done better with headers – but we had one or two chances of our own and at no stage did we just sit back and invite them on to us. I played a slightly more withdrawn role, just off Big Al, and in the hole, similar to where Gatesy would normally play, but Bobby didn't want the front men dropping too deep because he always wanted an out ball.

The gaffer was pleased with how we played in the opening forty-five minutes, and within twenty minutes of the second half he soon became delighted.

Frans Thijssen was fouled by Stephan Engels and the referee awarded us a free-kick midway inside the Cologne half, to the right of centre.

It was a simple free-kick routine, one we'd attempted many times before – Millsy looking to float one just inside the box for Big Terry to attack – but rarely did it work as well as this. Big Lofty is six-foot-four, the tallest player in our team, and you would think they'd at least try and mark him. But Terry got a free run and met the free-kick perfectly, heading home from twelve yards for a priceless away goal.

The funny thing is we'd been awarded a free-kick just a few minutes before the goal in exactly the same position following a very similar foul by Stephan Engels on Frans Thijssen – the same two players involved again – but on that occasion Arnold

Mühren tried to play it quickly to Thijssen and the ball went all the way through to Harald Schumacher.

We rode our luck at times in the second half, Engels hit the post just before we scored, but Terry's goal seemed to knock the stuffing out of the Germans who, by that stage, needed three. And we nearly scored a second goal but Warky couldn't quite redirect Millsy's mishit shot and the ball went over the bar. Just like the quarter-final, another fine result and performance away from home in Europe and we were through to the UEFA Cup final.

> I'm delighted. We've revived ourselves and played the game with a lot of spirit, just like we did after the [FA Cup] semi-final when we lost to Manchester City then went on to beat Aston Villa. Great defensive play, and on the break we got players up in good numbers and we deserved to win. I think the team have played absolutely splendidly here today.
>
> I knew that they would push people forward and they only left two at the back which suited Paul Mariner and Brazil because the ball into space was always on. We could always hit them and we had floods of people coming up to them and that's why on the break we played so well because we had lots of space.
>
> The direction to the players was that we had to try and score. We felt to always be on the threshold and defend and defend and defend was going to be a risk and we felt we could score here. We knew they would lose players coming through the midfield and if we could get in behind them we might punish them. And we did.
>
> **Bobby Robson, speaking post-match to BBC**
> **commentator John Motson**

UEFA Cup Final – beat AZ '67 5-4 on aggregate (3-0 at home and 2-4 away)

Going into the first leg of the UEFA Cup Final – our sixty-fourth game of the season – just four days after losing the league title, it was going to go one of two ways. We would either bounce back – just like we did at Villa after losing in the FA Cup semi-final and just like we did in Cologne after losing to Norwich – or it would be third time unlucky.

We may have been walking wounded – Frans Thijssen was struggling with a groin strain, Paul Cooper hurt his arm at Middlesbrough the previous weekend, Eric Gates had just recovered from a calf injury and my Achilles had started to flare up – but none of us wanted to miss such a big occasion.

Keeping the spine of the team intact that season was so important. Marrers up front, Warky in the middle, me at the back and Coop between the sticks. That meant even though replacements came in from time to time it didn't weaken the backbone too much. It's just a shame we didn't have a stronger squad to help us manage the fixture congestion, which became ridiculous especially after the Easter period. I'm very proud that I was able to play in every match – all sixty-six of them – that season but there were a few games that I probably shouldn't have played. But you sort of back yourself and you think, well, if it's just a pain threshold thing then that's not really a problem. And I think most of the Ipswich boys felt that way. Yes it was a long season, and we were all mentally exhausted, but we had to make sure we won something and if you can't push yourself to play in a UEFA Cup final then what's the point?

Russell Osman

Since competing in European competition for the first time, against Floriana in the European Cup in 1962, Ipswich Town had never lost at home in Europe. Played twenty-two, won twenty and drawn two. The likes of AC Milan, Real Madrid, Lazio and Barcelona (twice) had all lost at Portman Road, as had AZ'67 in round one of the European Cup Winners' Cup in 1979 when I scored in a two-nil, second leg win. Two years later and the Dutch side were back in Suffolk at our place, this time with a piece of silverware up for grabs over two legs instead of a place in the second round.

We were the favourites to win and had beaten better teams to reach the final but they were fresher, having played fewer games, and they'd just clinched the Dutch title the previous weekend. Ultimately we had better players than they did and, thankfully, we played like favourites in the first leg.

Wednesday 6th May, 1981

Ipswich Town 3-0 AZ'67

I've spoken to many referees over the years, predominantly when I was coaching, and some of the older generation used to say they didn't like to have to make big decisions – handing out red cards or awarding penalties – inside the opening few minutes of a big match. While it's true that players might get away with something at the start of a game when they would probably be punished for the same incident later on, I never understood how, in the eyes of some officials, the specific timing could determine the severity of the punishment. A foul is a foul regardless of when it happens.

So when Eric Gates, with less than two minutes on the clock, was brought down by Richard van der Meer inside the box it was as clear a penalty as you're likely to see. Not in the eyes of East German referee Adolf Prokop, though. Was he one of those officials who were scared to make a big decision early on? It certainly looked like it. A nonsense, regardless.

Privately, Bobby told us in his pre-match team talk that he was looking for us to score at least a couple of goals without conceding. "Let's take a good result with us to Amsterdam for the second leg." Bobby always used to try and identify the main weakness of our opponents – in this case AZ weren't great in the air when defending free-kicks or balls into the box – and we spent a bit more time than usual in training on trying to exploit that. And we nearly did when Big Lofty headed narrowly wide early on.

They offered very little in the first twenty minutes and most of the game was being played inside their half, but we were unable to capitalise on several corners. I didn't have too many looks at goal early on – they tried to surprise us by playing a high line and it took a little bit of time to work that out – but Gatesy was the one who'd come flying out the traps, he was everywhere, and the wee man had a shot saved by their keeper.

It seemed like it was only a matter of time before we opened the scoring, and that's exactly what happened. Arnold's smart header found Warky inside the box and although Jan Peters prevented Johnny from getting off a shot, my wee pal did really well and managed to redirect the ball across goal and it sat up nicely for me. I thought about taking it first time, but decided to let it bounce instead before driving it towards goal. It was heading for the back of the net until their captain, Hugo Hovenkamp, used his hand to prevent the ball crossing the line. Not even this referee could fuck this up. Penalty.

Warky had previously taken eleven spot-kicks that season. He'd been successful with all of them. So of course he scored and we had a thoroughly deserved lead with half an hour on the clock. It was also his thirty-fourth goal of the season, his thirteenth in the competition and meant he'd scored at least once in every round. He's my guy.

Wanting to keep the pressure on, because we knew they were there for the taking, we continued to push forward looking for a second goal and Frans Thijssen's effort wasn't too far away with five minutes left of the first half. Bobby was happy enough at the break – "keep doing what you're doing but just be mindful of any counter attacks" – and he was actually still doing a live television interview with commentator Gerry Harrison on ITV when Frans Thijssen scored our second goal just after half time, our Rolls-Royce of a Dutch midfielder nodding home from close range after his initial effort was only parried.

I think our biggest problem at that stage was complacency. They were offering very little but we had to be mindful there was still a second leg to play and more goals were needed. Gatesy came close once more with a shot from distance that went just over, but number three arrived ten minutes into the second half. Big Al was the provider – at times he was practically unplayable on the night – and he crossed it in from the left with the outside of his left boot. I made my favourite penalty box run, in front of the defender just before the ball came in, and managed to flick it beyond their goalkeeper for our third. It was also my sixth goal in ten games in the UEFA Cup that season, very pleasing, but still eighty-three goals fewer than Warky managed in the same period, or something like that!

The gaffer was pleased with the result, although he did say to us at full-time that he felt we perhaps took our foot off the pedal and should have scored more goals when we were dominant. But we would have settled for a three-nil scoreline before the game and it gave us a nice lead to take to Amsterdam for the second leg two weeks later.

> Before the match I would have settled for 2-0, but to win 3-0 is a bit of a bonus. In fact, they were lucky to get off with a 3-0 defeat because we tactically outwitted them. They never quite solved Eric Gates.
>
> **Bobby Robson**

Wednesday 20th May, 1981

AZ'67 4-2 Ipswich Town

With the title already lost, and no FA Cup final to prepare for, myself and Frans Thijssen were kept out of the last league game, at home to Southampton, to give us additional time to recover from injury, Frans with his ongoing groin problem and me with that bloody Achilles issue. A lot of people thought we had done enough in the first game to ensure the second leg would be a formality, but Bobby was at pains to stress that the tie was still very much alive because he'd twice been in charge of Ipswich when they lost after holding three-nil leads from the first leg at home – against FC Bruges in 1975 then again two years later when Barcelona beat us on penalties.

The second leg, however, was not the main topic of conversation when the gaffer spoke to the press in Amsterdam the day before the game.

> Bobby Robson yesterday underwent such a prolonged grilling from the British press about the prospects of his leaving Ipswich Town after 12 years that the second leg of the UEFA Cup final in Amsterdam tonight began to assume secondary importance. The Ipswich manager's future career has

become so closely connected in the public mind with both Manchester United and England in the post-Greenwood era that the task of defeating AZ 67 Alkmaar seems like a footnote. Fortunately nothing could be further from the truth as far as Robson is concerned. After a series of bitter domestic setbacks, Ipswich, who hold a 3-0 lead from the first leg, are just one game away from their first European trophy and consequently the manager is in no mood for a last minute upset. "The Dutch are capable of wiping out three goals in half an hour," said Robson, "so our minds mustn't wander for a moment, especially at the start of the match."

The Guardian newspaper, written by Robert Armstrong, Wednesday, 20th May, 1981

Our sixty-sixth and final game of a crazy season. With a bigger squad, and a bit more luck avoiding injuries, I'm convinced we would have travelled to Amsterdam looking to complete the treble. It wasn't to be, however, so we had to make sure we returned to Suffolk with the UEFA Cup for company. The build-up to the second leg was relatively problem-free; the only minor problem being eight of us getting stuck in the hotel lift on our way down to get the team bus! Thankfully the issue was rectified pretty quickly.

The support of more than seven thousand Ipswich Town supporters inside the Olympic Stadium was a huge help and they were in party mood when we emerged from the tunnel, although if you can't enjoy a few days away in Amsterdam then there's something wrong. And we gave them even more to enjoy inside four minutes. Gatesy swung in a corner from the left, Peter Arntz headed it partially clear but only as far as Frans Thijssen, who volleyed home beautifully from the edge of the box to give us the perfect start. An away goal, meaning they needed to score five, and a four-nil aggregate lead.

With absolutely nothing to lose they came at us and soon equalised, Kurt Welzl levelling the score on the night with seven minutes on the clock. A further goal from Johnny Metgod midway through the first half made things interesting, and really got their fans involved, but just after the half hour I flicked on a corner and Warky was there to do what he did so often, timing his run to perfection and planting the ball in the back of the net for his thirty-sixth goal of the season and his fourteenth of that UEFA Cup campaign, equalling José Altafini's long-standing scoring record in European competition. "Not bad for a defensive midfielder," as he's always keen to tell anyone who'll listen!

We conceded again five minutes before the break, meaning they led three-two on the night, but we were still ahead five-three on aggregate. At half-time, Bobby stressed to us to play smart, he knew they had nothing to lose and − needing three goals − would come at us right from the whistle to start the second half. And if we were to concede then don't panic. We were well prepared for the onslaught and played a little bit deeper in the second forty-five, happy to allow their defenders plenty of possession of the ball, then trying to deny them space as they came forward into our half. Paul Cooper made a couple of really good saves and with no change to the scoreline for the first twenty-minutes or so of the second period they were becoming increasingly frustrated.

AZ did manage to reduce the deficit even further when Jos Jonker scored a peach of a free-kick from way out with fifteen minutes remaining but they still needed to score twice. A subsequent header from Jonker that went wide was all they could muster and when the West German referee blew his whistle for full-time the celebrations started in earnest. I just remember being absolutely shattered at full-time, and I don't think I was the only one. We'd all put so much into the season, aches and pains everywhere, and it would have been a travesty if we had ended up with nothing. One last push in Amsterdam and thankfully we got the job done, a huge relief to win something but I still look back on 1980-81 as a what-might-have-been campaign.

> Marrers is spot on. Without a shadow of a doubt the UEFA Cup is the least we should have won. To this day I still can't believe we never won that league. We should have won the treble but we just didn't have a big enough squad, only carrying fifteen or sixteen players, and that's asking a hell of a lot of those players to play twenty more games than our title rivals Aston Villa. It was mainly because we had injuries towards the end of the season, players playing when they weren't really fit, but we were so close and not winning the title will stay with me for as long as I live.
>
> **John Wark**

When we went up to get our medals and lift the trophy I was nearer last than first in the line but I still managed to get a decent view of our Captain Fantastic – Mick Mills – raising the impressive silverware above his head. And who was standing right behind Millsy? Big Al, resplendent in a bloody white toweling bathrobe he'd brought with him from the hotel. If that bugger was any more laid back he'd be horizontal!

The celebrations were decent, if a tad muted, in the dressing room afterwards because we were all absolutely drained. It was almost a case of 'let's just go back to the hotel and just have a couple of beers'. Almost, but not quite. We were in Amsterdam, so there's no way that was happening, even if Big Al claims he didn't go out afterwards…

> Some of the lads were there with the wives and the single lads, of which I was one at the time, went out on our own. So the morning after contained a fair bit of 'what did YOU do last night?' Well, we were down in the red light district and the married lads went partying with their wives. The club hadn't organised anything so there was no big party back at the hotel – I think they were a bit apprehensive about doing something like that. I just remember it seemed like a long, long, long night.
>
> **Russell Osman**

* * *

Quizzed many years later on the events of that night, Paul was sparing with the details…

After winning the UEFA Cup in 1981 there are suggestions from some of your teammates that a good night was had by all in Amsterdam after the second leg of the Final. None of them, however, are prepared to elaborate. Care to enlighten us what you really got up to?
Just suppin'

Yeah, very good. So you were in Amsterdam and you were just supping ale after winning the UEFA Cup?
Yup

I don't believe you. Do these answers have anything to do

188

with the fact that you're currently sitting with two ladies in the room – your mum, Peggy, and your partner, Val?
Maybe

So it was just a quiet evening in Amsterdam with minimal celebrations?
Yup. An early night for us all…

* * *

A civic reception was held in Ipswich the following Sunday and while it was great to celebrate with around fifty thousand supporters, the biggest cheer of the day was reserved for the gaffer when Bobby Robson announced that he'd be remaining at the club for the following season. He confirmed he'd both rejected the chance to move to Sunderland and would not be applying for the role of Manchester United manager.

That decision said a lot about Bobby, and about the football club, and its owners, the Cobbold family. The gaffer could have earned significantly more money by going to Sunderland, and United are one of the biggest clubs in the world, but he'd helped create one big family at Ipswich Town over twelve or so years and wanted to build on our success. We knew he'd go on to bigger and better things elsewhere eventually, but at least his immediate future was sorted and that was a source of comfort for me and the rest of the players.

14

Hope And Glory

'Lord Nelson, Lord Beaverbrook, Sir Winston Churchill, Sir Anthony Eden, Clement Attlee, Henry Cooper, Lady Diana, vi har slått dem alle sammen, vi har slått dem alle sammen! (we have beaten them all, we have beaten them all!). Maggie Thatcher, can you hear me? Maggie Thatcher… your boys took a hell of a beating! Your boys took a hell of a beating!'

Bjørge Lillelien (radio commentator)

Yeah, about that…
Ron Greenwood did indeed survive as England manager after the disappointment of Euro 1980, leading the country into World Cup qualifying, but the two-one defeat in Oslo in September 1981 in our penultimate game put our chances of reaching the 1982 World Cup in jeopardy and left us having to rely on other results to qualify. And Ron was under pressure once again.

My son, Dan, lives in Norway – in Bodø, near the Arctic Circle – and a few years ago he put me in touch with the Ipswich Town supporters branch in Oslo. They wanted to have a chat about my time at Portman Road and also my international career, but the first thing they did when they called me was put on that bloody recording of the commentary! I can watch the highlights again now with a wry smile on my face, knowing we eventually qualified, but we certainly weren't smiling on the journey home. That was a rough Wednesday afternoon for us at the Ullevaal Stadium.

England had played Norway five times previously and scored twenty-four goals, conceding only twice, and we went into the game as hot favourites on the back of a decent three-one victory over eventual group winners Hungary in Budapest. With two games left to play in the group we knew that two wins – against Norway away and Hungary at home – would probably secure a top two finish and qualification for the World Cup in Spain. Woulda, coulda, shoulda.

> Arne Larsen Okland, into the area... finds Hallvar Thoresen... scores, scores, scores... Hallvar Thoresen, oh my God! It's two-one after forty minutes... after forty minutes... unbelievable... Ullevaal is boiling... Ullevaal is boiling. We are two-one up against England... four minutes left of the first half. It is unbelievable. England was one-nil up. Norway is now leading two-one. This is football history!!
>
> **Bjørge Lillelien**

I remember playing and scoring in the home game – our very first qualifier of the campaign – and we beat them four-nil at Wembley, but the press absolutely destroyed us the following day, calling it an unacceptable performance. I thought we played alright, yes we could have scored more goals against the team rated sixty-eighth in the world in 1981 (just behind St Vincent & Grenadines) however the campaign was off to a winning start and that's all most of us can ask for. But we certainly didn't expect to lose over there, especially after going a goal up inside fifteen minutes courtesy of Bryan Robson. They may be a decent side these days; back then, though, Norway was one of the whipping boys of international football. Even Norwegians considered the national team a bit of a joke. But the joke was on us.

The captain of Norway was Hallvar Thoresen, the man who scored their winning goal against us, and I knew Hallvar quite well from filming Escape to Victory with him the previous summer. I remember that bloody game like it was yesterday, just one of those that didn't go our way. Afterwards, Hallvar invited me out for a drink with him, 'and bring a couple of the boys if you'd like'. I asked Marrers and Millsy but neither of them were interested so it was just me and the captain of Norway out on the town after the match. He was treated like a Lord, people throwing champagne at him all night long, which I gratefully enjoyed having a glass of here or there to drown my sorrows. To hear the bloody commentator after-wards was farcical, but nobody expected them to win so I suppose the excitement was understandable. England was in a bit of a transitional period back then. And you know, with Kevin Keegan, he wasn't in his best form and was proba-bly being found out a little bit by a few people. Thankfully Marrers was coming into his own at international level and played in most games, but it wasn't to be for any of us that day. Just a forgettable afternoon for us all. At least the champagne was enjoyable.

Russell Osman

Thankfully group rivals Romania failed to win any of their last three games and that meant we faced already-qualified Hungary at Wembley needing just a draw to join them at the World Cup in Spain the following year.

* * *

We actually had Switzerland to thank for the final game against Hungary even being relevant. They came back from a goal down against Romania in Bucharest in October 1981 to win two-one, then drew nil-nil with the Romanians in Bern the week before we played the Hungarians. The qualification picture had completely changed from a few weeks earlier. Romania, Switzerland and Norway had completed their fixtures and England's fate was back in our own hands once again. Win and we were in. Draw and we would qualify on goal difference. Lose and we would stay at home, with Romania going to the World Cup instead despite only scoring five goals in eight qualifiers.

Wednesday 18th November, 1981
England 1-0 Hungary

Ticket sales for Wembley were sitting around the thirty thousand mark the week before the game, but that soon changed following the goalless draw between Switzerland and Romania and the remaining sixty-two thousand briefs were quickly snapped up ensuring a full house inside the Empire Stadium for the visit of Hungary. The capacity crowd also meant the match could be shown live on television, with BBC picking up the rights, and subsequent viewing figures showed that a third of England's population would be tuned in.

The pre-match warm-up reminded me of the FA Cup final

in 1978. Thousands already in the stadium with half an hour until kick-off, and that was the first time I heard them sing "If you all hate Scotland, clap your hands". I suppose it made a nice change from the Wembley crowd hating England around that time!

In fairness, we'd not really given them much to cheer about in the late Seventies and early Eighties.

It was twenty years since England had last qualified for the World Cup, getting there automatically in 1966 as hosts and in 1970 as holders. And it was one day short of an entire year since the last England player had scored at Wembley in a competitive fixture – that would have been me, against Switzerland in a two-one win, with a Roy of the Rovers-style header from Trevor Brooking's free-kick. The stakes couldn't be higher. The wait had gone on for too long. It was time to get back to where we believed we belonged.

1.Shilton, 2.Neal, 3.Mills, 4.Thompson, 5.Martin, 6.Robson,
7.Keegan (c), 8.Coppell, 9.Mariner, 10.Brooking, 11.McDermott

I was named in the starting line-up for the fourth consecutive World Cup qualifier, the only problem being I hadn't scored in any of the previous three. Thankfully I was playing well and scoring goals for Ipswich at the time so my confidence was high.

As far as the rest of the team selection was concerned it didn't contain too many surprises. Peter Shilton replaced Ray Clemence in the pipes – Ron Greenwood was forever chopping and changing between those two – while Alvin Martin made his competitive debut, coming in for Russell Osman from the team that lost the previous game in Norway and winning only his third cap alongside Phil Thompson in central defence. It was a blow to be without the injured pair of Trevor Francis and Glenn Hoddle – Trevor Brooking and Steve Coppell were chosen as their replacements.

The weather was miserable, it had rained for most of the day in London, but the atmosphere at kick-off was proper old-school Wembley, noisy and anticipatory.

Fifteen minutes gone and we were awarded a free-kick just to the right of centre about twenty yards inside the Hungary half. Terry McDermott floated it long towards myself and Alvin Martin at the far side of the penalty box, but the ball was in the air for what seemed like an eternity so Hungarian goalkeeper Ferenc Meszaros decided to come well off his line to try and collect. Knowing there wasn't enough pace on the ball to reach me I stood my ground, but the delivery was perfect for Alvin who beat the keeper to the jump and managed to head it back in the direction of Trevor Brooking, leaving Meszaros in no man's land. Trevor had scored twice in Hungary in the corre-sponding fixture five months previously, but this time he was slightly off-balance when attempting the shot from just inside the box. A good bad one as it turned out. As Alvin's header was rolling back towards Trevor, my instinct took over and I started running towards goal – a classic case of strikers always expecting the unexpected and being ready for all eventualities. With the ball coming towards me, I had a split-second to sort out my feet and managed to delay my stumble just enough to make contact with my right foot and guide it into the back of the net from about six yards out. Instinctive? Yes. Lucky? No.

We were well on top for the rest of the game, a few of the boys had decent chances to score and I also missed a couple of sitters. When the French referee blew his whistle for full-time the collective feeling was probably more relief than exaltation and the on-the-field celebrations were enjoyable but relatively low-key. I think that was mainly because we were so comfortable during the game and there were very few occasions when I felt the Hungarians were providing a goal threat. They'd already qualified for the World Cup and, to be honest, quite a few of them looked like they couldn't really give a toss and their minds were already thinking ahead to playing in Spain a few months later.

With a television audience of more than twenty million watching the action from Wembley it was one of the most-watched programmes on the BBC in 1981. English trio Jimmy Hill (hosting), Bobby Charlton and Lawrie McMenemy were understandably happy afterwards during the post-game chat in their studio in the stand, but former Arsenal and Scotland goalkeeper Bob Wilson was less praiseworthy for a certain England number nine...

> Paul Mariner got a goal there but really he should have scored three. I don't think anyone has scored a hat-trick or more for England since Malcolm Macdonald. He scored the first goal and dug it out from underneath him and then he missed the two easiest chances, early on in the first half when his control was awful and of course the header was even worse.
>
> **Bob Wilson on BBC television**

Harsh but fair from Bob. Saying the header in the second half was worse than awful is actually an accurate description. I still don't know how I didn't hit the target. Trevor Brooking's corner was chested down by Alvin Martin, Kevin Keegan – going away from goal – got in front of their keeper and managed to spin back round then cross it perfectly for me. And from six yards out, with the goalie on the deck and helpless, I headed wide of an open goal. No excuses, no complaining that the cross might have been slightly behind me, quite simply a header that was worse than awful and one that should have been buried in the back of the net.

It's funny looking back now at my post-match interview on television, and listening to my reply when asked whether or not the winning goal was lucky. "If you ask the twenty-two lads in the dressing room whether it was fortuitous or not I don't think they're too bothered. As long as it went in the net, that's all they're interested in," I said, in my rather-too-squeaky nasally tone. I should have gone into politics with that answer – give them something but say bugger all. I was in the right place at the right time and did the right thing. Who gives a fuck if it was lucky or not? It's all about the end result. You don't see diagrams on a golf scorecard, do you?

It was a good feeling to have the nation back on side and the headlines the following morning were the most positive we'd seen since England qualified for the European Championships in 1980.

"Don't look for heroes this morning – just salute them all" – Daily Express

"This morning it is indeed a land of hope and glory" – The Times

Plenty to look forward to, then, with qualification for the 1982 World Cup now secured and the opportunity to compete for a place in the England squad for the tournament had begun in earnest. And, of course, that's exactly when my injury problems began.

* * *

After scoring the winner for England against Hungary I played one more game for Ipswich, a two-nil defeat at Stoke, but then a stomach muscle injury kept me sidelined for six weeks. Looking back now, that was the start of my body breaking down. I was twenty-eight years old and, up to that point, had been relatively injury-free apart from that early leg break while playing for Chorley.

I made my comeback at the start of January 1982 in an FA Cup win at Birmingham City then, three days later, scored a couple of goals against the same opponents in the league at Portman Road. My stomach felt fine but I soon noticed a twinge, then a sharp pain stabbing the backs of my feet. I was starting to have problems with my Achilles. Nothing too severe at first, and I was able to keep playing thanks to a couple of cortisone injections to keep the inflammation under control, but then it flared up again after the four-nil league defeat at Liverpool at the start of February and I could hardly walk. Further analysis revealed that, partly because of the injections, the sheath had become stuck to the tendon and would not move. Surgery was required.

I was booked in for an operation on the eighteenth of February and my immediate thoughts turned to England's first group game at the World Cup in Spain, which was due to take place less than four months later. The operation at Addenbrooke's Hospital in Cambridge was carried out by Doctor David Dandy, a wonderful gentleman who went on to become the vice-president of the Royal College of Surgeons. It was a success but I was told the recovery period was going to be around eight weeks. It would have been a lot longer if I'd ruptured the tendon, so at least there was one positive to come out of the whole sorry saga.

After consultation with medical counterparts in the national team, the Ipswich Town doctor decided to send me to live in digs at Cambridge University for a month where I'd work with a track coach and a physio every single day to ensure I got the best rehab possible. They had me sprinting, they had me leaping into long-jump pits but, most importantly, the routine got me back on the road to full fitness. It bloody killed me, mind you, but it worked. Thank God I did it because in the following few months I was able to run faster, jump higher, I was as fit as a flea and played some of the best football of my career. Foolishly, later that year, like the idiot that I was, I decided I didn't need to continue the training regime any longer because I felt great. So I stopped, meaning my only source of daily exercise were the morning sessions at the football club. The additional time in the afternoon, instead of continuing with the extra training, was available for social activities again. That would come back to haunt me later in my career.

* * *

I knew I would have to be playing again by mid-April to have a chance of being named in the England squad so I initially targetted the home game against Manchester United on the twentieth of April for a potential comeback. With the rehab going very well I was back in light training at the beginning of April, a week or so ahead of schedule. I felt good and was able to step up the intensity each day.

Thinking – wrongly – the more games I was able to play for Ipswich the more chance I had of getting into the England squad I asked Bobby if he'd include me in the travelling party for the trip to face Spurs on the tenth of April. But after just a week back on the training pitch the gaffer said he didn't think I was ready to play in that match; he suggested the home game against West Ham the following midweek might be an option as long as I was straight up with him and "only tell me you're ready to play if you're actually ready to play".

I probably should have got another full week's training under my belt and looked at returning against Stoke City at home on the seventeenth, but I told Bobby I was good to go against West Ham. *'Ready or not. Here I come.'* The comeback was fine. I played the full ninety minutes against the Hammers, didn't score but suffered no after effects. After that I then played in seven of the last eight league matches, scoring against Stoke in my second game back and again at Brighton and Hove Albion on the seventh of May. The goal at Brighton was a big one for me because although I'd been back in the team for nearly a month I was still trying to find my feet and, more importantly, my sharpness. It was the only goal of the game and three days later Ron Greenwood named his provisional forty-man England squad for the World Cup. Thankfully my name was included as one of the forty.

Yes, I probably returned to action too soon but if football's a drug then I was suffering withdrawal symptoms. Could I have made more of an impact for Ipswich in those few games before the end of the season if I hadn't tried to come back as quick as I did? Probably. And if there hadn't have been a World Cup that summer then I wouldn't have rushed back to action and would have taken more time to ensure the recovery was complete, but every decision is easy after the event. The bottom line is this; I didn't want to miss out on going to Spain with England because – at the age of twenty-nine – I knew it was probably my last chance of playing on that stage. It's as simple as that.

* * *

Hope And Glory

The first warm-up game ahead of the World Cup was at home to the Netherlands towards the end of May, Ron Greenwood's final match at Wembley in charge of England. After failing to qualify in 1974 and 1978, the English public had waited a while to get behind our nation at a World Cup and there was a lovely buzz about the country in the build-up – an air of positivity for a change – and everywhere we went people would wish us good luck and have smiles on their faces. With the feel-good factor returned, more than sixty-nine thousand people turned up for the game against the Dutch and they saw a comfortable win. Tony Woodcock scored the first goal just after half-time and I scored the second five minutes later with a lovely finish into the top corner – possibly the best goal I scored for England – then jumped over the advertising boards and celebrated in front of the supporters. A nice way for Ron to bid farewell to the old Empire Stadium, although that didn't stop him pulling me up in the dressing room after the game and giving me a bollocking about my celebration, which he considered excessive: "We don't do that here, not when you're playing for England. You stay on the pitch and celebrate with your teammates." Okay, boss. Next up, a trip to Glasgow for my favourite fixture.

Back in the day there was no bigger game than England versus Scotland. Even now, every time I think of that fixture it always makes me smile. I played against the Scots three times – never at Wembley and always at Hampden by some strange quirk of fate – and I was on the winning side on each occasion. It was always the most pressurised fixture I was involved in; playing against a lot of lads who were either club teammates or you'd butted heads with them in opposition throughout the season. And this time not only would myself, Terry Butcher and Mick Mills be up against our Ipswich teammates George

Burley and Alan Brazil, but the Jocks had also qualified for the World Cup in Spain and they used to love nothing better than putting one over us. A game against England was their World Cup final. Hampden was an absolute bear pit for this game in the Home Championship and I absolutely loved it!

Of everything I did in football, all the matches I played and the goals I scored, you might be surprised to learn that playing against the Jocks in front of more than eighty thousand at Hampden in May 1982 is one of my best moments in the game. It was fantastic to score the only goal, don't get me wrong, but the whole occasion was one of the greatest days of my life. Ironic, when something that happened forty-eight hours previously was one of the greatest regrets of my life, but I'll tell you more about that shortly.

The bus ride to Hampden from the hotel, the inhospitable tartan-clad throng of humanity outside the ground, pipers and drummers resplendent and covering the whole field in perfect formation, the freshly cut grass of Hampden Park, immaculately painted white lines, Flower of Scotland being belted out, God Save the Queen being roundly jeered, then two hours of mayhem on the pitch involving two sets of players that care not a jot for each other once the white or the blue shirts are pulled over their heads. Unbelievable scenes, my kind of day out – proper rock and roll football – and an experience I will never forget. After all the problems I'd had with injuries in the previous few months, just to be out there was brilliant and I was able to enjoy every moment and take every single thing in – just as well because it would be the last time I played against Scotland. The excitement of a game against the Jocks in their back yard and a World Cup to look forward to in a couple of weeks; life was good.

Hope And Glory

When we were standing waiting for the anthems I had a little look down the line at the Scottish boys and one or two of their less experienced players looked edgy, certainly a fair bit more concerned than we were. The game might have been played in Glasgow but this was the [three] lion's den. Inexperience would not be tolerated. Terry Butcher was the only player in our starting line-up with less than twenty caps, but I would back Big Lofty even if it was his first battle so that certainly wasn't a concern.

We started the game well and had a couple of chances before the deadlock was broken inside fifteen minutes. Steve Coppell it was, I think, who delivered the corner, Bryan Robson headed it down, Terry Butcher flicked it on to the bar with George Burley on the goal line unable to reach it and I got there just ahead of goalkeeper Alan Rough to nod home from close range.

'...once again Paul Mariner is the Johnny-on-the-spot'

Barry Davies (BBC)

That was the only goal of the game — it was always sweet to beat the Jocks — and the third match in a row that I'd scored for England. Next up was a trip to Reykjavik and Helsinki for the last two warm-up games ahead of the World Cup. First of all, as promised, details of what happened on the Thursday night in Glasgow.

We travelled north on the Wednesday ahead of the game against Scotland and word quickly spread that the Rolling Stones were playing at the Glasgow Apollo the following evening. An invitation to attend was soon obtained and extended to all the England players. All the boys went, of course, except Paul fucking Mariner. As they were preparing to leave for the gig, Mick

Mills, my roommate, asked why I wasn't dressed and ready to go. "I'm staying here at the hotel, it's a big game on Saturday and I need to get ready for it so I'm not going to go". To this day I still have no idea why I turned down the invite – "I need to get ready for the game so I'm not going to go" must be up there with one of the worst excuses ever given. Later that night the lads came piling back to the hotel with all the stories of being backstage with Mick Jagger after the gig.

"Hey Mash – my nickname from Phil Thompson, who thought I looked like one of the characters in the TV show M*A*S*H – guess what? Jagger even apologised to us for wearing a Scotland top on stage during the concert!" One of many tales told that I didn't want to hear. At the time I didn't think much of missing the gig, I just blew it off, thinking I was doing the right thing by not going out less than forty-eight hours before a big game. But I soon realised how much of a fucking idiot I'd been for not going. I suppose the only *Satisfaction* I got that weekend was scoring the winning goal at Hampden...

* * *

With the squad just days away from being trimmed down from an initial forty players to the official number of twenty-two, Ron Greenwood split the group for games against Iceland and Finland – the so-called fringe guys played in Reykjavik, in what was initially classed as a 'B' international before being upgraded, and the rest of us were involved the following evening in Helsinki. Another England game – cap number twenty-one – and two more goals, taking my consecutive scoring streak to four games with five goals.

Thankfully I made the cut for England's official squad – I would have been well pissed off if I'd not been included, given the international goalscoring form I was in – and was handed the number eleven jersey for the World Cup in Spain, visually certainly an improvement on the number twenty jersey I wore at the Euros in Italy in 1980.

And here's me – in my late Sixties – only now realising that the phrase 'The rain in Spain falls mainly on the plane' isn't even a thing. Apparently the correct phrase, 'The rain in Spain stays mainly on the plain', is from a song in the musical *My Fair Lady*. You live and learn, even at my age. The point being there was no fucking rain in Spain when we got there ahead of the World Cup and it was bloody roasting.

I'd experienced pretty hot conditions at the Maracana in Rio in June 1977 as an unused member of the England squad that toured South America, a tour which was meant to be in preparation for the World Cup in Argentina a year later. But the stifling heat in Bilbao in Northern Spain was something entirely different. It had always been easy to use the conditions as an excuse for England's exit in certain previous World Cups, but this was heat that very few of the squad had ever experienced before.

Wednesday 16th June, 1982
Estadio San Mames, Bilbao – 5.15pm
England 3-1 France (Robson 2, Mariner – Soler)
Everyone knew what we would do apart from France. We used it a lot, the attacking long throw, we just didn't expect to get the chance to use it inside the first minute of the opening game. Steve Coppell would take, myself and Terry Butcher would come near post with Bryan Robson peeling off to the far post hoping for the flick-on. What happened? Coppell took it, Big Lofty flicked it on and Robbo – in acres of space not having

been picked up – scored from six yards out. Twenty-seven seconds gone and we're one-nil up.

What can I say about Robbo? We were joined at the hip for a long, long time with England. We were Pac-Man teammates, card school teammates, drinking teammates and having fun teammates. All the superlatives have been used to describe him as a player, but I would talk about Bryan Robson the man in a similar fashion. A very generous individual, an unbelievable player, and, when he wore the armband, a magnificent captain. You could not wish for a better leader on the field – the ultimate when it comes to leading by example.

That was one of two goals Robbo got that day inside a blisteringly hot cauldron in Bilbao – I always was in awe of his energy levels – and seven minutes from time I scored our third to complete a three-one win. Trevor Francis tried a shot which deflected off French defender Marius Tresor and fell perfectly for me seven or eight yards from goal. It was actually a pretty easy finish beyond goalkeeper Jean-Luc Ettori to extend my goals-in-consecutive-games-for-England streak to five and move level with my hero, Jimmy Greaves. That was a proud moment for me to equal Jimmy's record because it took a lot of hard work to get to that position, and eleven goals in twenty-two appearances for England up to that point was a very decent record. Unfortunately I was so tired I didn't really have much energy left to celebrate, settling for a simple both arms above the head while standing still. More than sufficient in the conditions.

France were a really good side who made the semi-finals that year so to beat them by three goals to one in the opening group game was impressive. Ron Greenwood's game plan worked, high-intensity pressing and denying their key men space and time to play, and it was very similar to when Ipswich won at St Etienne the year before when Roger Osborne kept Michel Platini quiet.

After the game Robbo and me were sitting in the dressing room and the pair of us were picked to do the drug tests. I lost eleven pounds that day and we were so drained of fluids, so dehydrated, that it took us a good few hours to produce a sample. The rest of the boys were long gone when we eventually managed to take a piss and we eventually got back to the hotel to celebrate with them over a couple of pints later on in the evening, rehydration of a different kind, but after the exertions of earlier in the day it certainly wasn't a late night for any of us.

A little side story for you – after the opening game against France a lot of us were all complaining about the jerseys we'd worn, those iconic Admiral shirts with the blue, red and white on the shoulders, because the thick material was anything but ideal to wear during a Spanish summer, never mind in the stifling heat and humidity of Bilbao. They were sweat-soaked before we'd even kicked a ball. So we asked the gaffer if we could get some jerseys made using Aertex fabric instead, the same material that Bobby Moore and the players wore at the World Cup in Mexico in 1970. It wasn't until we were in the hotel the morning after our final game of the tournament when we were getting packed up and ready to return home that we saw the lorry backing up with a delivery of special Admiral Aertek England tops. I wonder what ever happened to those shirts…

Sunday 20th June, 1982
Estadio San Mames, Bilbao – 5.15pm
England 2-0 Czechoslovakia (Francis, Barmoš own goal)

Speaking of pints, two second-half goals in three minutes was enough to see off the Czechs in our second group game and in the dressing room afterwards, Ron Greenwood, knowing most of the lads liked a drink, simply said 'replace fluids'. Next thing you know there's a scramble for the bus to get back to the hotel!

How we only scored twice in this game I'll never know. In fact Ron said afterwards that we should have been five goals up by half-time when, instead, it was nil-nil at the break. Trevor scored the first from close range after their keeper fumbled a corner. Then Jozef Barmoš put through his own net, diverting my cross intended for Trevor beyond his own goalie. My goals-in-consecutive-games-for-England streak was over, but two wins out of two for the boys and qualification for the next round secured with one game still to play.

Friday 25th June, 1982
Estadio San Mames, Bilbao – 5.15pm
England 1-0 Kuwait (Francis)
Shilton, Francis, Mariner, Francis. One-nil. A simple goal, really. Peter kicked it long to Trevor, he flicked it on to me, I back-heeled it to him and he did the rest. Another game when we should really have scored more goals, but a win's a win. I was just pissed off at the Colombian referee, Gilberto Aristizabal, who had a bloody annoying habit of getting in the way of play. Three times in the first half he failed to get out of the way in time, and on the fourth occasion, when I was trying to get on the end of a pass from Graham Rix, I found him wandering in front of me so I gave him a gentle push to get him the hell out of the way. The bastard booked me.

Three wins out of three, six points out of six, on to the second group stage, job done.

Hope And Glory

* * *

In addition to talent you also need a fair bit of luck to be successful at any major tournament. Two of our most experienced players, Kevin Keegan and Trevor Brooking, were never really fully fit and they only played once, both coming on in our final game against Spain. And our reward for winning Group Four, and securing a place in the second round, was a spot in Group B alongside West Germany and Spain. Meanwhile France, the runners-up, got to play Austria and Northern Ireland. There was absolutely no advantage given to initial group winners ahead of the second round. One of the other three-team groups contained Italy, Brazil and Argentina! It was a daft format, having a second group stage with only three teams after the initial groups contained four teams, and it came as no surprise to me to see it ditched for the World Cup in Mexico four years later.

Leaving Bilbao behind, we moved to a training camp in Navacerrada near Madrid ahead of games at the Santiago Bernabéu against the West Germans and the hosts, Spain.

I was lucky enough to be the lead commentator for ITV at the World Cup in 1982 and had the honour of covering all the England games. The players were in a jovial mood when I met up with them in Navacerrada, looking for any little nuggets ahead of the second round of fixtures, and I remember Paul being a great help with various tidbits. We sat down for ages and there wasn't a single question he wouldn't answer. But that was him, always helpful and jovial – he had that cheeky chappy nature and was impossible to dislike. I'd also spent a bit of time with the players in Bilbao during the first group stage and, as was the case in Navacerrada, Paul couldn't do enough to help. It was a wonderful tournament for me on a personal level and Paul Mariner played a big part in that. I'm very grateful to him for that.

Martin Tyler (television commentator)

Tuesday 29th June, 1982
Estadio Santiago Bernabéu, Madrid – 8.00pm
England 0-0 West Germany

Ron Greenwood decided to revert to the same starting line-up that beat France and Czechoslovakia which meant Glenn Hoddle, who'd started against Kuwait, found himself back on the bench. Once again Trevor Francis and myself led the line in a 4-4-2. It wasn't a must-win game but it was pretty much a must-not-lose.

The pre-match team talk focussed on being smart with the ball and choosing which moments to high press, the heat in Madrid meant that wasn't possible for ninety minutes. The West Germans played with a sweeper system – Uli Stielike behind three central defenders – and Ron wanted me in behind when possible to try and put pressure on Stielike and limit his time on the ball. The manager also spoke about their surprise opening defeat to Algeria and the changes they'd made since then – an extra man in midfield for the game against us with Pierre Littbarski now on the bench.

Unsurprisingly it was a cagey affair with chances few and far between in the heat and humidity of Madrid. We started better and they ended the game stronger, Karl-Heinz Rummenigge hitting the bar near the end. I partnered Tony Woodcock in attack for the last fifteen minutes after he came on for Trevor in a like-for-like change, Ron possibly preferring him to Glenn because of Tony's knowledge of the West German defenders he was used to playing against in the Bundesliga. But neither of us saw much of the ball in the last few minutes and the game ended all-square.

Monday 5th July, 1982
Estadio Santiago Bernabéu, Madrid – 9.00pm
England 0-0 Spain

Playing the World Cup hosts in their backyard in front of seventy-five thousand screaming fans – THAT is why you play football. The final game in the three-team group and with West Germany beating Spain two-one three days before we knew we had to beat the Spaniards by at least two goals to reach the semi-finals. Another hot and humid evening in the Spanish capital and just the one change to our starting line-up selected by Ron Greenwood; Steve Coppell was injured so Tony Woodcock came in for him and partnered me in attack with Trevor Francis dropping deeper and playing wider on the right. Meanwhile Kevin Keegan and Trevor Brooking joined Glenn Hoddle among the five substitutes.

A strange game, this one, with a lot of what I would call reasonable chances for both sides but not too many clear cut opportunities. With Tony Woodcock more through the middle I found myself playing a little bit wider, coming in from the right a fair bit in the first half. Shortly before the break a cross from Graham Rix, intended for Tony, went over him but I couldn't get my header on target coming in at the back post and it remained goalless at half-time.

The introduction of both Kevin Keegan and Trevor Brooking after sixty-four minutes – for Tony Woodcock and Graham Rix – gave us an immediate spark as Ron threw caution to the wind, and Trevor came close to opening the scoring within two minutes of coming on but his shot was saved. Then the chance of the match in the seventieth minute. By this stage I was now playing more on the left of our attack to accommodate the changes. I picked up the ball from Bryan Robson at the corner of their box, took four touches while moving back infield to create space then played a reverse pass back to Robbo who I saw was unmarked inside the area. He stopped the ball with his left, pushed it towards the goal line with his right then, with his left foot, hung up a beautiful cross for Kevin Keegan. Luis Arconada, their goalkeeper, had covered his near post to prevent Robbo initially taking a shot and was slow to get back across goal so the net was pretty much empty with the exception of one of their defenders on the line. Anything on target would surely have gone in, and given us the lead with twenty minutes still to play, but Kevin headed wide of the left post.

I picked him up and just said to him, "Come on, we'll get another chance." That's the way you've got to think as a striker, that another opportunity is just around the corner, because you'll quickly lose focus if your mind is preoccupied with a previous miss. Kevin was someone I really looked up to. He's one of the greatest guys you could wish to meet and he was always a big help to me when I was on England duty. I just wanted to return the favour, even though it was only helping him back to his feet. As it happens we didn't really get another chance, well nothing clear-cut, and the game finished scoreless. West Germany topped the group and went on to beat France on penalties in the semi-final before losing to Italy in the final.

'Robson... Mariner... and Robson, the flag has stayed down... KEEGAN... well the picture tells the story.'
I remember my commentary very clearly because I

was convinced that Kevin was going to score. Even Jack Charlton alongside me got up off his chair. Seeing Paul help his teammate back to his feet was just the sort of thing that he would do. It wasn't surprising because he's such a lovely person. Normally you'd hear things about players – he's a bit this or a bit that, he's lively in the bar or whatever – but Paul was sociable without being stupid. It was easy to be stupid back then but at that stage of his career he knew where the line was and he knew not to cross it. I think Bobby Robson at Ipswich had a lot to do with that, the perfect father figure, and I think Paul was very lucky to have him in his life. We've all heard the stories about Bobby getting names wrong, but Big Jack was with me in the commentary box throughout that tournament and he had Brian Rix playing on the left wing for England instead of Graham while Ray Wilkins was referred to as Ray Wilkinson on more than one occasion. The best one of all was the Spanish goalkeeper being called Anaconda instead of Arconada! It was all harmless fun, though, and Big Jack was just like Bobby, warm-hearted and very passionate about the game.

Martin Tyler

* * *

England's record at the 1982 World Cup – played five, won three, drawn two, lost none, scored six and conceded one. We didn't lose a game and only let in one goal but that still wasn't good enough. Yes the format was shit – with no advantage whatsoever for initial group winners – but we knew what we had to do in our last game against Spain and the bottom line is we didn't get the job done. That's on us. Were the tactics against the West Germans and the Spaniards in the second round of group games perhaps a bit too cautious? Maybe. However, we played for three hours in total against two opponents and failed to score. It's easy to question Ron Greenwood's tactics or team selections but he's not the one who couldn't put the ball in the back of the net. I started every game, scored once in the opener against France and provided a couple of assists. That's all. Could I have done more? If we're talking physically then no, I gave everything I had. My fitness was at a decent level thanks to the training programme from the guys at Cambridge so I was happy with that. Of course I could have been a bit sharper in front of goal but that's going down the road of examining things to the nth degree. Can't change things now.

Overall, I look back on the tournament with great joy and I think we gave a really good account of ourselves. There was camaraderie and togetherness among the lads and I have some incredible memories. The team spirit was fantastic, in spite of injuries to Kevin Keegan and Trevor Brooking, and if they'd both been fully fit I think we would have gone very close indeed to winning the whole thing. Kevin, especially, was a big loss. Even when he came on against Spain we saw the impact he was able to make. He may have been thirty-one but he'd won his second Ballon d'Or only three years previously and was still a fantastic player who had qualities that nobody else had. And that's what you need in the big matches, you need your game-changers to step up and we just didn't have that without him.

Having Kevin available for the first four games, I'm sure, would have made a massive difference – it's like taking Cristiano Ronaldo out of the Portugal team – but he was flying back to Germany for treatment on his back problem. The England staff initially tried to keep it all hush-hush – obviously as players we knew what was going on – but it wasn't long before the press and media found out what was going on and it became a pretty big story back home. But I wouldn't say it had any impact on us because we didn't pay much attention to any outside noise and the players were fully focussed on every game. Sadly, we just didn't have enough when it mattered to reach the last four.

That game against Spain was kind of the end of an era. It was the last time Kevin Keegan, Trevor Brooking and Mick Mills played for England while Ron Greenwood's time as manager was over and he'd be replaced by Bobby Robson. It was also the last tournament I would be involved in – I only played nine more times for my country – and just seven members of that particular England squad travelled to the World Cup in Mexico four years later after we missed out on qualifying for the European Championship in 1984.

The times they were a-changin'.

15

End of an Era

All good things must come to an end. Winning the UEFA Cup with Ipswich Town in 1981, following on from the FA Cup success in 1978, was the pinnacle of my club career. I would have loved nothing more than to be a league champion – something that escaped me throughout my career – but that ship sailed in 1980-81 when it was so close to docking in Ipswich Harbour. Speaking of which, just imagine the fun Gillan could have had with a league trophy as part of his nautical tomfoolery…

We finished second, again, in Division One the following season, 1981-82, when Liverpool came out on top after recovering from a slow start. Another case of what might have been, certainly for the first few months of the campaign. We were top of the league at the end of September, level on points with Manchester United but with two games in hand after the October games had taken place then, by the end of the year, in close pursuit of leaders Manchester City along with Southampton, Swansea City and United. January ended with Southampton on top – the fourth different team to lead the division at the end of the month – but we were only two points behind them and we had three games in hand. Then we hit the skids. Three wins in twelve games between the end of January and the middle of March – including a home defeat to Notts County and an embarrassing FA Cup exit at Shrewsbury Town – meant we were playing catch-up in the league and were out of all the cups (our UEFA Cup defence having come unstuck against Alex Ferguson's up-and-coming Aberdeen in the first round). Winning eleven of our last fifteen games ensured we finished second, four points behind Liverpool, but we were never really considered a title challenger following that poor run of form in February and March.

It wasn't the best season for me; a stomach muscle injury keeping me on the sidelines for six weeks at the end of 1981, then the Achilles injury – which first surfaced just before the UEFA Cup final against AZ – flared up again at the beginning of February following a heavy defeat at Liverpool. I'd been playing through the pain barrier thanks to cortisone injections before matches but the pain became excruciating after that loss at Anfield and I could hardly walk. That's when the surgery took place. I subsequently had both my Achilles operated on – probably because of the battering I used to take from defenders because back in those days they would go right through you and their only punishment would be a reprimand from the referee and a 'don't do it again' warning. So defenders just used to take it in turns to target opposition forwards.

I have some regrets as my career went on, mainly that I didn't learn from some of the more senior players when I first joined Ipswich and I think I lost focus a bit too often. I should've been a bit more grounded and I just wish that somebody would have pulled me up in my mid-twenties. It took a really bad injury to make me really knuckle down and become fully committed to rehab; I trained like a madman at Cambridge University with a track coach and a physio and that allowed me to get back into the groove. I was faster, I could jump higher and those guys helped me reach a fitness level I'd never achieved before. Then, inexplicably, I stopped following the bespoke training schedule; I felt great so I thought I didn't need to do it any longer when, of course, the routine was the exact reason why I was feeling great. I could have prolonged my career, no doubt about it. But no, I was a daft bastard who thought he knew best. I definitely should have done better looking after myself, and if I had done then who knows how much longer I could have played at the highest level?

It was during times like that when I wish I'd had some kind of personal mentor – someone in addition to Bobby because there was only so much he could do. Someone to bounce thoughts and ideas off. Someone to perhaps tell me no when I thought yes. Just someone to make me think about decision-making. I think of someone like Arsene Wenger and what he did for the likes of Tony Adams, Steve Bould, Lee Dixon and Nigel Winterburn. I wouldn't be surprised if he had a word with them at the start of his tenure at the club – "Look, I can extend your career but I need you to take more care of your body, don't drink as much and watch what you eat." I think that kind of guidance would have helped me prolong my career. In saying all that, who's to say I would have followed that advice!

* * *

I explained earlier in this book about my narcissistic tendencies and lack of humility as a younger footballer – 'when I was twenty-five I was at my worst. I didn't like myself back then or who I'd become. I just didn't know it at the time' – but thankfully those particular traits didn't hang around for too long and with maturity came a more thoughtful guy who was far more self-aware. Don't get me wrong I could still be a dick at times, and I retained an obstinate trait, but overall I was a better person.

Doing something you love in life means you're very lucky. Maybe I appreciated it more at the very start of my career because of where I came from, playing semi-pro while studying mechanical engineering and not turning professional until I was twenty. My previously-discussed attitude aside, I tried to enjoy every single day of my football career, even the shitty ones because a bad day as a footballer is probably still better than a good day in a normal job. I'm pretty sure every single supporter would want to swap places with us – taking the adulation of thousands after scoring a goal, making headlines in the news-papers (for the right reasons!), there's nothing like it. But when you love training as well, and enjoy having a laugh and a joke with the lads, it's extra special and is the best job in the world. I say job. It's not. It's a hobby you get paid for. I just wish I had shown a lot more humility in my mid-twenties but, thankfully, my narcissistic tendencies only lasted a year or so.

I get asked quite a lot if I'd rather be a top striker playing in modern day football and earning huge wages but I was quite happy with my lot. Of course the money the decent players get these days would be lovely, but at what cost? The camaraderie and team spirit we had back in the day was priceless. I'll be amazed if, in the future, football autobiographies of present day players will contain even half the number of funny or daft stories as most of the guys playing when I did. That's not their fault – in return for the riches, those in the public spotlight these days live their lives under a very intrusive microscope – and I certainly wouldn't want all that attention, even if it meant earning astronomical amounts of cash. Work hard, play hard was our motto. Going out to the pub after training isn't an option for professionals these days, but that was where a lot of our team bonding took place. I'm sure my style of play would still fit in to today's football but my lifestyle off the pitch wouldn't!

I was twenty-nine years old at the World Cup in 1982, feeling the best I'd ever felt in my career thanks to the help from the guys and girls at Cambridge, and with Bobby Robson taking over from Ron Greenwood as England boss my international outlook appeared decent – the press viewed me as England's main striker at that stage. And my relationship with journalists was a lot better than it had been four or five years previously, mainly due to my more refined and mature character...

Calming down, Mariner transformed into something of a media darling, with ghostwritten columns in the papers. When journalists would travel abroad, they'd often form their own teams to take on the football press corps from other nations. Mariner came in as a ringer for the English press side, says former Sunday Mirror editor Bob Harris, and "took that game as seriously as a regular game." He was also helpful to younger players, easy with advice, shunning the hazing rituals beloved of veteran athletes when rookies join the team.

From The Player by Jonathan Vankin, originally appearing in Metro: Silicon Valley's Weekly, July 1992

From a personal perspective 1982-83 was decent, and pretty much the opposite of the previous season. I stayed fit and had a good campaign – winning the Ipswich Town Player of the

End of an Era

Year award for the first time – and was made club captain in November 1982 after Mick Mills joined Southampton, but from a collective viewpoint our results were nowhere near as good as the previous year and we were far too inconsistent. Bobby Robson had been replaced by Bobby Ferguson, Arnold Mühren left for Manchester United, Big Al joined Spurs in March 1983 and we were only able to finish ninth in Division One, failing to qualify for Europe for only the second time in ten years.

The players were never privy to who was in the fray to replace Bobby Robson and become the new manager, and when the board decided to promote Bobby Ferguson there were a few raised eyebrows, including mine. Bobby [Ferguson] was a fantastic coach – I mean one of the best I've ever worked with – but we did clash a fair bit over various things. A lot of that was on me because as I got older I became a little bit more headstrong. I was still the first choice number nine for England – starting in each of Bobby Robson's first three games in charge – I'd scored for my country at the World Cup in the summer and I was now captain of Ipswich after Millsy left. Yes, I was sort of hanging on a little bit, but they were all still facts.

There's something about turning thirty. It's only a number, but when your age begins with a three instead of a two it just feels different. I'm sure it doesn't bother a lot of people, but I started to think more about my future – how long did I have left playing football at the top level, potential financial investments I might look to make and various other things, a lot of which were inconsequential. I hadn't scored for England for over a year: was I washed up, past my best, stupid things like that. Maybe I felt the need to think 'adult' thoughts because my age began with a three instead of a two, I don't know, but the additional thinking helped trigger a specific decision I still regret to this day...

* * *

I was earning a basic wage of around one thousand pounds per week at Ipswich Town plus appearance money and a goal bonus, a decent amount back then, but I was now thirty and the team was starting to break up. Bobby Robson was no longer in charge, Millsy had gone to Southampton and Big Al has joined Tottenham Hotspur while Arnold and Frans had moved on to Manchester United and Nottingham Forest respectively. It just wasn't the same. So I spoke to Warky and we came up with a plan.

> We put in a transfer request at Ipswich in the very same week. Players were getting sold and the club wasn't the force it was before. Marrers and me talked about things one weekend then I put in my request on the Monday and Marrers submitted his on the Thursday or something, so it made the headlines and we got a fair bit of stick from a lot of the fans. I wanted to try to win the league, luckily I went to Liverpool and I did. That's the reason I put my transfer request in.
>
> **John Wark**

Let me fill you in on the backstory to this. In early February 1984 – a couple of days after I'd scored in a three-one win over Coventry, our first league win that year – I went to Bobby Ferguson and asked him if I could stay at Ipswich Town for the rest of my career in return for a pay rise. "We'll go and we'll ask," he replied. I just wanted the club to pay me what I felt I was worth at that time. I'd not had a raise for a while so, after finding out that a number of the England players I played with on international duty were earning more than twice as much as me, I asked for an additional ten grand per year, a rise of less than two hundred quid a week. I felt that was a reasonable request. Then, as I got a little older, I could transition over to the coaching side at the club and work my wages down.

The response came back pretty quickly; 'there's no more money available'. The club had just finished constructing the Pioneer Stand and, clearly, the timing of the request wasn't the best. A bit like my response…

"WELL, FUCK IT, I'M LEAVING". This was the perfect case of opening my mouth without engaging my brain first. I didn't want to leave. Had no intention of doing so. I loved the club. But my alter ego, Mouthy Mariner, had other ideas and I was now in a rather awkward predicament. And I remember driving home that afternoon, thinking, 'Jesus Christ, what have I just done?' My mind was full of things like 'Who's going to come in for me?' and 'What sort of club will want a player who is nearly thirty-one?' By that stage of my career I'd already had surgery on my Achilles, which in those days could be quite a major injury, and my best days were probably behind me.

The more I thought about it the more I tried to convince myself I'd done the right thing – even though I hadn't – but the damage had already been done. So I handed in a transfer request. Fortunately Arsenal came in for me later that month and I got my move. But it remains a massive disappointment that I didn't spend the rest of my career with Ipswich Town, and that goal against Coventry City was the last one I ever scored for them. Mouthy Mariner had struck again.

With hindsight, I wish I had cooled my jets a bit. I should have sought some external advice first but it just wasn't around at the time and very few players had agents. So me and Warky tried to resolve the situation by forming a brains trust (!!). We thought we were being underpaid and both of us would have committed to the club long-term if the money was right, but neither of us got a wage increase so we both handed in transfer requests. Warky was twenty-six and in his prime – 'FUCK IT. I'M LEAVING' was not a required part of his strategy to force a move – and Ipswich knew they had a valuable commodity on their hands. Johnny joined Liverpool for 450 grand just a few weeks after Arsenal paid Ipswich 150 grand for me. I was thirty with a rather suspect Achilles so I suppose they got a good deal for me in comparison. On the surface it worked out really well for the pair of us, but I would have had no qualms about staying at Portman Road if the money was right. Even if Ipswich would have been willing to negotiate I'm sure we could have found a compromise. Lesson learned. Bull in a china shop never ends well.

* * *

I was away from my family a lot, especially during my time with Ipswich. I checked the European games I played away from home; in 1977-78 I was in Sweden and twice in Spain, in 1978-79 it was Holland and Austria, then Norway and Switzerland in 1979-80, and when we won the UEFA Cup in 1981 I played in Greece, Poland, France, Germany and Holland again for the final. Not to mention my last European game against Roma in Italy in 1982.

And when you factor in all the league games we played, plus the thirty-five times I represented England, including at a World Cup, that's a lot of travel, that's a lot of football and that's a lot of time away from home. Ipswich isn't exactly in the middle of England so we were also on the bus for a decent chunk of time for most away games.

I was fully focused on playing football, that was my entire life back then, and when I think about it now I don't actually have any friends from outside football from that era. None at all. As for my family, I'll always treasure the time I spent with the boys when they were growing up. Ali immersed herself in the education of the kids, home-schooling the boys until they were thirteen or fourteen, which I initially thought was a bit excessive, but I really appreciate it now and our lads have all turned out great. I'm so proud of George, Dan and Joe and the fantastic men they've become. There were, however, occasions when I may have been there physically for my loved ones but mentally I was elsewhere because I couldn't really get football off my mind. My work definitely put a massive strain on things at home.

* * *

Wednesday 16th November, 1983
Luxembourg 0-4 England

Thirty-three of my thirty-five England caps were won during my time with Ipswich Town. This was the game when I scored the last of thirteen goals for my country and also the final time representing England while playing for Ipswich. But was it actually my goal? Well it was certainly scruffy, to say the least, and I don't even know if it was legal. Sammy Lee, in the middle of the park, hung it up for me to attack but I honestly can't remember how much contact I made with the ball. It definitely hit an arm, maybe mine or maybe the defender, and that flummoxed their goalkeeper who didn't even bother making an attempt at a save. I didn't really know at the time what happened and I'm still no further closer to the truth several viewings later. It was either an own goal or the ball went in off my arm. Regardless, the Dutch referee allowed it to stand and I doubt anyone is going to try and take it off me now!

My last two England caps came when I played for Arsenal, following my 150 grand move from Ipswich in February 1984. Later that year, in my penultimate game for the national team, I was replaced by Mark Hateley – pretty much a changing of the guard – against East Germany at Wembley in a friendly at Wembley, incidentally the last time I ever played there. And my final appearance for England, a last hurrah, took place in May 1985 in Bucharest in a World Cup qualifier against a Romania side containing a twenty-year-old midfielder called Gheorghe Hagi. I played eighty-four minutes of the goalless draw before being replaced by a twenty-four-year-old who was winning his third cap. His name? Gary Lineker.

I think it was actually Chris Waddle a few minutes earlier who got to the byline and cut the ball back. I'd made a near-post run – I loved that near-post run, I think it changes so many things for other players – but my effort went just the wrong side of the post. And as I was splayed out on the ground, with mud all over my shirt, I turned my head to the right and saw Gary warming up just a few feet away from me. That's when I thought to myself that my time with England was up.

Overall, I look back on my international career with nothing but joy. Thirty-five caps for England, some people would say that's not too many, but for me it's thirty-five more than I thought I would get. I'm a humble type of a bloke, I was as proud as punch to play for my country and whenever I got called up I was absolutely elated.

16

Me and Charlie and Tony and Viv

Don Howe had done his homework. He knew all about Paul
Mariner from our time together with England but he just
wanted an Arsenal player's viewpoint about whether or not
Marrers would fit in at Highbury. I told Don he would be a
great addition; "If we've got a chance to get Paul then sign
him straight away."

Tony Woodcock

S o... Arsenal. A few months before my thirty-first birthday and I finally plucked up the courage (!!) to give the
London life a try, seven-and-a-half years after rejecting
the chance of a move to the East End with West Ham United.
Fortunately for me, Don Howe was the gaffer at Arsenal and
I'd known him for a long time having played for England when
he was one of the coaches. He knew me as a person and as a
player so when he asked me if I wanted to sign I simply told
him: "I'm there".

People talk about 'The Arsenal' being one of the biggest
clubs in the country and I'd never witnessed anything like it,
even in those days back in '84. The star quality, the constant

spotlight from the press, the attention to detail, Arsenal-Totttenham games, everything. It was properly ridiculous, but in a good way. We were treated like royalty. I made my debut at home to Aston Villa in February 1984 playing alongside Tony Woodcock and Charlie Nicholas. And a certain Brian Talbot was part of our midfield that day, just like he was when I made my debut for Ipswich back in 1976. We had a laugh about him asking me "Who the fucking hell are you?" after I'd just joined from Plymouth Argyle. As I'd done at Ipswich, I scored my first goal in my second game for my new club. This time it was a late winner at Nottingham Forest, getting on the end of a through ball from Paul Davis and nipping in ahead of goalkeeper Hans van Breukelen.

That entire day was a real eye-opener for me. I remember getting on the team bus in the morning and seeing these two older gentleman sitting up at the back. I didn't have a clue who they were so I asked around – it turned out they were chefs and would be providing food for the players on the bus, "And they'll be making us afternoon tea before we get to Nottingham," said Tony Woodcock. I loved Woody, and we always had loads of fun together on international duty with England, but I wasn't having it. "Okay, sense of humour with the new boy, very good, well done, tell me what really happens." Sure enough, two or three hours into the journey, the white tablecloths came out followed by "Mr Mariner, what would you care to have?" I was actually a little bit embarrassed and for the first time in my life I turned down food. That was until I saw the rest of the boys scoffing away – especially Woody – and I had to sheepishly approach one of the gentlemen and ask for a couple of sandwiches.

This was next level. At Ipswich we'd get a steak and kidney

pie each and would have to share a crate of Carlsberg on the way back from an away game, and that's if we were lucky. But there's more. When I got back on the bus after the match against Forest the individual tables were all set up with a selection of healthy food – prawn cocktail, melon, various fruit, you name it – and you could request whatever else you wanted as well. That was the way you were treated at Arsenal. From the minute you arrived in the morning to the moment you left, it was absolutely phenomenal.

Everything about the club was first class. Sometimes we would train at Highbury on a Friday and when we did you'd go through the front door and the apprentice who was assigned to each player would take your training gear to the kit man who would warm it, beautifully fold it, then the apprentice would return with the warm gear. Spoiled rotten we were.

I did really well early on at Arsenal and scored seven goals in the first fifteen games I played between February 1984 and the remainder of that season, including two against Ipswich at Highbury in a four-one win in just my fourth game. I was directly up against Big Lofty, Warky and Russell for the first time in my career. The three of them tried to wind me up but, of course, they knew it wouldn't work and Ipswich had no answer for the lethal trio of Mariner-Woodcock-Nicholas and all of us scored.

One of Paul's two goals was a powerful header at the Clock End. He rose majestically above his former teammates to get on the end of a cross before planting the ball in the back of the net beyond Paul Cooper. We were all pleased as punch for Marrers and went to go and celebrate with him. But he was offski. As he's landed, he's carried on running; he ran past the goalpost, got to the byline, ran around the corner flag, made his way towards the halfway line, around the flag there then back along the halfway line into the middle of the park. We just let him run, thinking he'll stop in a minute, and he did eventually – just standing there in the centre circle waiting for us to come to him. All hail the messiah!

Tony Woodcock

I felt very comfortable at Highbury. The gaffer was playing a system with Charlie Nicholas in the hole so it was very similar to my Ipswich days, with Gatesy playing the number ten role and Brazil and myself up front. At Arsenal it was Woody and me up top and Charlie Nic in behind. When Tony was anywhere near the goal he just came alive. His nickname was 'lash' because he loved to smash one. Charlie, meanwhile, had a great eye for a pass, and so much guile, top drawer, if he had another yard of pace he could have been one of the very best. And magnificently flamboyant. I have seen that young man wear varying degrees of exotic attire, let's put it that way, and I still love him to bits.

* * *

I'd been at Arsenal for about nine months before Marrers joined. Before that, the team was very defensive and even when I got there I felt the ball was just being launched over my head most of the time. We went through a bad spell and Terry Neill, the manager, eventually lost his job in December 1983 with us sitting twelfth in the table. Don Howe, who'd been a coach under Terry, took over as caretaker-manager. I used to talk to Don a fair bit anyway, but now he had far more clout so I explained that I wanted the ball played in to my feet more. I didn't think the old tactics played to my strengths and they weren't getting the best out of me. It was during one of our chats, in February 1984, when Don told me he was bringing in Paul Mariner from Ipswich Town and he wanted me to play just in behind Marrers and Tony Woodcock. After Ipswich, I think we were one of the first teams to formulate that specific triangular system. It was great for me; I enjoyed being a centre forward but I was probably more of a number ten than a number nine, and Paul not only helped me adapt to a slightly deeper role but his style of play really helped the new system flourish.

I remember this loud, very happy character coming in and he knew Tony Woodcock and Kenny Sansom from England get-togethers. When he was signing I was speaking to Woody and he said to me, "Oh, you'll love him, Jock". I had played against Paul previously in a testimonial when he was at Ipswich and I was at Celtic and we'd met up for beers after the game so it wasn't like we'd never crossed paths before. As soon as he walked in the room, it immediately put a smile on my face. I would say I'm a younger version of Marrers. I'm a happy guy. I like to get on with people although there can be a shyness within me. And I think even sometimes Paul probably had that when he was young, but you blast your way through it with a bit of bluster to get you over the line. He already knew a number of the guys so he got into it quite quickly. I loved him and as soon as he walked in the door I was all over him – Paul Mariner was basically an extension of me.

The three of us – Mariner, Woodcock and Nicholas – played together for the first time at home to Aston Villa and that was the start of a run of league games in which we only lost once in fourteen matches. I'd already scored a couple of goals against Spurs at White Hart Lane that season in a four-two win on Boxing Day, but had yet to experience playing a North London derby at Highbury. And neither had Marrers. He made such a difference in those types of games. Physically we were much stronger up front, with him right up there rather than me. A lot of the newspapers at that time claimed Spurs were a better team than us. Strange, because we'd already beaten them twice that season – at their place in both the League Cup and the league – and then we beat them at Highbury as well on that sunny April afternoon.

Glenn Hoddle was one of the finest talents I ever played against but he was injured and didn't play in that game. Defensively they had the likes of Graham Roberts and Paul Miller and I remember, particularly on that day, Marrers just wasn't having any of Roberts. Graham was seen by some as a bit of a bully boy, and I'm sure he thought of himself as a tough nut, but he was like a pussycat with Paul in that game. I'm not saying he was frightened of Marrers; he respected him but certainly didn't try as much of the physical stuff that he used to try on with me. Both Woody and me scored that day, but Paul played a big part as well with his strength and power keeping the Spurs defenders on their toes. There was a potency when the three of us played together. Me and Tony always linked up well, but Paul gave us a physicality and an honesty that the team hadn't had before. It worked really well for the last three or four months of that season, Marrers would be winding you up and slapping you on the back of the head in the dressing room before games, it was total non-stop motivational stuff. That's just the way he was. And that three-two win over Spurs was when I really learned what Paul Mariner was all about, and I remember the conversation we had after the game.

"You're not frightened of anything, are you?" I asked him.

"Nothing. Why should you be frightened? Just go after it."

That's just the type of player Paul was. In fact I can actually picture Paul Mariner as a modern day front man being Jürgen Klopp's perfect number nine at Liverpool – rock and roll football led by a rock and roll footballer. Imagine Marrers getting on the end of crosses from Trent Alexander-Arnold or Andy Robertson whipping them in from the other flank?! He'd score a minimum of twenty goals a season easily.

Charlie Nicholas

* * *

I played a lot of matches for Arsenal in 1984-85 – my first full season – but only scored seven goals in the league. I'd managed the same amount at the end of the previous campaign in just fifteen games and I definitely wasn't as sharp as I would have liked so I changed my game slightly. I was thirty-one and wasn't able to cover as much ground, but still had a good touch, was decent at hold-up play and linking with teammates so I tried to become more of a provider, more of an all-round striker as I got older.

I probably should have learned a lesson from Kevin Beattie, when Kevin came back too soon from surgery on his cartilage at Ipswich, but once I realised I was starting to get on a bit I tried to minimise the time I wasn't playing and maximise the time I was. Not a good idea when injuries are involved.

Although I made a full recovery from the first surgery I had on my Achilles, what I didn't realise at the time was that I was actually trying to balance my weight off elsewhere to compensate for the repaired Achilles and all that was doing was putting additional strain on other parts of my body.

As far as the football was concerned, finishing seventh in the First Division was disappointing, but not as disappointing as our record in the two cup competitions in 1984-85. A third round loss in the League Cup at Oxford United from the Second Division was bad, but nowhere near as embarrassing as our performance in the FA Cup. We needed a replay to get past Hereford United from the Fourth Division in round three before being drawn against York City from Division Three away from home in round four.

The game should never have been played, the pitch was icy and absolutely rock solid, but we were in cruise control at nil-nil with time running out. Take 'em back to Highbury and we'll give them an absolute spanking, just like we did with Hereford in the previous round when we beat them seven-two in the replay. It sounded simple, but then the roof caved in. As David O'Leary went over to try and prevent Martin Butler from getting a cross in, Steve Williams was jostling with Keith Houchen just outside the box. The nonsense continued inside the penalty area then Houchen went down after being tripped and the referee gave a penalty.

Most people remember Keith Houchen scoring that spectacular diving header in the 1987 FA Cup final for Coventry City against Tottenham Hotspur but I doubt as many will recall Keith scoring the spot-kick for York that knocked us out of the cup at Bootham Crescent. An absolute shitshow. Don went through us after the game, rightly so, and although he survived that result, it was probably the beginning of the end for him as Arsenal boss.

> ...where were the centre halves? Where was the organisation, the shape? It summed up my early months at the club I loved. York was a microcosm of the problem. I was the 'culprit' but I still don't think I was. The club was disjoined. The team all over the place.
>
> **Steve Williams –**
> **from www.arsenal.com in March 2016**

Don was a magnificent football coach and an excellent assistant manager, and a super guy, but I'm just not sure if being the main man was for him. There were a lot of egos to massage at Arsenal when I was there, including my own, and I'm not sure he quite knew exactly how to deal with us if/when any of us stepped out of line. He was a rigid disciplinarian – I do like that trait in a boss – but by God did we keep him on his toes. We had loads of characters in the squad who just lived life to the full. They trained as though it was their last session then, after training, made sure they enjoyed themselves to the fullest when going out on the town. I should know, I was part of the gang on many occasions.

When I moved to Arsenal I stayed in Winchmore Hill, close enough to central London if I wanted a night out but far enough away not to get into too much bother. I say that, but I did get roughed up a little bit at times when I went out on the town with Charlie Nicholas. When he was single I was usually his plus one. It may or may not have got messy once or twice, and when it did it was only right for me to repay the favour at the next possible opportunity...

I had been left out of the team at Arsenal by Don Howe. I loved Don, but he'd decided that my form wasn't up to speed and I'd been slacking. So one Tuesday after training he said something to Marrers and Pat Jennings. Now my best mates were Graham Rix and Kenny Sansom but Don knew I really looked up to Paul and Pat because they were two of the senior figures in the dressing room. Next thing, I'm in this room with Don, Paul and Pat. The gaffer said he didn't think I was behaving very well and, in his opinion, it was showing in my training. According to the boss I wasn't putting in the effort that he thought I should be putting in. Then Don explained why Marrers and Pat Jennings were in the room as well – because 'they're the two players who you really respect'. Paul and Pat played Good Cop, Bad Cop, one of them sticking up for me and the other having a pop at me. I got a telling off and was fined a week's wages. Pat left the room but Marrers stayed put and asked Don if he could have a word. I went to leave as well, but was told by Paul to stay put because it involved me.

Charlie Nicholas

"Gaffer," I said to Don. "Now that you've fined Jock a week's wages, and because you dropped him from the team last week, any chance the two of us can go down to Plymouth and play in a charity match tomorrow night?"

"But you're injured?!" Don replied.

I told the boss I was only planning to play for five or ten minutes, and explained it was important for us to be there to support the charity. Wednesday was our usual day off anyway. He looked confused, but not as confused as Charlie was! He grudgingly gave permission, but told me I had to have Charlie back in time for training at eleven o'clock on the Thursday morning. "And that's non-negotiable."

I didn't have a say in any of this by the way – he was basically kidnapping me because he wanted a drinking partner. Not that I would have complained if given the choice…

Charlie Nicholas

I arranged for a chauffeur-driven car to pick me up in Winchmore Hill then go and get Charlie at his flat in London. The pair of us in the back seat, feet up, with champagne flowing and off we toddled for some drinking in Devon with a wee bit of football thrown in.

The charity match may have broken the record for the most number of drunk people on a pitch at any one time, and it wasn't just footballers taking part. Ian Botham was playing and Viv Richards was also there.

The plan was to head straight back up to London after the game, but Beefy decided he wanted us to join him and Viv at a random party in a random house with a load of random others. Well that was an experience. Charlie, becoming increasingly concerned, enquired, "What the hell have you got me involved in here?" and made sure, for the umpteenth time, that I knew he had to be back at training in the morning nearly 250 miles away.

I got that big daft grin of his in return. He was injured and wasn't playing the following weekend so didn't have a care in the world. In fact, he was more concerned with trying to get me to sing with him, while Viv Richards was sitting in another corner of the room puffing on something rather interesting – I'd hazard a guess whatever it was wasn't made by Marlboro...

We ended up staying over following the random party at the random house, but couldn't make contact with our driver again until seven o'clock in the morning. I had to be at training by eleven o'clock. It was a four-and-a-half hour drive. Not happening. I told Paul that he'd got me into that mess so it was up to him to get me out of it, and I wanted him to phone Don Howe to explain what had happened.

"Sure, no problem!"

After breakfast he called Don's house phone, made light of the situation and explained that we'd been diverted – I still don't know what he meant by that – but the gaffer wasn't to worry because he was taking care of me and we'd be back in London later that day. Paul Mariner virtually kidnapped me for two days, but it's as good a two days as I had in my football career. A small price to pay for being left out the team again the following Saturday!

Charlie Nicholas

That's just one of many stories involving Charlie. My favourite involves some horses and plenty of chickens. I'll let Charlie fill you in...

One of the craziest experiences I had in football was with Marrers when we went to the horse racing at Newmarket. We'd been given the following day off: "Jock, come on, let's go, you're coming to stay with me and Ali in Newmarket and we're going to the racing." We ended up having a few bevvies at the racing with a few of the Ipswich boys; big Terry Butcher, Mick Mills and Alan Brazil and you could tell straight away that Paul was loved by so many people. At night we went back to his place. I had no idea it was a bloody farm with chickens running amok and animals everywhere. The bugger got me up at half past five in the morning feeding the fucking chickens! I couldn't believe what I was doing. I'm thinking to myself, 'I'm a bloody superstar in London yet here I am at half five in a coup surrounded by poultry – certainly not the kind of fouls I was used to!'

At no point the previous day did he tell me this was part of the plan. He didn't ask me. No warning, nothing. He just burst into the room, opened the curtains and literally dragged me out of bed and threw me in this thing with a bucket of feed. It was the weirdest experience, but I've loved him ever since that. I wouldn't say he was a father figure to me, but he was someone, both as a person and as a footballer, that I can honestly put my hand on my heart and say is one of the best. There's probably four or five people in everyone's life that tick all the boxes and Marrers is one of my five. I could never, ever understand anyone having a bad word to say about him if they ever played with him, trained with him or were just around him. He's that good a guy.

Charlie Nicholas

One of the most embarrassing things that happened during my time with Arsenal took place following a proper major league drinking session. I'll get to the specifics of what happened in the wee small hours shortly but the backstory needs to be told first. Our all-day 'sesh' got underway around one o'clock when the players arranged to meet up in Central London for a liquid lunch before going out on the town. While I can't recall the exact name of the establishment, I do remember it was also hosting a promotional event for Hofmeister Lager at the same time when we were in there. Now back in the mid-Eighties there was a television commercial for Hofmeister featuring 'George the Bear' in which a furry mascot wearing a pork pie hat and a shiny yellow jacket urged drinkers looking 'for great lager' to 'follow the bear'. In this particular instance, and having tasted the product, I'm not sure the word 'great' was absolutely necessary in said tag-line. (Thankfully it was rebranded in the mid-2010s with a new recipe and a much better taste…)

Anyway, following the conclusion of the promo event 'George' removed his head and placed it on a chair at an adjoining table while the rest of the bear went to the bar to order a drink. My eyes lit up and, after waiting a few seconds to check the coast was clear, I told Viv Anderson, who was sitting beside me at lunch, to 'follow me'. I stood up, swiped the furry head and made a beeline for the front door, with a bemused Viv not far behind.

The bugger just handed me the keys to his Porsche 911 cabriolet and told me to drive. As we jumped in the car I tried to ask him what the hell was going on but AC/DC started blaring from the speakers when I turned the engine on and with the bloody bear's head on, anything he tried to say was muffled. So I just drove around central London for ten minutes while he waved at confused strangers on the pavement. When we stopped at a red light a bus pulled up alongside us so Marrers, or was it George, stood up and started dancing in the car, much to my embarrassment but to the delight of the passengers in the bus. I don't ever recall a dull moment when out with Paul!

Viv Anderson

...sprint away after scoring a goal in the first leg of the UEFA Cup final at Portman Road that made it 3-0 ahead of the return match in the Netherlands

Lifting the silverware with John Wark after our 5-4 aggregate victory over AZ 67 Alkmaar in the Olympic Stadium in Amsterdam

Climbing the football ladder meant I was able to afford a better car than the Mini 850 that blew its head gasket when I first drove to Ipswich! Here I am with my shiny sports car in 1981

Locked in an aerial battle against Wolves at Portman Road. Bobby said I had 'vision in the air'

My instinctive finish in the decisive game against Hungary (below) secured England's place at the 1982 World Cup in Spain – relief all round among the players and a noisy Wembley crowd. (Above) I scored again in our first World Cup warm-up game against the Netherlands

WEMBLEY STADIUM

Association
nal Match
p Qualifying)
GLAND
ERSUS
NGARY
NOV. 18, 1981
OFF 7.45 p.m.
ADVISED TO TAKE UP
SITION BY 7.15 p.m.

No ticket genuine unless it carries a Lion's Head watermark below

TURNSTILES
ENTRANCE B

22
EAST
UPPER
STANDING
ENCLOSURE

CHAIRMAN
WEMBLEY STADIUM LTD

DING   £3.50
AINED   ISSUED SUBJECT TO THE CONDITIONS ON BACK

1376

One of the moments England fans always remember me for. Socks rolled down in a blisteringly hot cauldron in Bilbao after scoring the third goal in a 3-1 World Cup win over France. This was the only celebration I had the energy to do!

In action against Spain in the second group stage and (below) playing the waiting game with the Spanish police during a break in play

With strike partner Tony Woodcock and Ray Clemence outside the team hotel

In action for Arsenal. Signing for the Gunners at the age of 30 was an eye-opener. We were constantly under the press spotlight

Joining Portsmouth in 1986 – we had some strong characters at the club

'Alright Jim?' It was always fun being assistant to Stevie Nicol at New England Revolution

A spell in the dugout at Plymouth Argyle saw me mixing with big names like Steve Ogrizovic, Gordon Strachan, Neil Warnock and Roy Keane

enjoyed my time at Toronto FC and it opened up doors to the next chapter in my life

With book writer and close friend Mark Donaldson, my commentary partner here for EURO 2016 on ESPN

I loved working in the media, being paid to talk about the game I love!

(Far left) a recent snap with my good pal Warky. (Left) trying out an old England cap for size and (below) with my mum Peggy – always by my side

(Left) with Val in Bermuda in 2019 and (above) rock and roll and football – the perfect combination for a good life

Me and Charlie and Tony and Viv

After returning George's head to its rightful owner, and apologising for the inconvenience, the liquid lunch continued and soon day turned into night which then turned into early morning. I was absolutely plastered by this time so Viv and the rest of the lads threw me in a cab, sent me back to Winchmore Hill and I then fell out of the taxi outside the house. Could not stand up. Tried but failed repeatedly. So I crawled up the pathway. How I got through the front door I do not know. My wife and the kids were upstairs in bed so I chose to fall asleep on the sofa downstairs beside the dog, Moss, my faithful border collie who I loved dearly. Now you know when you've had a little bit too much to drink and the pit of your stomach comes up along with everything else, a proper toxic barf? Well here comes the embarrassing bit. I proceeded to be sick all over the fucking dog! Poor old Moss had an orangey/yellowy stain on his coat which was there for weeks. When I woke up in the morning the dog was gone. And so was the wife. The kids were nowhere to be seen either. It transpired they'd all fucked off back to Suffolk, leaving a rather fragile me to contemplate how to tidy up this pool of fragrant, toxic mess. I'd love to say I learned a lesson that night, however…

* * *

One word to describe Marrers? Loud. But surely everybody says that. I don't know anyone who's got a bad word to say about him, though. As soon as you mention the name Paul Mariner to anyone: 'Oh what a great lad he is'. Always friendly, always jovial, he gives you a big massive bear hug as soon as you see him and that laugh, always that laugh. What a man. He could be a rascal, but most of the time he was just daft. The pair of us were playing for Arsenal against Leicester City at Highbury in April 1984 and in the first few minutes – when the ball was up the other end of the pitch – he came and stood beside me, knowing the two Leicester centre-backs would swiftly follow. Even though I was standing right beside him, he shouted, "These two idiots are going to be following us for ninety minutes – fancy going for a wander?" Marrers then proceeded to mimic Max Wall's silly walk. The poor Leicester boys didn't know what to make of it.

Then, later in that game, in the second half I think it was, someone caught him in the face and he had to go off for treatment. His lip was cut and there was also damage to his eye, or something like that, and he looked like he was in the wars a bit. After a few butterfly stitches he came storming back on to the field and ran straight towards me. "Right, which one was it?" I told him I didn't know exactly who'd done it, all I knew was that it was one of the central defenders. He bided his time then, with the ball in the arms of Pat Jennings, Marrers put his hand in the air then nodded to our goalkeeper indicating he wanted the ball played up to him. As requested, Pat launched a clearance up the field towards Paul who proceeded to absolutely rattle the centre-half, fully, and the guy's on the floor in a heap. The defender, holding his face, looked up from the deck and said, "Fucking 'ell, Mariner, it wasn't me, it was him," then pointed to his mate! Paul then apologised profusely to the stricken innocent victim, helped him back to his feet then shouted across to the other guy, "You've got away with this one, you have." It might have been an aggressive moment at first but it wasn't going to be dragged on. Marrers had got his own back, or at least he thought he had, before realising he'd targetted the wrong player, and then it was a bit of a laugh all round with the situation easily defused by some Paul Mariner humour.

Speaking of which, there are plenty of examples of that, including the day he scored his first goal for Arsenal, against Nottingham Forest at the City Ground. On the pitch before the game, the pair of us standing next to each other waiting for the Forest players, Marrers started singing the Robin Hood theme song that the home team ran out to and began dancing away to the music without a care in the world. He's as daft as a brush.

And going back a couple of years, to October 1982, during Paul's time at Ipswich, I'd just joined Arsenal from Cologne that summer and we were playing against each other at Portman Road. It was the first time I'd seen Marrers in a few months since we were together as part of the England squad at the World Cup in Spain that summer. As our coach pulls in to Portman Road and we get off the bus to go inside I hear this loud voice. There's a little window to the Ipswich changing room. And of course Paul has stuck his head out. I could see he was with Terry Butcher and Russell Osman, who I also knew from England duty and we all got on well. So he shouted through the window, "See you out there, Woody," then Butcher added, "We'll be coming for you," before Osman chimed in with "Better watch out," and daft stuff like that.

Forty-five minutes or so later we were out on the pitch warming up when Paul, Russell and Terry signaled me over to them. "What's the matter?" I asked. "Hold your hand out," said Marrers, so I put my hand out and he then reached into the groin area of his shorts and gave me a piece of pork pie. The three of them then ran off, sniggering. There's less than twenty minutes to kick-off and I'm in the middle of the pitch at Portman Road holding part of a bloody pork pie in my hand that had spent goodness knows how long stuffed inside Paul Mariner's underpants. Now I love my food but I drew the line at this. Watched by the three of them, I took the offending item over to the sidelines and one of their staff thankfully took it from me, I think it might have been the kit man, and the boys told me later that he ended up eating the pork pie!!

They weren't finished yet, by the way. About ten minutes before kick-off there was a knock on the Arsenal dressing room. One of our guys opened the door: "This is for Mr. Woodcock." It was a box containing a pair of large shin guards and a note: 'You'll be needing these today. Love Mariner, Butcher and Osman xx'. Very amusing. We beat Ipswich one-nil that day and guess who scored the winning goal?

Tony Woodcock

* * *

I was playing in Glenn Hoddle's testimonial at the beginning of August 1985 when Chris Hughton accidentally stood on my Achilles tendon in the first twenty minutes. I had to go to hospital to get it fixed and the doctors were initially concerned it might be gangrenous, but they did a remarkable job to patch me up and I was back on the pitch by the end of the month, albeit in a rather different position from which I was used to playing.

The league game against Luton Town at Kenilworth Road was only five minutes old when David O'Leary had to go off injured after being caught accidentally by one of Mick

Harford's pointy elbows. I was sat on the bench and Don Howe turned to me and told me to get ready because I was going on. We didn't have a replacement centre-half on the bench. "And you're playing alongside Tommy Caton at the back," said Don. Well fuck me, not what I expected to hear. I've even been asked by some Arsenal fans about playing in central defence but for the life of me I don't know why the boss did it − I can only assume it was to try and counter the aerial threat of Mick Harford. That would make sense, but I also played at the back four days later against Leicester City at Highbury because David hadn't recovered in time yet there were plenty of other options. Unlike the two-all draw at Luton, this time we kept a clean sheet and beat Leicester one-nil, but I was delighted when David returned to the side for the trip to face Queens Park Rangers the following midweek, even though it cost me a place in the starting line-up.

I have a high regard for central defenders. I never did in the past when I was playing centre forward, but now that I've experienced playing in defence it's a much harder role than it looks because it's a totally different game back there. It makes me laugh when some managers or coaches talk about players being a nine but they can also play as a six or an eight or a ten. What a load of rubbish. The pictures that you see on the football field, whether you're playing full-back or right up top, it's totally different to what managers see from the dugout. As a number nine leading the line I knew exactly what my job was. And if I ever had to drop in the hole, maybe play the ten role, then I wasn't as confident. And I certainly wasn't comfortable playing as a five, you know, at centre-half. I remember Alan Ball at Portsmouth a few years later asked me to play at the back in the big local derby against Southampton and mark Colin Clarke.

He rag-dolled me from start to finish, scored both their goals in a two-all draw and, thankfully, my central defensive career lasted only a handful of games.

Returning to action within a month of suffering that Achilles injury in Glenn Hoddle's testimonial seemed at the time like a rather quick recovery, given what appeared initially to be a pretty serious injury, and although I was given the green light by the club's medical staff and felt fine, I clearly wasn't one hundred per cent fit. Then the other Achilles went at the end of September and I was out for more than four months, the end result being I only started three league games for Arsenal in 1985-86. I played a total of fourteen times that season including cup competitions – six starts and eight substitute appearances – and my only goal of that campaign, in fact the last one I ever scored for the club, came in a League Cup defeat against Aston Villa at Highbury in February 1986. That's my biggest regret about Arsenal, being injury prone. I was never like that previously. I couldn't wait to train, I couldn't wait to play and for the first ten years or so of my career I rarely missed more than a handful of games in a season. So to only start sixty competitive games for Arsenal in two-and-a-half years at the club was one of the biggest disappointments of my career because I was desperate to make more of an impact at that club and give the people there everything I had.

It was no surprise when new boss George Graham let me go in the summer. My contract was about to expire when he came in to replace Don Howe in May 1986 and I knew my time was up. George wanted to build something special and I wasn't part of his plans. No problem whatsoever with that. Time to move on to new pastures and, fortunately, one of my heroes, Alan Ball – who, like me, was also born in Farnworth in Bolton

– wanted to sign me for Portsmouth. Mick Channon had just left and Bally wanted me to fill that void and play alongside Mick Quinn. Next stop: the south coast.

17

Play Up Pompey

The summer of 1986 was the first time since I turned professional in 1973 that I found myself unemployed. My Arsenal contract expired in May and it was a weird feeling waking up the following morning knowing I wasn't attached to a particular club and didn't have a job. I had no idea what was around the corner. A friend put me in touch with a contact of theirs in New Zealand; the television company over there who had the broadcast rights to show the World Cup in Mexico that summer were looking for analysts to cover the tournament. I'd received a few telephone calls from managers wondering if I wanted to sign for their club, but I put that on the backburner for a month and flew to Auckland to do some commentary and studio work when England were playing. It was the first time I'd done something like that in the media, and I'm pretty sure I wasn't great, but it allowed me a foot in the door and the experience was extremely helpful in later years.

Although my body was starting to break down, at the age of thirty-three I still felt I had a few years left in the legs and wanted to continue playing. The interest from back home was flattering but I knew I couldn't return to England having gone two months or so without doing any fitness work and still be in proper shape to get a contract, so I played two or three games for a semi-professional team in Auckland and took part in a few training sessions to keep myself ticking over.

That proved to be a wise decision and I felt pretty good when I got back. Now I just had to make another wise decision and pick the right club. I reckon there were four or five teams interested in signing me and I quickly narrowed that down to two after hearing the various proposals – my next destination, after holding initial talks with Mick Mills and Alan Ball, would either be Stoke City or Portsmouth.

"Fancy coming up here to play for me?" I was player-manager at Stoke when I called Paul shortly after he'd been released by Arsenal. I'd taken charge the year before but had lost a couple of experienced players – Mark Chamberlain and Alan Hudson – and I thought Marrers coming in would be an ideal fit for our football club. He could be the captain and leader on the pitch. I was thirty-seven and didn't really want to play anymore, having appeared about thirty times in 1985-86, and thought PM would be perfect as my on-field replacement.

"I've got interest from a few teams, Bomber, but I'm happy to come up for a chat when I get back from New Zealand," he told me.

It was pretty clear from an early stage that the maximum weekly wage that I was able to offer Paul – 450 pounds – was unlikely to be enough, with more money available elsewhere. But I was desperate to sign him, and thought I had an ace up my sleeve when one of the Stoke directors offered to add the use of his cottage in Staffordshire, rent-free, to the package so that Marrers and Ali wouldn't need to search for somewhere to live. Paul may have just turned thirty-three but he was around the same age as I was when I went to Southampton in 1982, and I went on to play more than one hundred times for them. And I also discussed with Marrers the possibility of him even playing at centre-back if he wanted to, alongside Steve Bould, who I'd just moved to that position after signing right-back Lee Dixon. I did everything I could to persuade him to sign. After our third or fourth conversation he told me the bad news...

"Bomber, I would love to come and play for you, I really would, but I just can't afford to because of what's on offer elsewhere."

For me, that meant Portsmouth were offering a package that Stoke City couldn't get near. He was very apologetic but I totally understood, although I did tell him he better not get promoted with Pompey. Of course they ended up finishing second and going up while Stoke were eighth in Division Two and missed out. I was gutted not to be able to sign him, but Paul's decision had absolutely no impact on our friendship in the years that followed.

Mick Mills

Playing for Millsy, one of the best guys you could ever meet, would have been magic, and I appreciated the package the club was able to put together as well as the effort Mick put in to try and sign me, but the offer from Portsmouth was nearly twice as much to play in the same league as Stoke – Division Two – and I was impressed by what Alan Ball had to say and his plans for the football club. By the way, being wanted by both the former England captain and an England World Cup winner – an iconic Boltonian – was humbling and something I was very proud of.

Bally was building a 'team-to-win-now' at Pompey – rather than signing players for the future – and told me if I signed for him he was confident we could get promotion. "I've got this kid up front, Mick Quinn, who we got from Oldham Athletic – a Scouser who loves to put himself about – and I think you'll be the perfect foil for him."

Sitting down with Alan Ball before signing for him and just talking football, chewing the fat, was an absolute joy. We had some great conversations – our best times, our worst times and our regrets. My biggest regret was not sticking to the training regime that was put together for me prior to the World Cup in 1982 after I'd recovered from my Achilles injury. Discarding that routine was actually the beginning of the end and that really stuck in my craw. The specialised plan was designed to help me look after my body better and minimise the risk of injury, and I followed the routine for a few months before getting lazy and cutting corners. Instead of 'right, after training, I've got to do a specific stretch routine for a certain number of minutes' it soon became 'well, I suppose I'll stretch for a couple of minutes after training then head down the pub'.

Injury prevention in 1982 was still in its infancy. I spent a fair bit of time running on one of the tracks at Cambridge with only a physio for company, but they would work on things they knew would help my body. Everybody makes a big deal about sports science these days, and quite rightly so, but I think the experts I worked with were – probably without knowing it back then – way ahead of their time. They made me faster, stronger, quicker and I could even jump higher. In fact, I could do everything better. So my decision not to continue with that extra-curricular training is my biggest regret in football.

Those discussions with Bally got me thinking, and those chats helped me appreciate the game – and my role in it – a lot better. I was heading back down the other side of the hill rather rapidly – it seemed as though someone had tampered with the brakes – and I was determined to make the most of the time I had left on the pitch.

We had a lot of strong characters at Portsmouth. Kenny Swain at right-back, who was a year older than me, and some other very serious chaps who you wouldn't want to mess with – Billy Gilbert, Noel Blake, Mick Kennedy and Vince Hilaire. A decent mixture of youth sprinkled with plenty of experience and we were probably the toughest side in the league. In fact, I don't think I ever played in another team throughout my career with as many hard bastards. And we were also very resolute in defence, extremely tough to play against and borderline vicious if I'm being honest.

'The necessity of living in the midst of the diabolical citizens of Portsmouth is a real and unavoidable calamity. It is a doubt to me if there is such another collection of demons upon the whole earth.'

General James Wolfe (writing in 1758)

The General was perhaps rather harsh on the lovely people of Portsmouth, but he certainly showed plenty of foresight when it came to the squad that Bally put together to try and get promotion.

The boys were great to have as teammates – a smashing bunch of lads – but I wouldn't have fancied lining up against us.

Play Up Pompey

I suppose we were like the Crazy Gang at Wimbledon before they made it fashionable to be unfashionable.

* * *

I first met Marrers in July 1986 when we were getting the boat to the Isle of Man for a pre-season tournament. He had just signed for Portsmouth, having left Arsenal, and was already on the ferry when we got on.

The Pompey boys had been on the piss in Blackpool the night before and, somehow, we all made it there in time for the eleven o'clock departure. Alan Ball was waiting for us at the gangway. The gaffer's trademark was a tweed flat cap so we bought twenty tweed flat caps and all turned up looking just like him.

Still half cut from the night before and wearing Alan Ball flat caps with our Portsmouth tracksuits, we introduced ourselves to Marrers at the bar. The poor lad didn't know what the fuck to make of things. Quite the first impression! I handed Paul an extra flat cap, he duly put in on and was now one of the lads.

The boat hadn't even left Heysham Port in Lancashire and we were on the pints again. Paul wasn't with us the night before so he was playing catch-up, but he quickly made sure that wasn't a problem for him. Things did get kind of rowdy after we set sail – a couple of the boys started having a scrap with each other and it got a bit out of hand, quickly going from a lighthearted few drinks to a bit Lionel Messi, but that was normal with us.

It must have been an eye-opener for Marrers – by the time we reached the Isle of Man he certainly knew what his new teammates were all about and who the 'characters' were in that squad, but Paul was a great character himself and he gelled brilliantly with the rest of the boys.

Micky Quinn

When that's your first experience of your new teammates, some players might have felt overawed or intimidated but I was a loud, rock music-loving thirty-three-year-old who enjoyed a drink, some fun and a decent bit of chaos so it was the perfect partnership. I felt part of the squad straight away.

* * *

I made my league debut for Portsmouth in the salubrious setting of the Goldstone Ground in Hove on Saturday, 23rd August 1986 in a goalless draw at Brighton & Hove Albion. It wasn't quite the glamour of Highbury – where I'd made my last appearance for Arsenal, against Nottingham Forest, back in April as a first-half sub for the injured David Rocastle – but that ship had sailed after I was given a free transfer.

It took me until our twenty-first game of the season – against Grimsby Town at Fratton Park towards the end of November – to score my first goal for Pompey, although I had missed a few games because of various knocks and niggles. No excuses, however, because I would have loved to score early doors – just like I did after joining Ipswich then doing the same after joining Arsenal – but it wasn't to be. Thankfully Micky was banging them in regularly and he went on to score twenty-two of Portsmouth's fifty-three league goals in the promotion season of 1986-87.

Don't forget Portsmouth had missed out on promotion to the top flight the previous season by just three points and on goal difference the year before [1984-85]. 86-87 was a big season for us and Paul was a great addition to our squad. He's up there as one of the two best strike partnerships I've had in my career – playing up front with Mark McGhee at Newcastle United and alongside Marrers at Pompey. He brought class to the table, of course because of his pedigree, but his ability to hold the ball up was outstanding. When I first joined Portsmouth in March 1986 I was playing up top with Mick Channon but his legs had gone. Now you could tell straight away with Mick's touch and his presence and what he was doing in training that he was class, a cut above, and it was exactly the same with Marrers. When Paul first arrived he might not have been quite as dynamic as he was with Plymouth, Ipswich and Arsenal but you could see with his touch, his awareness, vision and strength that he was quality. He was very aggressive. I think a lot of people forget that about him. Marrers could put himself around and look after not only himself but his teammates too. A class act, and I actually learned as much from Paul off the field as I did on it, just being in his company was a treat, and we hit it off straight away both on and off the pitch. He's a northern lad, from Chorley, and I began at Wigan so we had a bit in common there, plus the Portsmouth squad was half southerners and half northerners so we were usually in the same team at training as well. We were a great foil for each other. Marrers was also very kind. My mum and dad were down staying with me on one occasion and he also invited them to a barbeque at his house one Sunday – he didn't have to do that – but he got on with them brilliantly. That was Paul in a nutshell. He was the same with everyone. And he always looked out for me, whether it was giving some advice or just taking me under his wing, almost like a big brother, and that's why we gelled so well. He's a top man and Marrers was the final cog in that particular Portsmouth team.

Micky Quinn

When I look back at my playing career I was lucky to have some fantastic strike partners; Kevin Wainwright, Billy Rafferty, Trevor Whymark, Alan Brazil, Kevin Keegan and Tony Woodcock, then Quinny at Pompey. He wasn't your archetypal classic footballer – and he didn't look like one either – but who cares because he had this wonderful knack of putting the ball in the back of the net, and that is what it's all about when you're a striker. When we played together he scored most of the goals, I only managed to get five in total in the league in '86-87, but I was just as happy setting them up for the big man because I knew he'd find the back of the net more often than not.

* * *

Saturday 2nd May, 1987
Portsmouth 2-0 Millwall
1. Alan Knight, 2. Kenny Swain, 3. Paul Hardyman, 4. Kevin Dillon, 5. Noel Blake, 6. Billy Gilbert, 7. Kevin O'Callaghan, 8. Mick Kennedy, 9. Paul Mariner, 10. Micky Quinn, 11. Vince Hilaire

Nearly sixteen thousand fans were at Fratton Park for the Division Two game against Millwall at the start of May knowing a win for Portsmouth would take us back into the top flight for the first time since 1959. We'd actually hit a rocky patch in the league, winning only one of four games prior to the Millwall fixture, but knew if we won that match then we'd be promoted. The club had come close to promotion in the previous two seasons without getting the job done and the gaffer was determined it was going to be third time lucky...

> The boys are in great form. We had a good chat yesterday and they're very relaxed in there. After a couple of years of disappointments we're very, very close once again. It's what the people here want, it's what the whole ground wants, in fact the whole city wants it. Let's hope we can give it to them and I think the lads are ready.
>
> **Alan Ball, speaking pre-match to 'The Big Match'**
> **on ITV**

Bally had us well fired up and I'd like to think I set the tone for our approach to the game after just twelve seconds. The ball was played forward to me from kick-off and after taking two or three touches I then lost possession to Millwall left-back Nick Coleman and ended up falling over. Les Briley then tidied things up but just before he got rid of the ball I quickly got back on my feet and launched myself into a ridiculous two-footed tackle, catching Les at the top of his shin and sending him flying through the air. A quick 'peep' on referee Ray Lewis's whistle to indicate a free-kick to Millwall and everybody just got on with the game. These days Law 12 would ensure I saw red – for 'using excessive force' – but it was a different game back then, although I admit I was daft and shouldn't have been as reckless in such an important fixture. No harm done, thankfully, to either the wellbeing of Les or my chances of staying on the field.

We played pretty well in the first half and had the better of the chances – I should have done better with a shot which their keeper easily saved – and Bally was actually pretty calm in the dressing room at half-time. 'Keep it going' was the main message because the gaffer was convinced the goal would come in the second half. And it did, nine minutes after the restart. Quinny, the birthday boy who turned twenty-five that day, nodded it down for me just outside the box and I actually failed to control it initially but me doing that meant their defender Alan Walker was now facing the wrong way. I took a touch to take it beyond him, another one to set myself properly and then fired the shot past Brian Horne in the Millwall goal.

'Mariner... yes... Mariner... in with a chance of giving Portsmouth the lead... Paul Mariner's done it! They're going wild... and that was an England striker at his best.'
ITV commentator John Helm

Arms outstretched followed by both index fingers pointing skywards. Seven out of ten for the rather nonchalant celebration but a couple of marks automatically taken off for a soon-to-be-thirty-four-year-old attempting to be cool. It was only the fifth goal I'd scored in the league since joining Portsmouth but it's in my Top Ten of favourite goals. There's nothing better as a footballer than to score when it means so much to so many.

There was a nasty undercurrent throughout the whole match – not helped by the early Bruce Lee impersonation courtesy of the Portsmouth number nine – and things boiled over shortly afterwards when a certain Les Briley dished out some retribution on the Bruce Lee impersonator. Turns out Les had neither forgiven not forgotten my 'mistimed' attempt at a tackle inside the first minute, otherwise known as an attempted assault. In fairness to him, neither would I if the roles had been reversed!

Once again I lost possession of the ball – I did have a good first touch once upon a time, honest – this time when reaching around and trying to win it back I committed a foul, although not quite with the same ferocity as the one earlier in the game. But Les wasn't happy and as he tried to get off the deck he proceeded to perform the rarely-used 'donkey kick on a football pitch' technique. His left boot caught me square in the face and left me needing treatment to stem the flow of blood from the side of my left eye.

> 'Mariner's face is covered in blood. He looks like he's just gone six rounds with Frank Bruno.'
>
> **John Helm**

Soon after, just like Bruno, we delivered the knockout punch courtesy of the seldom-seen indirect free-kick inside the penalty box, awarded following an obstruction on Vince Hilaire. I handed the ball to Kevin Dillon, he placed it down, the two of us discussed what we were going to do while the referee got their wall back far enough, he tapped it to Kevin O'Callaghan and Kev smashed the ball into the roof of the net. Game over. Portsmouth had been promoted to Division One for the first time in twenty-eight years and the celebrations could begin in earnest.

We had an open-top bus parade through the streets of the city to celebrate promotion and all our kids were with us. My son, George, was just a baby at the time so I took him with me, then handed him to Micky to babysit when I needed to go and get another drink for us. My strike partner on the pitch and my babysitter off it!

That was some weekend. The civic reception first up on

the Sunday then on to the Guild Hall square with around seven-thousand fans waiting for us. We were introduced one-by-one on the steps and, just like the rest of us, Marrers was lapping it up. He'd been there, he'd won things, scored at a World Cup and been very successful in football, but it looked like that achievement meant just as much to him as it did to us.

Micky Quinn

For the Portsmouth fans it was so special. Absent from the top flight for all that time, and having come so close the previous two seasons, for their team to finally get to the big league again was magnificent and such a relief. That weekend still stands out now as a special memory in my career.

* * *

Pre-season during the summer of 1987 was anything but dull. We were at a training camp over in Jersey and after a particularly heavy night on the beers we got back to the hotel around three o'clock in the morning. I may or may not have been making the most noise in the foyer before we eventually headed to our rooms. Training was supposed to be at nine o'clock down by the beach so at least we'd get a few hours of kip. But we were woken at seven-thirty by Gordon the kit man thumping on everyone's door and shouting, "The gaffer wants to see you all downstairs now."

"We're in a bit of trouble, gentlemen..." said Alan Ball. "The owner of the hotel has called the police and he wants us all off the island. I've already ordered the biggest bunch of flowers for his wife but it made no difference whatsoever. He's given us twenty-four hours to get out of here and never return."

Thankfully Bally was also drinking the night before as well as the players so we weren't in too much trouble with him, but the length of our stay had been cut short and we only had one training session left. So the gaffer took us down the beach to do doggies – shuttle runs between cones – but he was marching, goose-stepping and placing these bloody big traffic cones twenty-five yards away, then fifty yards, then one-hundred yards. Normally they're just a few yards apart!

He knew most of us were still pissed so that session was torture, he absolutely pummelled us. Next thing we know the tide is coming in but we're still doing the bloody doggies. "Gaffer, the cones are fucking floating!" I told him. He then told me to go and retrieve every single one of them otherwise none of the boys were allowed to leave. Eventually we got back to the hotel and Bally gathered us all round. Fuck sake, what now? "Get upstairs for a shower then meet back down here in the bar in twenty-five minutes. It's our last night so we're all having a drink!"

* * *

It was great to be playing in Division One again and I scored Portsmouth's first goal in the top flight of English football since 1959 (when Ron Saunders netted in a five-two defeat at Arsenal as Pompey were relegated). It was nice to be back among the big boys, but it wasn't a particularly good season because my body was starting to break down and I knew the end was nigh. Bally knew it as well but he gave me another year so I could play in the First Division again and take me through to the age of thirty-five so I could get a pension which was very kind of him. I was a fringe player, he subsequently brought in other players to play that nine role, so it was a difficult season for us, but an enjoyable time for me surrounded by really good people. And at least I didn't have to train the day before a game more often than not. That's because on Friday mornings Kenny Swain and myself, two of the elder statesmen at the club, were excused a trip to the gym to join the boys who were playing five-a-side because Bally always used to send us to the bacon and egg shop down on the seafront at Southsea to get breakfast. That was our specialist training regime.

Instead of Bally giving the Portsmouth players who had won promotion a fair crack of the whip he went out and signed two strikers, Terry Connor from Brighton and Ian Baird from Leeds, and neither of them were cheap. Although Marrers and me started up front together in the first couple of games, I was replaced at half-time in the third league game at home to Southampton and the pair of us rarely played together again after that. Either he found himself sitting on his arse on the bench or I did. We helped get Pompey back into the top flight but, after a few games in Division One, it was as if the manager didn't trust us anymore.

I remember a midweek game at home to Spurs in November 1987 – I was on the bench and Clive Allen was on their bench. Now he'd scored forty-nine goals the previous season in all competitions and I think I got twenty-eight goals in total in our promotion season yet we couldn't even get a start between us in that game! I looked over to him, he looked at me and we both shook our heads and started to laugh.

I ended up getting back in the team because Terry and Ian were struggling for goals – with Ian being sold back to Leeds after just seven months with us – but Paul's days, sadly, were numbered. I can understand why because he was a thirty-four-year-old playing in the top flight but it was a shame because I still thought we had something together. I'm sure we could still have done the business if given more of a chance but Bally messed around with the team due to inconsistent results and in the end paid the price when we were relegated. Very frustrating for both of us.

Micky Quinn

There weren't too many personal highlights during my last season playing football in England but there were a couple of shockers, including being part of a six-nil thumping against Arsenal on my return to Highbury. That result happened just a week after another game to forget. We had a few injuries in defence and that was when the 'in case of emergency' mode was activated. Big Noel Blake had just had a knee operation so I played at the back against Southampton at Fratton Park in August 1987 and proudly (?) wore the number five jersey while new signing Ian Baird partnered Quinny up front. It was the first ever top flight meeting between the two sides and the build-up all week was intense. The atmosphere was sensational and it was the featured game of the week on 'The Big Match' on ITV. I'm doing my best here to talk about everything to do with the day itself without wanting to mention the game, a two-all draw, because I was hopeless.

It's quite an achievement in football to get booked inside sixty seconds; I managed to do just that by wiping out Gordon Hobson on the halfway line. I would prefer to call my attempt at a tackle clumsy and somewhat mistimed, others (including Millwall's Les Briley) may prefer the word 'assault', and they would probably be right. My instructions pre-match from Alan

Ball were simple – "You take care of Colin Clarke." I've had better days following orders… Colin ragdolled me throughout, scored twice and I'm surprised I didn't have to pay him rent because he absolutely owned me.

Let's start with the first Southampton goal. Goalkeeper Alan Knight rolled the ball out to me at the edge of our box and there was nobody within twenty yards of me. Under no pressure whatsoever, my attempt at a long ball to Quinny went straight to Saints midfielder Andy Townsend just inside his own half. No biggie, I still had time to make amends because Andy's header found Glenn Cockerill, who I wasn't far away from. But he waltzed past me like I wasn't there.

Meanwhile, the man I'm supposed to be marking – big Colin Clarke – is lurking at the edge of the box, Glenn laid it off to him and Clarkey scored the equaliser. Not great. Twenty-six minutes gone, I'd been booked within sixty seconds of kick-off and was responsible for our biggest rivals getting back on level terms. Things could only get better in the second half. Or maybe not…

Two minutes after the restart and we're trailing by two goals to one, and of course Colin Clarke scored the goal to put them ahead. Southampton had a free-kick inside their own half and looked to go long. Colin was the target and as the ball was in the air I made my move. However our left-back, Paul Hardyman, was a lot closer than I was and he was getting there first so I did an about-turn, but in doing so got caught out of position. Clarke flicked it on to Gordon Hobson, now the closest Saints player to me, but as I went to try and challenge him he played the return ball to Colin who put them ahead. Thankfully Bally realised I was more of a hindrance than a help at the back so he brought on defender Lee Sandford and pushed me further forward to fill the gap left by Mick Quinn, who'd been replaced by Kevin Dillon.

I wasn't directly involved in our equalising goal – scored by Clive Whitehead – but I did make a nuisance of myself and even though I wasn't able to get a touch on Ian Baird's header back across, I did enough by just being in the box to keep Kevin Bond occupied, allowing Clive to make it two-all. Probably best that I didn't bother trying to claim any kind of assist, mainly because I would have found a way to fuck that up as well.

* * *

Exactly a year to the day after we beat Millwall to gain promotion to the top flight – the second of May – we lost two-one at home to Newcastle United and Portsmouth were relegated from Division One after only twelve months, the briefest of stays. Seven league wins from forty games won't usually get the job done, and that season was no different. It was a sad way for me to end my career in English football. I couldn't really train at all during my second year at the club. My warm-ups were some stretching in the dressing room, and maybe a little bit of head tennis in the gym, but that was it. I'd never even heard of a warm-down. I was approaching my thirty-fifth birthday and found most things a struggle – four goals in just twenty-six league appearances not a very good return and, sadly, I went out with a whimper. Lenny the Lion had lost his roar.

18

Agent Mariner

I would be lying if I told you I could locate Wollongong on a map of Australia. In fact, I'd never even heard of the city in New South Wales until I received a phone call shortly after leaving Portsmouth at the beginning of May in 1988. An Aussie entrepreneur by the name of Harry Michaels was offering me ten thousand Australian dollars (equivalent to just over four thousand pounds at the time) if I would fly out and play two games for Wollongong City, the club of which he was an executive director. Within a few days I was standing at the baggage carousel at Sydney International airport collecting my suitcase. Alan Brazil had already been over there to play a few games – that's how Harry was able to get my number – and Trevor Francis went out to Australia for a brief spell shortly after I returned to England. They also agreed terms with Michel Platini to play twice for Wollongong, but I don't believe he ever made it over there.

* * *

Within a few months I went from not knowing what I'd do with my life after playing my final game for Portsmouth to hardly having any spare time. A feast followed a famine. Australia was never going to be any more than a couple of games so when I got back home I agreed a part-time deal with Maltese side Naxxar Lions. We agreed that I would fly over at weekends for their games, and I actually ended up playing forty-nine times for them between September 1988 and May 1991. That was Saturdays and Sundays taken care of, and during the week I had a new challenge to get my teeth into – full-time agency work, the seeds of which had been sown a couple of years earlier.

I was quite friendly with some of the Arsenal players in the mid-Eighties and that's when I first met Paul. I was in the players' lounge at Highbury after a game in 1985 when Tony Woodcock introduced me to Paul.

He was the embodiment of the fun Eighties if you like. He was loving life, he'd brought a great career with him to Arsenal and I just remember Marrers always laughing. That kind of character is attractive to most people. I'd lost my wife to leukemia in 1981 and four years later I still hadn't fully got over that. Paul was one of the people who helped me smile again after Lee died.

Having lived in America for a few years – I moved over there after selling my record company – I came back to London and was out having dinner with Paul one night. My background was music and entertainment and I explained to him that I wanted to do in England something similar to what they were doing in America.

For me Paul was a rock star who played football. My idea was to make our top players rock stars like they were in the States. Marrers may have been the wrong side of thirty during his time with Arsenal but he still had talent, plenty of charisma and, ultimately, was a performer. He was the ideal person to discuss my business idea with.

You've got to remember this was the mid-eighties and it was a bad time for football. Thirty-nine people died in the Heysel Stadium tragedy at the 1985 European Cup final between Liverpool and Juventus and English clubs had subsequently been banned from competing in Europe. However good the game was, it wasn't worth people's lives. I wanted to bring more of a family atmosphere to football. At dinner that night we spoke about violence that would erupt from time to time at matches yet most clubs had a 'family enclosure'. That summed up a lot of what was wrong with football. The rest of the place might be a shithole but you're in the family area so you're okay, you'll be safe in there? Things needed to change. I explained to Paul that I was setting up a business called 'First Artist', provided him with the details and said I wanted him on board, fifty-fifty. "Let's do this."

Jon Smith, agent

We agreed that I would provide the contacts and he would provide the cash. I put my phone book in and he put his cheque book in. Jon then set the wheels in motion and First Artist Management was born in 1986. Things started well with the agency. I managed to help get the England team account later that year and they were First Artist's first client. That came about after I told Jon about Harry Swales, a veteran agent who had looked after the England players for years but he was coming to the end of his time with the squad. Harry's tenure was very successful but he'd told me he wanted to hand over to someone a little younger – this was ideal for us because we wanted to offer fresh ideas. I won my last cap for England in

May 1985 but still knew all the boys so I arranged to meet Ray Wilkins, who was in charge of the players' committee, for a chat.

> We put together a presentation. I brought in some people who I knew and all the marketing guys that I'd had the record business with. We jazzed it up and made it very present day – all-singing and all-dancing. I wore a suit and tie, trying to be all professional and serious, and Paul was there just chatting with the players. He was more than a conduit. He pretty much said to them, "Trust me, I'm your mate and I know what I'm doing here." And they all did.
>
> Bobby Robson was England manager at the time so Paul took me to see him as well. And Bobby was lovely, I got on with him instantly. Again, it was Paul's charm and his irreverence that sort of won the day, because everyone knew that he was good at what he did. Add to that his wonderful attitude towards life in general – everybody loved him.
>
> Finally Marrers and I went to see Ted Croker, the general secretary of the Football Association. And we seemed to pass the sniff test there as well so we got the gig. We'd just set up our business and our first client was the entire England football team. And as good as I thought I was, it was because of Paul that we landed that account.
>
> **Jon Smith**

We also became the European representative for Diego Maradona after I gave Jon a contact number for Ossie Ardiles. Later on, I also helped negotiate boot deals for some of the less-famous England players who didn't have endorsements.

Paul Mariner

Paul was great fun to work with. And for someone who was kind of 'out there' he was quite a moralistic guy, which we all liked. He was very, very concerned about the racism that was thrown out at times to Viv Anderson and John Barnes during matches and Paul would regularly talk about it in public. He wasn't ahead of his time, because it shouldn't have happened anyway, but he was very vocal about everybody in football, and in life, being equal regardless of skin colour or where you came from.

Jon Smith

I didn't really do that much for the first couple of years with the exception of helping set up the England deal and providing Jon with additional contact details for potential clients because I was still playing football. But after leaving Portsmouth in 1988 I moved back to Suffolk and would travel down to the First Artist office near Wembley most days during the week. Suffolk to London on a daily basis was quite the trek, as was flying to Malta two or three weekends every month between September and April to play for Naxxar to help supplement the pension fund. It wasn't long before the extensive travel started to take its toll.

Unfortunately I also started to feel like a fish out of water a lot of the time once the initial excitement of the new role had subsided. I didn't like going to people and asking for sponsorship money. I wasn't cut out for it. And the travel was getting me down. I was leaving the house at six o'clock in the morning and not getting home until around nine o'clock at night. Then off to Malta most weekends. I was hardly seeing the children, which was a major concern of mine, and I lost a lot of weight. I looked ill. So much so that one day Ali asked me, "When was the last time you took a proper look at yourself in the mirror?" I couldn't remember. "Well take a look at yourself. You're doing far too much."

I cut back a bit on the travel to and from London and started doing some things more remotely, which certainly helped, then a chance encounter in April 1989 led to a new opportunity. We were at Bisham Abbey, where the England squad had gathered ahead of the forthcoming World Cup qualifier against Albania, and First Artist was hosting a party to launch our new instructional football video featuring four players from the England national team. Certain members of the media were invited, as were various age-level coaches plus some Football Association members. One of them was John Bramley, the FA's former national youth coach who'd moved over to the States the year before. He recognised me and asked what I was doing at Bisham Abbey. I told him about my role with First Artist, "But to be honest, I'm not enjoying it as much as I thought I would."

"Well I'm the head coach at Albany Capitals in New York State. How do you fancy coming to America this summer to play for me in the American Soccer League and see how you like it?"

I was really missing the game. Playing two or three times a month in Malta was okay but I was in and out of that country very swiftly on each occasion. I wasn't even training with my teammates before games. "I'd love to," I replied. Of course I had to tell Jon. "Look, I want to take the summer off and go and play in the States. To be honest, it's probably what I need to help recharge the batteries because I'm struggling a bit right now."

Jon and I continued to work together when I got back and although the travel to and from the office wasn't enjoyable, we still had fun when I was there, including that time I sent an internal memo to all the staff:

'*WARNING – I'VE JUST HAD A RATHER STRONG CURRY FOR LUNCH AND WILL SHORTLY BE VISITING THE TOILET ON THE DOWNSTAIRS FLOOR. PLEASE AVOID AT ALL COSTS AND AWAIT FURTHER INSTRUCTION!*'

If you can't laugh at yourself then what's the point. But as time went on I wasn't in the office as much. That was the trade-off at home because I needed to spend more time with the boys.

* * *

None of what we were able to do with the England account would have been possible without Bobby Robson. He allowed me a short time at every international get-together to talk to the entire team and update them on the various commercial activities. In those days we were earning seven figures for the players. When divided up, that might not be a lot of money for some of the top guys these days – but it was back then.

I'd negotiated a potential sponsorship deal with SEGA but needed the help of both Paul and Bobby. I sat down with Marrers in the office and explained the SEGA proposal to him. He laughed. "Not a fucking chance will Bobby agree to that. And if he does then I'll give you the money myself!"

So at my next briefing with Bobby I updated him on the various deals in place – such and such a player is doing this for Mars, another has Coca Cola commitments, we've got this newspaper and that television station doing whatever, oh and we're also about to do a deal with SEGA.

"What's the agreement with SEGA?" he asked.

So I explained what the finances were and told him how much it would be worth.

"And what is it they're asking for in return?"

I explained to Bobby that I'd run their idea past Marrers and he said it might be difficult – a rather more polite way of putting it than Paul did – but to ask you anyway.

"SEGA is wondering if it would be possible to get a full size Sonic the Hedgehog on the England bench in an upcoming game."

"Fuck off," replied Bobby.

Jon Smith

* * *

The 1989-90 campaign in Malta started in September, just a few weeks after the season had ended in America. If I'd gone back to spending several days each week in the office in London, as well as flying to Malta at weekends, it would have been exactly the same as before and that just wasn't working – both for my family life and for my health. That summer in the States reignited my love for football. I was only thirty-six and still felt my legs had some life left in them, even though the rest of my body was kind of patched up. But, at the same time, my three months away in America had re-enforced my view that agency work and selling sponsorship wasn't really for me in the long term. I wouldn't say there was one particular incident that made me feel that way, although something that happened towards the end of 1989 was rather unfortunate.

First Artist had agreed a deal with Ford and Budget rent-a-car – I think it was something like the first player to come on as a substitute for England in each game would get the use of a Ford XR3i for a week or two. The deal itself was a nice little earner for the players and the money went into their pool – this was before the England squad was full of millionaires with various endorsements. If I remember correctly the fall-out was after the game in Poland when the boys secured qualification for the 1990 World Cup in Italy following a goalless draw in Chorzow. David Seaman, Paul Parker, Mike Phelan, Alan Smith and Paul Gascoigne were all unused subs – it was unusual for five lads to be on the bench without a single one of them getting on – so none of them were eligible to get the Ford XR3i, according to the terms of the deal we'd agreed with Ford and Budget rent-a-car.

Gazza wasn't happy and confronted me. I tried to reason with him but he was having none of it. Inside I was thinking 'Fuck this, I'm not having anyone speak to me like that,' but externally I was still trying to play the role of peacekeeper. That was not my kind of scene. Gazza may have been right – what harm would it have done to hand over the keys – but the way he spoke to me left a bad taste in my mouth.

Ultimately I was like a fish out of water in the agency game. Most of my life up to that point had been on a football pitch, and that's where I was happiest. Not trying to placate angry young footballers. Looking back on it now I can see the bigger picture. It was more about me no longer being a part of the inner circle with the players – the old guard had started to pass on the baton in the late Eighties – and my relationship with the younger boys in the squad was nowhere near as good as my relationship with the experienced guys I played with and against. I was yesterday's man. That hurt me more than any words said to me by Paul Gascoigne. Let's be honest, I wasn't cut out for that lifestyle anyway. However, despite incidents like that, I really enjoyed the time I actually spent when I was with Jon and we had plenty of laughs. This is one of my favourite stories, let's just call it 'Lost in Translation...'

Agent Mariner

After agreeing a deal with Trebor, making them the official mint of the England Football Team, Paul and I held a brainstorming session aimed at maximising publicity for our new clients. Fred Street was the England physio and Norman Medhurst was his assistant. The Umbro logo should have been plastered on both sides of the medicine bag they took on to the pitch, but we managed to persuade them to get the Trebor logo printed on one side. And we told Norman that when he and Fred ran on to treat an injured player to make sure the Trebor logo was facing away from the player and towards the cameras; Fred and Norman then became part of the players' pool, something which both we and the squad were delighted to do. Whenever play was stopped for an injury it meant the television match director had very few shots to choose from so more often than not they would just give the viewer a close-up of the player receiving treatment. And that also meant Fred and Norman and the Trebor logo getting some air-time. But we came badly unstuck in Oslo during a World Cup qualifier in 1993 by trying to be too clever.

We thought it would be a good idea to put a slogan – 'Trebor: suck on a strong one' – under the Trebor logo on the side of the physio bag, except have it written in Norwegian. So we were put in touch with someone who claimed to speak Norwegian and asked them to translate it for us. What appeared, however, was 'Trebor: suck on a hard one'…

Jon Smith

* * *

We were in the office in London one day when I told Jon exactly how I felt: having been on the inside looking out for so many years I now hated being on the outside looking in. It was a simple 'That's it, I'm done' and we agreed to a friendly parting of the ways.

> When our company really got into its stride we were creating all sorts of good stuff. So good, in fact, that in 1994 the Football Association took their commercial activities in-house through their new marketing director, Trevor Phillips, and created Team England with us before taking it on themselves. We went on to spread our wings across many sports, eventually becoming a public company, but Paul was not overly keen to be part of a PLC because his life was now in the States and was still very much football-centric.
>
> We ended the association very amicably – Marrers continued to earn from deals already in place – and the two of us remained close friends.
>
> **Jon Smith**

Jon was a fantastic partner with an extremely sharp business mind who went on to do very well for himself, and good on him for doing that. He's a top lad and deserved his success. Me? In the end I wasn't cut out for it, it wasn't my cup of tea. I walked away from a lot of money but it was my decision to pack it in. I needed to get out. I needed to get back into football.

19

Reborn in the USA

My love affair with the United States of America began in July 1976. I went there on holiday for their bicentennial celebrations and loved it. A few months later, after swapping Home Park for Portman Road, I got friendly with an American lad called Kurt Kuykendall. He was third string goalkeeper with New York Cosmos and came to train with us at Ipswich Town for a few days after their season had finished. We were roughly the same age and just hit it off.

I hadn't long arrived at Ipswich and was still staying at the Copdock Hotel so after training I used to spend a bit of time with Kurt and his partner Sherry, and they invited us over to stay with them at their Long Island home in New York. The following summer, after returning from England's three-game tour of South America, I went back over to the States and we did all the tourist stuff – Empire State Building, the Statue of Liberty, Times Square. That's when I started to fall in love with the country and, especially, the way of life over there.

I've always loved travelling and seeing different parts of the world. It seemed like we were in a different country every second week when Ipswich were playing in Europe. Then the trips abroad with England followed by the chance to explore the world, especially the United States, once I'd hung up my boots. As I approached the end of my time at Fratton Park on the south coast I didn't really know what I wanted to do next and a lot of my decisions were made on a whim. So here's a whistle-stop tour of life after Portsmouth...

The very brief spell at Wollongong in Australia in 1988 kept the bank balance ticking over nicely and although flying to Malta most weekends between September and May from 1988 to 1991 was rather unusual, it also paid well and kept me in the game. Playing every summer in the States from 1989 to 1993 – firstly in upstate New York then latterly in California – gave me the chance to sample the way of life over there and the lifestyle suited me. I was successful as both a player and player-coach at Albany Capitals, where we managed to reach a final, then I transferred to the San Francisco Bay Blackhawks in a similar role of player and assistant coach. I was approaching my fortieth birthday and while the legs may have been going, the football brain was still sharp and I had a great time on the pitch with the boys. Not content with that, I also spent a fair bit of time in Tokyo from 1993 onwards helping Tom Byer launch his first soccer school focussing on the 'Coerver Method' for youth development. I came back to England later that year and played a handful of games for Chorley and Bury Town – and a guest appearance for Sunday amateur team Byhams Dairy – before finally hanging up the boots once and for all at the age of forty-one.

I was Director of Football at Bolton School for a while, worked with the strikers at Preston North End when Davie Moyes was in charge and did a bit of commentary on BBC

Reborn in the USA

Radio Lancashire for a couple of years. The lifestyle was colourful, and I enjoyed myself doing that, but the money wasn't great and, after getting divorced from Ali, I couldn't really make ends meet so I decided to start looking for a new challenge. And the opportunity came in late 1996 to get involved in youth coaching over in Arizona. I'd loved my time in New York State and California a few years earlier – the American way of life was one I enjoyed – so I upped sticks once more and headed to Phoenix. After a few months I formed my own club – SC Del Sol – and over time ended up with more than two thousand kids as members. Swapping Phoenix for Boston in 2003 and a role as John Kerr's assistant coach at Harvard, then, after six months, it was on to the New England Revolution to become Steve Nicol's assistant manager. And apart from a brief spell back in Plymouth for a couple of years – 2009 to 2011 – I remained in North America, living on both the west and the east coast as well as in Toronto, until moving back to England in 2019. Nomadic, yes? Enjoyable? Sure. But there's no place like home.

* * *

Let's rewind things a little bit – slow down the pace a touch – and go back to my time with the Albany Capitals. Speaking of which, that was the first thing that struck me when I arrived in the United States – just how much slower the game was. A lot of my teammates at Albany were exceptional young athletes, their conditioning was top drawer, but there were a few who didn't quite have the same speed of thought. That's probably why I got away with playing sweeper towards the end of my spell there.

When I first started playing for Albany in May 1989 there was no dressing-room banter for the simple reason that there was no dressing room. We had to turn up at the ground – a minor-league baseball park called Bleecker Stadium – with our kit already on. It was just like it used to be when I was a teenager playing for St Gregory's in the Chorley and District Alliance League so I suppose you could say my football career really had come full circle. But the Capitals had a good group of lads who were eager to learn, and in John Bramley the team had a coach not only with great experience but someone who was also a motivator and a mentor.

In 1989 I was going into my senior year at the University of Virginia and the football team was coached by Bruce Arena. I was only twenty-two but I'd already made my debut for the United States national team and represented my country at the Olympics in Seoul in 1988. The next step was qualifying for a World Cup, something we'd not done as a country for forty years. Bruce explained to me that the United States Soccer Federation wanted all prospective World Cup players to be playing regularly at club level to give us a better chance of qualifying for Italia '90. Around that time international soccer in the States was basically us training in Florida and playing friendlies and qualifiers – there was very little structure – so the USSF wanted to make things more professional and requested that their players sign full-time contracts with clubs.

I ended up going to Albany Capitals in upstate New York and I was getting to know everybody at training the day before my first game when I saw this lad with long hair. He looked familiar. I was like 'wait a minute, no way is that Paul Mariner, that can't be right.' I recognised him from playing at the World Cup in 1982, a tournament I remember watching with my Scottish parents, but I still couldn't get my head around the fact he was playing in Albany. "Hey, how's it going mate? Good to have you here." Paul was such an upbeat and positive person, as he always has been, and while I knew about his scoring attributes and how lethal he was as a striker, I now had the chance to get to know him and see what he was like off the pitch.

Paul was a good leader in our team and brought a calming kind of influence to the group. I remember a very positive person, always positive, and I looked up to him. Any time I was looking for a bit of advice – whatever it may have been – I'd ask him and he always made time for me. He reminded me of a gypsy, an English gypsy who'd somehow managed to get lost while travelling: 'What the hell is he even doing in Albany, New York?' But he still had quality, even at the age of thirty-six, and as a young player trying to qualify for a World Cup it was great for me to have a player of Paul's experience in the same team as me.

There's a specific play I remember from 1989 that still stands out to me. I was running down the wing and he had made a decent run into the box but there was another player coming in late so I cut the ball back to the edge of the box and the other player's shot found the back of the net. As we were celebrating Paul came over and asked me why I hadn't passed to him instead. "Look, we just scored, relax." I explained I played it into an area where there was more open space. He was having none of it and told me that he was in a better position in the box and therefore the better option, despite our teammate having scored. If it wasn't Paul, perhaps someone less experienced, then I would have put it down to a typical striker always wanting the ball. But the point Paul was trying to make was to weigh up all options, if possible, before choosing the best one. Of course he wanted to score, but that was another good lesson for the kids in our team – never lose that hunger, whether you're twenty-two years old, like I was, or thirty-six like Paul. That passion, that respect for the game and that love for football, it grows with you from a young age and never, ever leaves you.

John Harkes, former United States international
(1987-2000)

* * *

I flew out to New York a couple of weeks prior to the 1990 season because my dad, Jim, was with me. I just wanted to spend some quality time with him and have some fun before the football got underway again. Dad and me were joined at the hip until he died. I loved that man. And he loved his football. He even had a spell as the Albany Capitals kit man!

We played a couple of pre-season friendlies – away from home where the opposition had actual dressing rooms – and in the second of those I put him to work and told him he was responsible for arranging the tops, shorts and socks and putting them out before the game. Kit man for a day. He was in his element. My family is the most important thing in my life. I'm extremely close to my mum, Peggy, who's an incredible woman, my boys mean everything to me and Val is an angel sent from heaven. I'm a very lucky guy.

* * *

Albany Capitals had a good season in 1991, but it also turned out to be their final season. We reached the final of the American Professional Soccer League playoffs for the first time – I was player-coach by this stage – before losing to the San Francisco Bay Blackhawks. With John Bramley, our coach, on the verge of retiring, the club owner, Armand Quadrini, offered me the chance to replace John. At that stage I had no idea the team was going under. I travelled to New York in December to do some television work at the qualifying draw for the 1994 World Cup and the trip also included a meeting with the owner and negotiations about becoming the new head coach of Albany Capitals. But the talks didn't go well. 'I got the feeling that something ain't right...'

I was always due to fly back to England at the end of the American season, but this time I did so without knowing exactly what I'd be doing the following summer. The phone went dead for a couple of weeks after I got home then, one morning, I received a call. It was from Laurie Calloway, a former defender with the likes of Rochdale and Blackburn Rovers, who was the head coach of the Blackhawks in San Francisco. We'd exchanged contact numbers after the APSL final and, as fate would have it, met up in New York when I was there for the World Cup qualifying draw. He'd heard things weren't going well in Albany and the future was bleak. Laurie was offering me the chance to sign for his San Francisco Bay Blackhawks. I wouldn't be head coach, he was, but I would have the chance to continue playing and also join his coaching staff. I was very appreciative of the offer and told him I'd let him know within a couple of months.

As it turns out, Laurie was right. Armand Quadrini could neither afford to comply with the league mandate to improve the amenities at Bleecker Stadium or expand the team's budget. Quadrini let me know at the start of 1992 that the role of head coach was no longer available. That's because the fucking team was no longer available. Thankfully Laurie's offer was still on the table and I spent the summer of 1992 in San Francisco playing for the Blackhawks and assisting Laurie on the coaching staff.

* * *

The following is part of an article entitled 'The Player: Paul Mariner shoots for one more goal' by Jonathan Vankin, which originally appeared in Metro: Silicon Valley's Weekly in July 1992.

ON THE EVENING of June 25, 1992, Paul Mariner sat on a splintery bench watching the San Francisco Bay Blackhawks play soccer against the Tampa Bay Rowdies in a park built for baseball. Approximately 4,000 spectators sat on a wooden grandstand that curled behind home plate and extended down the left-field line. Grass sown over the infield sand stood noticeably taller than the rest of the grass on the field. On the Blackhawks team bench, 10 yards and a four-foot drop from the grandstand, a fidgety Mariner sat on the second letter 'O' of the word 'Broncos', painted on the bench in fading red letters. 'Broncos' referred to Santa Clara University's [American] football team, which also played in this baseball stadium.

A lifetime of playing soccer in sun, frost and fog has weathered a toughened and sandy complexion into Mariner's face. His black hair falls over his forehead, and when he brushes it back with his hand, a lump of scar tissue peeks through, just above his right eyebrow. A smaller scar notches the skin above his upper lip. Character-revealing creases define his narrow face: frown lines, smile lines, squint lines, holler-at-the-ref lines. He has angular features, though a thrice-broken nose throws off the geometry. From the grandstand, Mariner could be identified by his rock 'n' roll-length hair, flowing over the collar of a heavy black parka. He wore the coat to defend against a biting Bay Area summer breeze because he could not keep warm by playing: his hamstring muscle was sore. After working out with the team on the baseball-cum-soccer field that morning, he showed up at a nearby restaurant with an ice bag fastened by an Ace bandage to his right thigh.

"He can't admit he's 39," grumbles the Blackhawks' head coach, Laurie Calloway. "He keeps playing that all-out style that he used to play. But when you do it at our age, your muscles go pop."

Mariner is at a transitional point in his life. A superstar of English and international soccer, he's travelled around the world, played in front of 100,000 fans and on TV viewed by millions, won championships, fraternized with rock musicians, started a sports-marketing firm – basically all the things sports superstars do. Mariner's appearance on an American soccer field therefore begs the question: What is he doing here?

The short answer: he is doing another thing sports superstars do. He's hanging around. Playing until his body will no longer allow it while understudying the coach's role. Last winter in New York, at the World Cup qualifying draw, Mariner spoke to Laurie Calloway. Within a few weeks Calloway had created a job for Mariner – assistant coach – and offered it to him.

"He reinforces what I do," says Calloway of Mariner. "Lots of hard work. We're from the same school of thought about soccer."

Calloway – stocky and bearded – appears at first a dour sort of fellow. Really, he's quite friendly once he sits down to talk, testifying effusively to the superiority of his sport over all other sports. He motivates his team through training drills with outbursts of cursing in a Birmingham, England, accent that adds a touch of elegance to the profanity. His worst frustration, he complains, is adjusting his disciplinary standards to leisure-loving American athletes, just enough so they don't revolt. Now in his seventeenth year of playing or coaching soccer on the west coast of the United States, Calloway signed with the late San Jose Earthquakes of the equally deceased North American Soccer League in 1974, one year after Mariner signed his *first English pro contract. When Calloway called, Mariner had just lost his first American soccer job. Nothing to do with him. The team folded. The Blackhawks play in San Jose State University's Spartan Stadium most of the time. Except when Spartan hosts a very important event, then the Blackhawks move to the baseball field at Santa Clara University. In the case of this scheduled Rowdies game, the very important event that deemed Spartan Stadium unavailable was a hiatus between a motocross show and a rock concert by The Cure: the field required reseeding.*

Homeless or otherwise, the Blackhawks occupy first place in the five-team American Professional Soccer League – the lone surviving pro soccer circuit in America. The Major Indoor Soccer League, which featured a six-man, made-for-TV version of the sport, collapsed July 10, 1992. Like most of the U.S. soccer culture, Mariner waits for the stateside arrival of the 1994 World Cup tournament to effect a Frankensteinian resurrection.

"I look at this as the closest I can get to European soccer without actually having the competition day in and day out," he says, in rolling northern-English inflections (a Beatles accent, more or less, to an untrained American ear). "It's a great apprenticeship for me. Learning from Laurie Calloway, learning from people in the front office, the owner, how to think about the business side as well as the soccer side. And I'm just hoping that after the World Cup in 1994 the league will grow and grow and become strong, and I'm going to be one of the premier coaches in that league. That's what I hope. Whether it happens or not, I don't know. I'd like to stay in America, because England's changed a hell of a lot over the past ten years. It's gotten more materialistic. It's gotten more violent. It's not as nice a place as it used to be.

"I earned a lot of money in the Thatcher years, so I'm not knocking the Thatcher years, they were great to me. But I was just sort of blinkered in those days – it was all about playing football and earning lots of money. Therefore because it's so intense you tend not to pull the blinkers back, to look at the broader perspective. It was hurting a few people – a lot of people

in fact. They were getting trampled upon and the network of our society started pulling away a little bit."

Looking back now I find my comments in that piece very interesting. First of all I think England is a better place now than it was thirty years ago. It's certainly not as violent and people are more aware culturally of what is and isn't acceptable, although we're definitely not as patient a society as we were back then. Secondly, the comment about 'hoping to be one of the premier coaches in that league' after the 1994 World Cup suggests I saw my future at that point a) in the United States and b) in management – fifty per cent correct when it comes to forecasting the future isn't too bad, I suppose. Not having any previous managerial experience was certainly a hindrance when it came to looking for jobs ahead of the inaugural Major League Soccer season, but in truth my personal life wasn't exactly in a great place and my marriage was in trouble in the early Nineties.

Playing and coaching in America during the summer, helping Tom Byers set up Coerver Coaching in Japan and working as an agent most of the time when I was back in England meant I was spending far too much time away from home. That was on me, and although Ali and I stayed together for a few months after I'd finished my playing career, we eventually broke up. I was away on one of my many trips away – this time in San Diego, California – so Ali said she would come out to visit me. I picked her up from LAX [Los Angeles Airport] then we drove back down to San Diego. I can't remember any specifics of the conversation but things weren't great between us around that time. We subsequently had a big blow up and she flew back to England. Game over.

* * *

I played in many different countries during my time in football although never in Mexico, however that's nearly where I finished my playing career. Let me explain. Deep-pocketed real estate lawyer Dan Van Voorhis was the owner of the team I played for, San Francisco Bay Blackhawks, and a man whose thought process when it came to soccer was actually way ahead of his time. Dan knew that the game at club level in America was a mess so he made enquiries about applying for guest status in the Mexican top flight. And the President of US Soccer at the time was also on board...

> "We're having serious discussions with the Mexican Federation on the subject and I think there is a realistic possibility it could happen. I believe both the Blackhawks and the Mexican league are interested in testing what would be a new marketing concept."
> **Alan Rothenberg, speaking in 1993 (quotes taken from an article in The Guardian, January 2016)**

Ultimately Dan's plan remained just that, an ambitious idea but no more, and nothing came of the move to the Mexican Primera División. By this stage the league we played in – the APSL – had shrunk to five teams and three of them played in Florida. As if I wasn't doing enough travelling...

So the owner decided to make some changes. The San Francisco Bay Blackhawks were renamed the San Jose Hawks and Dan also struck a deal with the San Jose State University Foundation giving him full control over all soccer-related events at Spartan Stadium. Van Voorhis also told the APSL he was withdrawing our team from the league and instead joining the USISL, a 43-team minor league operation. If playing in the United States Interregional Soccer League wasn't enough to tell me to hang up the boots at the end of the season then I don't know what was!

* * *

The start of 1994 was when I decided to press life's reset button. I moved back to England because I wanted to live closer to my mum and dad again – a child is never too old to either want or need the love of their parents – so I bought a little terraced house in Chorley. Quite simply, I was just trying to rebuild my life after the divorce from Alison. Take stock, re-assess and be a better father for my boys. I wasn't as wealthy anymore and was just trying to make a reasonable living, hence working for BBC Radio Lancashire and at Bolton School, although I really enjoyed both roles and got on very well with the people I worked with.

After spending nearly three years back in England sorting my life out, I came back to the States in late-1996 after the opportunity arose to get involved in youth coaching in Arizona. Managerial positions for those with practically no managerial experience are usually scarce so I knew that wasn't an option but I wanted to stay in football. I chose to do something I love, coaching kids. And why not do it with the sun on my back every day. I'd previously had plenty of discussions with various people about the untapped potential of coaching youth soccer in America. I thought it was worth the risk because of the possible reward. Speculate to accumulate, Rodney.

As far as money is concerned, I wasn't sacrificing too much by giving up roles at Bolton School and BBC Radio Lancashire and to be honest the coaching opportunities at club level in

England were few and far between. Certainly nothing you could make a living from. While it may have been a gamble coming back to the States without guaranteed employment, I'd already fallen in love with the lifestyle over there and I was hoping a change of scenery would mean a fresh start.

I came back to Arizona in 1996 after playing professionally in Germany and was asked by one of the bosses, Gus Brose, to start a skills programme for Paradise Valley soccer club, where I worked with former Trinidad and Tobago national team player Leroy DeLeon. It wasn't long before Gus told me they were bringing someone in to fill the role of Director of Coaching. "What am I, chopped liver?"

I was introduced to Paul Mariner and not once at the beginning did he mention his background or his many achievements. He didn't need to. Within minutes of working with him I realised straight away this guy was big time. My respect for him was instant, and I loved that he respected me as well. Paul told me all about his career over a beer following that first session, but only because I asked, and just as importantly he wanted to know about my life in soccer and my role with Paradise Valley. The most unassuming person and one of the nicest people I've ever met. It was like a gift from the gods when Paul Mariner arrived in Arizona and began working here.

Tamera Hatfield, President and Director of Coaching at Arizona Soccer Academy

I settled in to the Arizona way of life pretty much immediately and Tamera was a huge help. I was able to combine my experience of playing the game and coaching the Coerver Method in Japan and she brought so many other required attributes to the table. Between us and a few others at the club we were able to spread the word about our coaching and our club and, over time, we eventually reached a point where we had more than two thousand members once Paradise Valley merged with Moon Valley to become SC Del Sol.

I'd become good friends with Paul after working with him for a couple of years on BBC Radio Lancashire and he invited me out to stay with him in Phoenix, Arizona, for a couple of weeks in the summer of 1997. A fair bit of that time was spent helping him coach the kids, and what a great job he did putting together that youth academy. It was still in its infancy when I was there and he basically had a bag of balls and was trying to coach kids the Coerver Method in a public park. Due to the heat, boys and girls would begin arriving around seven-thirty for training starting at eight o'clock, and this took place most mornings. It wasn't long before tens of kids became hundreds of kids which ultimately became a couple of thousand kids as registered members within five or six years.

Paul was most proud when he got the chance to showcase his talented players that were part of S.C. Del Sol. I remember going to London Colney in 1999 to watch his under sixteens take on Arsenal under sixteens. Paul had been in touch with Liam Brady, the Arsenal youth coach, to help organise the fixture. Arsenal were producing so many young players around that time – the ones who would play in the League Cup every season then Arsene Wenger would never pick them again – and Liam had put together a brilliant youth team. I knew Paul was really pumped for that fixture because he went into game-mode before kick-off, wouldn't speak to anybody other than his players and was fully focussed – this was an opportunity to come back to England with a team that he coached and try to prove that his lads were on a par with one of the best youth teams in England. He stood on the touchline, head-to-toe in Adidas gear and saw this as a chance to make a statement. I'm not sure to who, maybe himself, but he was certainly taking it seriously. This was the culmination of three years' hard work – he'd certainly not brought his boys all the way over from Arizona just to make up the numbers. The game finished one-all and Paul was so proud of that result. He was proud of what the academy had achieved in a short period of time and he was also proud of getting his players to a level where they could compete with one of England's best youth teams.

It says a lot that a former England international decided to start a new life in Arizona, sourcing then coaching a handful of kids in a public park at the beginning, but that was Paul. He was just looking to make a name for himself along a different career path, which he did very successfully. I'm sure he would have had a few offers from teams if he'd decided to stay in England, but Paul chose to go into an alien environment and to actually do what he did, in many ways, is even more impressive than, say, staying put and trying to get a job here in the United Kingdom.

Nigel Adderley, football commentator for Premier League Productions and talkSPORT

I absolutely loved my time in Arizona. Constant sunshine from five in the morning until around eight at night and working with the kids every day was magic. And having my son, Dan, coming out to Arizona to live with me for a couple of years to finish his schooling was the icing on the cake. To start something from scratch with Tamera Hatfield – who's still one of my best friends – and build it up to where we had over two thousand children taking part was extremely rewarding for both of us. When I got the opportunity to become assistant coach at Harvard University in 2003 I think the time was right to move on, but that was only because politics was starting to creep in to the running of the soccer academy. One or two things behind the scenes were becoming problematic, including plans to take the club to the next level, so it was probably best that I left when I did.

20

Horwich to Harvard

One of the first Americans to play league football in England was a guy called John Kerr, a forward, who arrived at Portsmouth in 1987 on the recommendation of former Chelsea striker Peter Osgood. Poor John was like was a deer caught in the headlights initially – he'd never witnessed anything like the ferocity of the tackles every Friday morning in the gym – so I put my arm around him and said I'd show him the ropes. In the end it didn't work out for John at Pompey and he went out on loan to Peterborough United after only playing six games for us. I liked John, he was fun to be around, and we stayed in touch. Just as well, because in 2003 I got a call out of the blue when I was in Arizona:

"It's time for you to come back to the east coast – I want you to be my assistant coach at Harvard University."

* * *

I don't mind admitting that the butterflies in the old stomach were fairly fluttering ahead of my first day in the new job. Prior to my arrival, I'm pretty sure the only time the words 'Bolton' and 'Harvard' ever appeared on the same page was when the homeowners of Harvard Road in Bolton, Massachusetts wrote their address on a letter. But the boy from Bolton was going to Harvard, proving that a Horwich County secondary school education can open doors anywhere!

It's funny how certain things happen in life. This was the right job at the right time with the top school in the Ivy League – eight American presidents have graduated from Harvard. You're coaching football but you know the students aren't there to become footballers; these kids are going to be big timers on Wall Street or in politics. It was an incredible opportunity.

I arrived in Boston from Arizona on the Friday night and John Kerr called me the following day to tell me about the Monday morning meeting at eight o'clock.

> I explained to Paul that the annual soccer meeting takes place on the eve of every new season, attendance is compulsory and the dress code was formal because the Principal of Harvard University would be attending.
>
> **John Kerr**

So I went into Boston on the Sunday to buy a bloody suit – it cost me about a grand – because I hadn't brought one with me from Arizona. The next morning I was all whistled up for the meeting and looking really sharp. Kerr rolls in to the car park and gets out of his motor, but he's still got his training stuff on.

"Where's your gear?" I asked him.

"In my office. I'm just going inside to get changed and I'll see you in there."

The bastard had played me like a bloody fiddle. He was waiting for me at the entrance with a big smile on his face. The Principal was nowhere to be seen because the meeting was just for coaches, assistants, trainers and staff. It was like a walk of shame going past all the secretaries in my three-piece suit accompanied by Kerr and his childish, sniggering ways. I didn't know whether to punch him or walk out – and I sincerely considered both options! There must have been over one hundred people in the room and needless-to-say I was the only one wearing a suit. Quite the first impression.

* * *

The job consisted of two parts. Assistant coach at Harvard University and also Technical Director for the Greater Boston Bolts, one of the top youth teams in the country, of which John was affiliated. And part of that role involved coaching the under ten boys and the under eleven girls. Believe it or not, that's actually one of the most rewarding things I've ever done.

> Getting Paul to do something was probably harder than him actually doing it. He only wanted to do something if he felt he could make a difference, and when I initially told him that he needed to coach eleven-year-old girls he looked at me like I had two heads. But I explained that I was trying to rebuild the club, starting with the youngest age group, and the best way to do that was by building from the bottom up. 'Let's show we care'. And what better way for me to do that than by getting former England international Paul Mariner involved. So I think if you can explain to Paul and reason with him that doing something was going to be beneficial to both himself and to the kids then he was in. And once Paul was in he was always fully committed. That's what I loved about him.
>
> **John Kerr**

I'd only been at Harvard for one full semester – about four months, hardly enough time to even get my feet wet – when John Kerr said that former Liverpool defender Steve Nicol wanted to discuss the possibility of me becoming his assistant coach at New England Revolution. All I had to do was meet Stevie at Desmond O'Malley's pub in Framingham, Massachusetts, the following Sunday.

I won't lie, I thought that was a bloody prank as well. Fool me once, shame on you. Fool me twice, shame on me. It took some amount of convincing to get me to go. And even when I got to the pub on the Sunday I still wasn't convinced.

"Where is he?"

"What are you talking about?" enquired Stevie.

"Kerr, where is he? The bastard must be here somewhere. Is this a wind-up?"

"No, I promise you, it's not a wind-up. I'd like you to be my assistant."

"Okay, I'll tell you what we'll do. If this isn't a wind-up then absolutely, I'll be your assistant. But if it is then you two can go and fuck yourselves. Last chance… is Kerr here?"

"No."

"Right, I'd love to be your assistant. Thanks for asking. What are you drinking?"

And that exchange in an Irish pub in Framingham – about twenty miles west of Boston – on a freezing cold Sunday afternoon at the beginning of January 2004 is how my relationship with Stevie Nicol began.

I have to admit, doing what Paul did – potentially telling a new employer to go fuck himself – was pretty ballsy and could have backfired spectacularly. But from that day forward I don't think there was a single occasion when we were together that we didn't laugh. Partners in crime; Statler and Waldorf; as thick as thieves; like an old married couple – you name it, we were called it, but we had so much fun over the next six years or so.

Steve Nicol

I hadn't been in the spotlight for nearly sixteen years and although I wasn't complaining about not being in the spotlight for nearly sixteen years, the opportunity to return to a position of relative prominence was too good to turn down. This wasn't me when I was in my mid-twenties – when the dormant ego needed to be awoken if not enough attention was being paid – but instead it was the fifty-year-old version of me, content to play a part without needing to be at the forefront of decision-making.

That meeting in Framingham was the first time I'd seen Stevie in person since October 1987 when his Liverpool side thumped my Portsmouth team four-nil at Anfield. We hit it off straight away, following my initial skepticism of course, and we even discussed potential draft picks in the pub with the 2004 MLS SuperDraft taking place the following week. And that allowed me to provide him with contact details for Doug Allison, Clint Dempsey's college coach at Furman University. Further digging over the following few days unearthed a potential attitude problem with Clint, but it was an attitude we liked. He was a winner and did not like losing. We knew this twenty-year-old midfielder was a gem but were worried that another team would select him with one of the first seven picks in the draft. Thankfully he was still there when it was our time to pick and we were absolutely delighted to get him.

* * *

5th February, 2004

New England Revolution News Release

FOXBOROUGH, MA – The New England Revolution announced today the hiring of former England international Paul Mariner as assistant coach. Also joining the Revolution coaching staff as goalkeeper coach is Peter Simonini, who served in the same capacity with the Revs from 1996-98.

"I am delighted to add both Paul and Peter to the technical staff here with the Revolution," said head coach Steve Nicol. "Paul obviously brings tremendous experience and credentials to the job, and Peter is well known to New England soccer people as a guy who understands the game at every level. I know both men well and look forward to their contributions as we build toward our goal of a league title."

Two of my most important signings were made at the beginning of 2004. I took 20-year-old Clint Dempsey with the eighth pick of the MLS SuperDraft and added 51-year-old Paul Mariner as my assistant (on a free transfer!) from Harvard University, where he'd been coaching. The man who brought me over to the States, John Kerr, had played with Paul at Portsmouth and thought he'd be a good fit as part of the Revs coaching staff. I'd played against Paul a few times back in England but didn't really know him that well, however from our first meeting at an Irish pub in Framingham, Massachusetts, we got on like a house on fire and he was the perfect choice to be my assistant.

Steve Nicol

It wasn't long before we had nicknames for each other. I called him Jim and he called me Jim. The start of any subsequent telephone conversation was always the same.

Him: "Awrite Jim?"

Me: "Aye. Alright Jim?"

Him: "Aye."

We'd just finished a pre-season session on the island of São Miguel in the Azores in March 2004 – I've had worse spring-training campaigns – with Clint once again a stand-out when I suggested to Stevie that we alter the system to get this kid Dempsey into the team. He'd just turned twenty-one but it was clear from the moment he joined us that he was an exceptional talent. Clint went on to start twenty-three of twenty-four matches for us that season, scored seven goals and was named 2004 MLS Rookie of the Year. It came as no surprise to me whatsoever when Clint went on to achieve bigger and better things and had a great career.

> Aye, but me and Paul never called him Clint. We used to call him Clit, and did so for three years right until he joined Fulham. Absolutely nothing against Clint, he was a joy to work with and a super player, it's just that we were really childish and got away with it because of our accents. And you know what, I wouldn't be surprised if, even to this day, Clint still has no idea that we called him what we did!
>
> **Steve Nicol**

Stevie's a fantastic coach and we went on an incredible run, with New England Revolution reaching the MLS Cup final three years in a row between 2005 and 2007. All the Liverpool methods came out and we had some very good players, but I think our success was all down to my wee pal Jim and the way he ran the club. Sadly we lost all three finals but Stevie created an atmosphere at the Revs in those days that was reminiscent of my time at Ipswich when we were doing well. You couldn't wait to go in to work every morning and there was an edge in training, with the players desperate to impress so they didn't get left out on a matchday. We had a combination of talented guys, a good system and a real desire to win, but I think if you asked all the other coaches at that time they would have said we were a team they did not enjoy playing against. In important games we played on that big time. All our players bought into our way of thinking and entered the field believing they already had an advantage over their opponents.

＊ ＊ ＊

It was the day before the 2008 MLS All-Star game against West Ham United in Toronto – Stevie and myself had been chosen to coach the team – and we were working on set-pieces during a training session. We knew what David Beckham was capable of when taking free-kicks, but what about blocking them? Would he put those good looks on the line for the good of the team? Stevie set up the wall, telling every player where they should go, then I explained to David that when the ball was touched to the side he should be the one to charge and block it and, if needed, take the full force straight in that handsome face of his. To his credit he strolled into position without once complaining and was ready for action. Meanwhile the looks on the faces of the other players was priceless when David was doing this – it was like they'd seen a ghost – but when me and Stevie started laughing out loud just before the free-kick was taken the game was up. It was a wind-up.

By the way, that was quite the journey Mr. Beckham had been on since the last time I worked with him during his loan spell at Preston North End in 1994-95. I used to cover Preston games for BBC Radio Lancashire and got to know manager Gary Peters and club captain David Moyes pretty well. It wasn't long before I was asked to help coach the strikers and I used to go in every Wednesday after training to work on finishing with players who wanted extra practice. Then, in March 1995, a nineteen-year-old kid arrived on a month's loan from Manchester United. His name? David Beckham.

Nigel Adderley and me were commentating on the Third Division clash between Preston and Doncaster Rovers at Deepdale when David came on as a substitute for Graham Lancashire at the start of the second half to make his debut. Beckham had been part of the group on the Wednesday working on their finishing and I told Nigel during commentary that the lad "certainly knew where the back of the net was". David went on to score direct from a corner. I tried to claim that I taught him how to do that during the week, but I'm not sure Nigel or BBC Radio Lancashire listeners believed me...!

* * *

I thought the team we had at the Revs was coming to the end of its lifespan during the 2009 season and needed breaking up. Stevie didn't agree with me. But I was right. I also thought it might be time for me to move on to pastures new as well. As it turned out, the team did start to break up at the end of that season, not long after I resigned as assistant manager in October 2009 to go back to England to join Plymouth Argyle.

I'm not sure I've enjoyed my time as much at a football club as I did during my six years with New England Revolution.

Playing the game is very different from coaching, and I had a blast at all the clubs I played for, but it's different when you're part of the hierarchy barking out orders while still trying to keep the squad on your side. I think Stevie and me managed to maintain an element of fun throughout our time together with the Revs and I hope the various players we coached over the years think the same way. Never a dull moment with those guys, and three MLS Cup finals in six years isn't a bad return. So many memories to look back on fondly, I just wish we could have won that trophy because those lads and our supporters deserved some silverware.

* * *

I've got Jürgen Klinsmann to thank for my return to North America with Toronto FC at the start of 2011. We first met in July 2003 at an Adidas Elite Soccer Camp in Wilmington, North Carolina, when I was Director of Coerver coaching systems, the pair of us hit it off straight away and continued to keep in touch.

Just a couple of months after Jürgen was hired by Toronto as a technical consultant to advise on an overhaul of club personnel, they appointed former Dutch international Aron Winter as the new head coach and I came in the same day as Director of Player Development.

> I was asked to recommend one or two people for the role, which I did, but I knew straight away that Paul was perfect for the role of Director of Player Development because of our personal relationship and the way he conducted himself, especially around people in the game. He's also a fantastic person and very knowledgeable about football having played

the game at the highest level, coached at grassroots level and had plenty of experience at pretty much every other level in between, either as a player or a coach. I tried my best to get him into the club and thankfully he crushed the interview, resulting in his hiring by the club at the start of 2011.

Jürgen Klinsmann

Ten games into the Major League Soccer season, and with the team only winning once and losing the other nine games, Aron stepped down and I was asked to take over as head coach at the beginning of June. The only way was up but I knew I had to make some changes to be able to do that. Confidence was low among the squad, understandably so given the run of results, so I gathered them all together and asked what they felt was required to turn things around. I got the impression the players weren't overly keen on the strict discipline from the previous regime so I reduced the number of formal team meals, relaxed the dress code and promised them we'd have more fun. I'm not saying that's what I would do if taking over the reins at any other club and starting from scratch – I do like an element of discipline – but things needed to change at Toronto and I wanted the squad to have a say and, more importantly, enjoy coming to work. They were the ones who would ultimately decide if my time in charge was successful or not and it made a lot of sense to have them on board right from the start.

In the next ten games we were unbeaten in eight of them, winning four and drawing four, and things had definitely picked up after an awful start to the season. Then a few injuries, coupled with a small squad, totally derailed the momentum and we failed to win any of our last fourteen matches. Quite the rollercoaster ride. I gave it my best shot but it wasn't good enough and I was eventually sacked by Toronto on the seventh of January, 2013. And that was the last time I was directly involved in professional football either as a player, a coach or a manager, just short of forty years after signing my first semi-professional contract with Chorley in 1973.

21

No Place Like Home

The congregation at Durham Cathedral for Sir Bobby Robson's memorial service in September 2009 was like a Who's Who from the world of football and entertainment. Bobby's death from cancer at the end of July at the age of seventy-six hit everyone hard and more than one thousand people were in attendance to pay their respects. Catching up with old pals from my Ipswich and England days was comforting, giving us all an opportunity to exchange so many great stories about the gaffer, and it was great to see the boys again, albeit in such sad circumstances.

As I was driving back to my hotel following the service my mobile phone rang. It was an old friend of mine from Plymouth telling me that Argyle executive director Keith Todd wanted to speak to me "urgently". He passed on Keith's number so I called him and explained I was flying back to Boston the following morning. Keith asked if I could change my flight and divert to Bristol instead to meet him and manager Paul Sturrock. After receiving sufficient guarantees that I would indeed be interested in what they had to say, and that it would be worth my while, I re-booked my flight back to the States and flew to Bristol first.

No Place Like Home

There wasn't a job offer per se, but a change of managerial structure at Home Park was discussed along with the possibility of me potentially working for Paul Sturrock. He would stay on as team manager and I would take over as head coach.

That's about as far as we got with the talks but after hitting it off with Paul straight away I said I was definitely interested. I was due back in the country a couple of weeks later to firm up my role as an ambassador for Plymouth's bid to become a host city for the 2018 World Cup (if England's bid was successful), and we agreed to have more talks on my return.

One of the first things Paul did when arriving back in Boston was tell me about the interest from Plymouth. I don't recall one single occasion during the time we worked together with the Revs when we kept something from each other. We might have disagreed about certain things – one of them being whether or not the 2009 Revs team needed to be broken up – but we were always honest with one another. I knew Luggy [Paul Sturrock] well, having played with him for Scotland. Marrers returning to Plymouth to work with Luggy sounded like an ideal setup to me and there was no way I would ever stand in his way, especially when there appeared to be a decent chance of Paul eventually taking over as manager at Home Park.

Steve Nicol

Sometimes in life you encounter people who, for whatever reason, you just have a bond with. I must have sat with Paul Sturrock in his house for about eight hours basically chewin' the fat over a few bottles of wine before I realised the time. Paul didn't have to invite me to his home and it was very much appreciated.

The local press were aware that I was back in England to promote Plymouth's bid to become a World Cup host city and I wasn't in the country long before I had to answer the inevitable questions about a potential coaching role with Argyle. I tried not to give too much away and this was my reply that subsequently appeared in the newspapers...

"I have been asked many times whether I would like to work in England but I have never had the opportunity. When the opportunity comes along, I will make that decision. At the present moment, I have got a couple of things in the States that are different to the MLS and they are on the table. I have got a decent reputation out there. I love Boston and everything is hunky-dory, but I'm probably in the house for half of the year. I'm always travelling, scouting and looking at players. It's a nomadic life whatever you do in football."

It's like a statement written on my behalf by a public relations executive! The old line 'people used to ask me why I'd never managed here and I told them that nobody had ever asked me' was resurrected once again on a trip back to England, but this time I think the journos got the hint and over the next few days the wheels turned on my return to Plymouth Argyle.

Further talks were held with the club and we eventually reached an agreement that I would become the new head coach, working under Paul Sturrock, so I flew back to the States to tie up some loose ends over there and prepare for my final game as assistant manager of the Revs.

It's funny how life works at times. I was only back in England to attend the memorial service for Sir Bobby but it eventually led to my return to English football, and with Plymouth Argyle as well, a club near and dear to my heart. I just felt this was Bobby's way of looking after me.

* * *

Tuesday 13th October, 2009

New England Revolution today confirmed that Paul Mariner has spoken to Argyle about a possible return to Home Park. Lizz Summers, director of communications for the Revolution, said: "Plymouth asked for permission to speak with Paul, which we granted. At this point, nothing is final and Paul and the rest of the coaches are concentrating on a key match against Chicago."

Three days later I handed in my resignation, effective after the fixture with Chicago Fire on the Saturday night, and that gave me a chance to say farewell to the boys and thank the fans for their support during the previous six years.

Saturday 17th October, 2009

Following the goalless draw with Chicago at Gillette Stadium, I asked the New England Revolution to release a statement on my behalf...

"I've had six wonderful years with New England Revolution and will take with me many wonderful memories. But Plymouth Argyle is in my blood. I'll be in Bristol on Monday night, ready for the game on Tuesday. In football, there is not much sentiment. But, if sentiment is involved in this scenario, then they gave me my very first chance as a player, so I grabbed it with both hands. The teams you're associated with are the ones you look for every week, and, when they came knocking on my door asking me to be employed there, I was delighted. I have a lot of friends back there, old friends, and old players. When I went back there last time it was fantastic. So hopefully I can do a decent job for all the supporters and the board."

And that ended my direct involvement with Major League Soccer, which began in January 2004, although it wasn't the end of my relationship with New England Revolution...

Sunday 18th October, 2009

Plymouth Argyle statement:

Chairman Roy Gardner said: "On behalf of the board, I am pleased to announce that we hope to confirm soon the appointment of Paul Mariner as Head Coach, working for Paul Sturrock. Paul Mariner is not only an Argyle legend, but has established himself as a highly respected and leading coach in American Major League Soccer and internationally, including in Japan. He will bring his own style and a wealth of experience to the club, supporting the development of the football side of the club. Paul Sturrock is already charged with working to complete the review of all aspects of the football side of the club, including: coaching, training facilities, the scouting system, medical and physiotherapy, and youth football. He will now be supported in this work by Paul Mariner. The board are appreciative of the co-operation that New England Revolution have shown in releasing Paul Mariner. The two clubs have agreed a first step of a potential ongoing relationship with a plan that a number of the New England Revolution younger stars will join Plymouth for a few weeks for joint-training sessions later in the season. This is an appointment which will cause a tingle to run down the spine of any Pilgrim. Paul Mariner represents a past, present and future that is the very essence of what Argyle should be about: a beloved ex-player who knows and understands the Greens and its fans, who has carved out a post-playing career as a respected coach and who now passionately wants to put something back into his former club."

It was quite the whirlwind start to life back in England. I arrived in Bristol on the Monday evening, met the players for the first time on the Tuesday morning and was in the dugout at Ashton

Gate for the three-one defeat to Bristol City in the evening. I was then formally introduced by the club on the Friday before the boys faced my former team, Ipswich Town, at Home Park on the Saturday. What a quirk of fate; my first home game as an employee of Plymouth Argyle since I played for them against Cardiff City in October 1976 and, of course, it had to be against the team Argyle sold me to that very same month.

The reception from the fans was so special – including the 784 visiting supporters who'd travelled from Suffolk – and I think I used up just as much energy jumping up and down like a dafty on the touchline that day as I did when I wore the green and white number nine jersey with pride back in the day. Carl Fletcher gave us a first-half lead before Ipswich substitute Jon Stead equalised in the second half and the game finished all-square.

So a defeat and a draw to begin with, but we'd only won four league games in the Championship by the first week in December. Following the midweek defeat at Swansea City, chairman Roy Gardner announced that Paul Sturrock was moving upstairs and I would be taking charge of the team 'with immediate effect'. Fifty-six-year-old Paul Mariner finally getting the chance to be a manager; I thought that ship had sailed ages ago.

I was lucky enough to bring in John Carver as my assistant. Bobby Robson's former assistant manager at Newcastle United, John had been out of work since leaving Toronto FC – where he was head coach – and I considered his appointment a bit of a coup. He subsequently turned down an approach from Burnley to become assistant manager to new boss Brian Laws and that meant a lot to me.

We won three out of four league matches after Christmas

but the results overall were too inconsistent, never going more than three games in a row without losing at least one of them. So we tried to change the team around a little bit. Rather than build it out from the back we went a little bit longer, trying to use the pace up front of Bradley Wright-Phillips and Yannick Bolasie to better effect. Bradley was back in contention following a serious knee injury and Yannick had returned from a loan spell at Barnet, and both of them started in the two-nil win over Ipswich Town on my return to Portman Road in March 2010, one of the few positive results we managed that season.

I was euphoric after the game. We'd played some bright football, the reaction from the Ipswich fans to me was absolutely remarkable before the game and I was on cloud nine. I remember after the final whistle going over to salute the Plymouth supporters in the upper tier of the Cobbold Stand and when I was over there a young girl, who was standing with her dad in among the Ipswich fans, asked if she could have my training top so I took it off and gave it to her. It wasn't until I was back in the dressing room that I realised my designer reading glasses that I'd paid five-hundred pounds for were missing. I'd taken them off at full-time and put them in one of the pockets of the training top I'd just given away. In every post-game interview I did I mentioned that I'd lost my specs and then explained what had happened, which led to talkSPORT broadcaster Danny Kelly putting out an appeal live on air. Amazingly, within half an hour they'd been returned to the reception at Portman Road and I had them for the journey back to Plymouth!

That was the first time I'd been involved in a game at Ipswich since playing there for Portsmouth in February 1987 so understandably there were a lot of people I wanted to see after the game, including several who were at the club way back when I played for Ipswich in the Seventies and Eighties. It wasn't until a couple of days later when reading the newspapers that I found out Roy Keane had hit out at me for not accepting his invitation to have a drink with him after the match. I have nothing but respect for Roy and would never intentionally snub him; three or four members of my coaching staff spent nearly half an hour with his staff because they knew I would be a while but unfortunately I just never got the chance to join them. I also didn't have an opportunity to apologise to Roy directly, but I certainly didn't mean any harm. I was already responsible for the late departure of the team bus that Tuesday night, it wouldn't have left until after midnight if I'd also socialised with Mr. Keane!

Sadly that win at Ipswich was one of the few high points during my time in charge. We never managed to get out of the bottom three at any stage and sadly we were relegated, finishing second bottom of the Championship. Four days after the final game of the season – a two-one home defeat against Peterborough United – my spell in charge was officially over when Plymouth announced they were looking for a new manager. I was well aware my position was being reviewed by the Board at the end of the season and it came as no surprise when they reached that decision. I could argue that a lot of the damage had already been done when we took over. I could also claim that in the end we just ran out of fixtures. Both, however, are just excuses. We lost our last five league games and finished eight points behind Crystal Palace, who just managed to stay up. That's probably a better indicator as to what went wrong.

I was brought in as manager to keep Plymouth Argyle in the Championship. We were second bottom when I took over and we finished second bottom, twenty-third of twenty-four teams. I can't have any complaints, especially because the club allowed me to stay on as Peter Reid's head coach when he took over as manager. But the opportunity to move back to North America at the start of 2011 and join Toronto FC as Director of Player Development brought to an end my second and final spell at Home Park, although I'll forever be grateful for everything that the club and the supporters did for me.

I've known Paul for a long time – from his early days at Chorley because I was in the youth team at Bolton – and working with him has been fantastic. When my Everton team beat Southampton in the FA Cup semi-final at Highbury in 1984, Paul ran across the players' lounge after the game and gave me the biggest hug, he was so pleased for me. And at Plymouth he used to invite me round to his house and would cook for me. Marrers also loved his horse racing and would organise days out for the staff at Exeter racecourse and we'd have such a great day. A great personality and someone who is a legend with the fans at this football club and I'm sure he'll be successful in everything he does in the future.

Peter Reid

* * *

I was very lucky to achieve a lot in football. The kid who worked in an engineering factory and went to night school while playing part-time football then signed his first professional contract a few days after his twentieth birthday. A big move to a high-flying First Division team was next, followed by an England debut at Wembley, then winning the FA Cup and the UEFA Cup before scoring at a World Cup and moving to Arsenal – all in the space of thirteen years. Somebody also told me that, somehow, I scored more goals for England than Trevor Francis, Teddy Sheringham, Stanley Matthews, Peter Beardsley, Robbie Fowler, Ian Wright, Paul Gascoigne and Jackie Milburn did. I still find that hard to believe. But being inducted into the Ipswich Town Hall of Fame in April 2011 is one of the things I'm most proud of in life.

To join Doug Moran, Andy Nelson, John Compton, Russell Osman, Roy Bailey (posthumous), Sir Alf Ramsey (special merit award) and the title-winning team of 1961-62 as new inductees was an absolute honour, our names alongside Ipswich greats who'd previously been inducted:

2007: Mick Mills, Ted Phillips, Ray Crawford, John Wark 2008: John Elsworthy, Frans Thijssen, Kevin Beattie, Jimmy Leadbitter (posthumous) 2009: George Burley, Arnold Mühren, Billy Baxter, Allan Hunter, Sir Bobby Robson, Pat Godbold, Roy Stephenson (posthumous) 2010: Larry Carberry, Terry Butcher, Cyril Lea, Roger Osborne, Tommy Parker (posthumous), John Cobbold (special merit award)

Just like Plymouth Argyle, Ipswich Town is a very special club and one that knows how to look after employees, not only on the playing and coaching side but also behind the scenes. And I just want to give a special mention to Pat Godbold, Bobby Robson's former secretary, who in total worked for nine managers during her time at the club, which stretched back to Alf Ramsey in the mid-Fifties. Pat was inducted into the Hall of Fame in 2009 and is one of the sweetest, kindest and most caring people I've ever known. She's one in a million.

The first person to contact me after Bobby Robson died in July 2009 was PM, all the way from America. Paul was very upset but he still wanted to check in with me and make sure I was okay. That's the type of person PM is. I promised him

I'd let him know the details of the memorial service for Mr. Robson as soon as I had them and I'm so pleased he made it over to pay his respects. It was lovely to see him again.

Pat Godbold, Ipswich Town legend

* * *

While things didn't work out the way I would have hoped at Toronto, being back on that side of the pond did open a few doors for me and I was lucky enough to get involved in the media side of things with ESPN in Bristol, Connecticut, where I worked with Steve Nicol once again.

"Awrite Jim?"

"Aye. Alright Jim?"

"Aye."

I also kept in touch with Brad Feldman, the New England Revolution radio and television commentator who used to call games when Stevie and me were in charge, and he helped facilitate my return to the Revs in 2014 working alongside him at games as an analyst, a role I was lucky enough to keep for six full seasons. We travelled all over North America with the team – a lot of the time on Robert Kraft's plane that was used by the New England Patriots – and working with Brad was always great fun, a throwback to my days as colour commentator with BBC Radio Lancashire in the mid-Nineties.

I learned about more than just football from Paul. His straightforward, honest, maybe honest-to-a-fault way of doing things is a lost art and, sadly, there's less of it in today's world. One of the reasons why Paul is a working class hero, or maverick, or whatever you want to call him, is that he speaks from the heart. He does things his way. That's the takeaway from all my experiences with him over nearly two decades. They even started calling him Sir Paul Mariner on the local television station here in Boston, but I don't think being a Sir suited him. He wasn't really about manners or titles or niceties. He probably swore and cursed a little too much and didn't go out of his way to kiss certain behinds. He didn't get his coaching badges either, it just wasn't his style, because he was like 'I'm gonna do it my way'. He was Paul Mariner and never pretended to be anybody else. That's why everybody loved him.

Brad Feldman, play-by-play voice of the New England Revolution

My nomadic ways continued at the end of the 2019 MLS season when I decided to finish my broadcast duties with both New England Revolution and ESPN and return to England. Time was getting on and I wanted to spend more of it with my mum, Peggy, and be closer to the boys and to Val. My long associa-tion with football – either as a player, a coach, a manager or a broadcaster - had finally come to an end for the simple reason that there really is no place like home.

POSTSCRIPT

Fighting To The End

Wednesday 14th April, 2021

A message from Val on WhatsApp reads *'Today is a good day if you want to call him.'* A time was subsequently arranged for later that day. This was the first time Paul had felt well enough to have a proper chat following intense chemotherapy and radiation therapy treatment for glioblastoma. It was also the last time we spoke. What follows is an abridged version of our one hour and thirty-four minute conversation, the only one we were able to have since agreeing to write the book together in February.

Mark Donaldson:
The last time I saw you was in the office at ESPN in October 2019 because you moved back to England the following month. Everything happened so quickly with the move, didn't it?

Paul Mariner:
It did, yeah, and sadly I didn't get the chance to say a proper goodbye to the people I worked with. And those six years at ESPN were some of the most enjoyable in my life. But there was a lady back home who was pushing to make things happen and get me to return to England.

That lady was Val. What's the history between you two?
We were friends from my days with Arsenal but lost touch after I left the club in 1986. I flew back to England in February 2019 to attend a nostalgia night in Clacton in memory of Kevin Beattie. Val was there too and that was the first time I'd seen her for more than 33 years.

Val Parry:
I lived in Clacton and my son-in-law asked if I was going to Kevin Beattie's do at the Royal Hotel. I remembered reading in the local paper a couple of months earlier that Paul was planning to fly over from America so I decided to attend in the hope that I'd get to see him and say hi. Paul was standing chatting at the bar just before the event started so I waited until he'd finished speaking then went up to him…

"Oh hi, do you remember me?"
"Give me a clue," Paul replied.

Val said two words, and my face lit up. We started chatting and I asked Val if she was married. She said she wasn't. I had to get back to my seat so I told her not to leave until I'd spoken to her again later that evening.

The pandemic began around March 2020. How did you spend the time prior to your diagnosis?
Val bought a house near Sudbury that month and we moved in just a couple of weeks before the first lockdown. She had to work from home and I think we were the only two people in the country who weren't unhappy at not being able to go out! The area was new to both of us so we just spent time exploring. I went out on my bike a lot, visited a few local pubs before they

got told to close and generally just tried to keep fit. I also cleaned the house regularly in my yellow marigold gloves while Val was working from home. There are no pictures before you ask! It was a complete lifestyle change and I loved every minute of it.

And then the brain tumour diagnosis in October 2020. What were the first signs that something wasn't quite right?

I started to get headaches, quite violent headaches, so I told Val about them. She's in the medical profession and initially thought they might be tension headaches, perhaps due to the stress of this ongoing divorce. So Val reported the headaches to my doctor, one of her best friends, and the doc was able to see me within a couple of hours. On the way there we stopped off at the chemist and Val bought me some extra-strength headache tablets. The doc carried out a lot of tests and did some blood-work, something wasn't right so she arranged an emergency appointment for me to get a scan. The nasal endoscopy wasn't fun – a long thin tube with a tiny camera put up my nose to check for anything abnormal. I remember asking the doc why the tube was so long and Val making a smart-arse remark that it had to be because of the size of my nose! I was also referred to the local headache clinic. Thankfully another doctor that Val knew worked there and I'm sure that helped me get seen quicker.

Over the next few days the headache medication seemed as though it was only marginally working. It was taking the edge off the pain but there was still a lot of discomfort. I told Val, she knew something wasn't quite right so we arranged to get more tests done.

Fighting To The End

Thursday 15th October, 2020

Val:

I was mostly working from home but on this day I'd gone in to work. My friend, the headache doctor, mentioned that she was seeing Paul soon and asked how he was. I told her that something was definitely not right. I'd noticed a slight personality change in Paul over the previous couple of evenings – normally after dinner he would get up from the table and help me with the washing up, but the first night he just sat there staring at the television and the night before he was just staring blankly at his phone. I asked him on both occasions if he was going to get up and give me a hand, he said yes then continued just to sit there. It may only have looked like a small change in behavior but to me it was massive. It's what we call a red flag, when there's a distinct personality change. As I was telling my doctor friend all this she got called away on an emergency. She tried to ring me later but I was unavailable – I later found out she was going to tell me that she thought it was a brain tumour, but due of the nature of the conversation she didn't want to leave a voice message and preferred to chat to me directly.

That evening we were all sitting round the table when Paul dropped his water bottle lid on the floor and leant sideways to pick it up. He fell off his chair, bashed his head against the wall and proceeded to be sick so I called an ambulance. They took him in to hospital: the bloodwork was fine but they also did a CT scan. The whole process seemed to take forever. I wasn't allowed in to the hospital due to COVID protocols so I was hassling them over the phone for any information while also reaching out to my own friends who were doctors to see if they could find out any more. Eventually Paul got the results of the scan and all they said to him was that it showed something, but they didn't tell him what it was. I got all my medics involved and it turned out to be a lesion on his brain and Paul would need to have to an MRI scan. It just went full steam ahead from there, involving Queens Hospital in London, and everything was like really quick, wasn't it?

It was incredible, Mark. Everything happened at double speed, culminating in the brain surgery on the 29th of October.

I'm just thinking, Paul, had it not been for Val and how quickly she was able to get things done then we might not be sitting here talking right now?
Correct. And that's what I said to her. Everything was done so fast and Val's friend, Maria Parsons, who is my doctor, was amazing and jumped on it straight away. The headaches started around the 9th or 10th of October, Val noticed the personality change a few days later, I had the fall on the 15th and the operation took place on the 29th.

Val:
We've talked about if Paul was still in America, and this happened, that he wouldn't be here now.

The whole process seemed to unfold really quickly?

Val:
Often the first sign of a brain tumour is a seizure and a CT scan is carried out at the hospital and the diagnosis is made very quickly. However, in Paul's case because I knew that he didn't normally suffer with headaches I was concerned and made an appointment with his doctor. Many tests had already been carried out by the time he had that first fall and we were waiting for an MRI scan date. He fortunately only had one seizure which was after his radiotherapy had finished.

As a player you were a brave, strong and fearless striker, Paul. How much have those traits helped you deal with all of this?

Well I could blow my own trumpet and say that's been the case but if I'm honest, having Val with me every step of the way and listening to what she says is how I'm coping. The doctors that she's put me in touch with are of a ridiculously good standard. I'm staggered. When we had the first episode – and I had to have all the tablets – I couldn't believe how quickly I got myself feeling better and that was all thanks to Val. It was remarkable.

Val:
Paul had the surgery at the end of October 2020, then there was a gap of four weeks before the radiotherapy. That lasted for six weeks, and he was also on chemo tablets – shedloads of medication and some of them caused him to be violently sick. The sickness lasted a couple of days at which point I got in touch with Paul's consultant, Dr. Jenny Collins. I advised that the anti-sickness medication was not working and suggested we tried a different one. Once the tablets were switched the sickness stopped. But then constipation became a real issue...

Marko, it was the worst. Jesus! I hope you never get constipation, it's horrific.

Val:
I told you it was going to get incredibly painful if the next lot of medication didn't work and it got to the stage where I just went out and bought Fybogel. That eased the discomfort a little bit but not enough, so I had to ring the hospital and ask for suppositories because nothing else was working. The line had to be drawn somewhere so I gave Paul the suppositories, some lubrication and a pair of gloves and told him he was on his own! "Get on that bed, bend your knees, slam it in and you can't go for fifteen minutes!"

This might sound like a daft thing to say, but is it

possible that Val going to the Kevin Beattie tribute night might just have saved Paul's life?

Val:

We've said that many times, haven't we? It's strange when I think of the set of circumstances that led to me going that evening. I'd just come back on the Monday night from a skiing holiday in Italy. The weather out there had been bad and we'd not been able to ski for a couple of days, my friends suggested we stay for an extra day because the forecast was improving but I knew I wouldn't be home in time for the Kevin Beattie tribute if I stayed, so my decision was an easy one.

Then the following day just a few hours before the event in Clacton, I seriously considered not going, I had a bit of a meltdown, wondering what to wear, and what was I going to say to him. I had previously contacted a friend from years ago when I first met Paul and asked her if she would come with me to the event because there was no way I was going on my own. Thankfully she said yes, but I know if she'd changed her mind after initially saying yes then I wouldn't have gone alone. So thank you Bev!

Can you compare life with Paul before and after the diagnosis, Val?

Val:

I'm sure I can speak for Paul when I say that our time spent together until the diagnosis was among the happiest of our lives, with memories I will forever cherish of such a wonderful, kind and truly amazing legend. His mother Peggy must take great comfort in knowing she and Jim raised an incredible son – the man of my dreams. The saddest part is that we had so many plans, nothing lavish, just making up for lost time and enjoying each other's company. We were really looking forward to spending time with family, friends and our new grandchildren, Parker and Poppy.

Fighting To The End

How big a fight is this, Paul?
For this cancer stuff? The biggest I've had. It's the fight of my life.

You've won every fight you've had before.
I'm gonna win this as well, mate. And just wait 'til you see the piss-up when I do.

Tributes

A selection of tributes from the world of football following the announcement on 9th July, 2021 that Paul had passed away, aged 68...

'He was my best mate. As a footballer he was unbelievable. He came into the club and made a difference immediately. He could hold the ball up, score goals. He'd take all the knocks for us. He made us a better team – and he helped me so much as well.

'As a person, he was even better than he was as a player and that is saying something. Bobby [Robson] put us together as room-mates and it just went boom from there. He was so bubbly. He was the loud one in the dressing-room, the one that got everyone going. The boys loved him, we all did.

'He called me his 'brother'. That's how close we were and we stayed in touch, even when he went to America. I can't speak highly enough of him as a footballer but even more so as a person' – **John Wark**

'I remember him standing there, his chest was out, his chin was high, he was standing to attention. He was just perfect. That's the example I wanted to follow. What it meant to him to play for England was everything. He was totally committed for England' – **Terry Butcher**

Tributes

'I'll remember Paul as someone who was always positive, always encouraging, always selling the game. The most empathetic person I know. He had such a positive outlook on life and never criticised players when they made a mistake – because everybody makes mistakes – or coaches even if they'd lost ten games in a row or had a bad stretch. Paul always looked for the positive sides of things and encouraged everyone, whether he was broadcasting matches or doing his thing on ESPN FC. 'The next game is always around the corner' he used to say. I admire that so much because it's so easy for all these journalists, pundits or commentators to go off on what they see and think they know better, but that was never Paul's way. He would always encourage everyone to look forward to the next game, win or lose.

'His main interest over here in the States was New England Revolution, the team he coached along with Stevie Nicol then commentated for, and I loved listening to him call games. I used to send Paul text messages during the match and he would always reply straight away, even though him and Brad Feldman were in the middle of a broadcast!

'We've lost an amazing personality in Paul and a fantastic human being. It just shows you how appreciative you have to be for life. He was such an outstanding personality because he made everybody around him smile and feel good and feel better. It's a very sad reality that he's not with us anymore' – **Jürgen Klinsmann**

'Ipswich Town were a team to be feared and Paul Mariner was a big part of that. He was the type of striker I admired growing up, he was a fantastic footballer' – **Tony Cascarino**

Paul Mariner

'Paul Mariner was one of THE strikers when I grew up' – **Jan Aage Fjortoft**

'Paul Mariner was an outstanding footballer' – **Chris Sutton**

'Paul was a superb player for Arsenal and will be fondly remembered as a great player in the club's history' – **Arsenal FC Supporters Club**

'I can't tell you how much everyone at ESPN loved Paul Mariner' – **Don Hutchison**

'Football hero, giant personality, heart of a champion, and also just a great guy' – **Brad Feldman**

'I was nine. This (Ipswich) team were legends and Paul Mariner was my God' – **Renaissance Statman**

'We talk about the years of hurt. But the 12 years between 1970 and 1982 when England couldn't even qualify for a World Cup were the worst. And Paul Mariner ended them' – **Dan Hodges**

'Very stylish and effective striker and the only opposition player who shook my hand immediately after I scored a goal' – **Terry Gibson**

'When you're too young to have seen the great (Ipswich) side of the '70s and early '80s play, all you have is the stories from the older generation. Paul Mariner's name was always on their lips with a glint in their eyes as they spoke. A true legend' – **Matt Clayton**

Tributes

'We were all his friend. We love you Paul' – **Ipswich Town Norway**

'The greatest Ipswich Town striker there will ever be' – **Craig**

'It's always been a source of great pride in the town that such a distinguished footballer began his career at Chorley FC. I hope his story inspires another promising footballer to make the journey from Victory Park to glory' – **James Walsh**

'Wonderful target-man, fine coach and just one of the loveliest people you could meet. Privileged to have watched you and known you' – **Henry Winter, The Times**

'The outpouring of affection for Paul Mariner from fans of all the clubs he played for says so much' – **Nigel Adderley**

'We know class when we see it' – **Highbury Canaries**

'Everyone wanted to be Paul Mariner, playing at the park or in the playground' – **Shaun Watson**

'His partnership with Billy Rafferty was the greatest ever seen at Home Park' – **Simon Speare**

'Will never forget the opportunity he gave me at 16' – **Jordan Berry, UEFA B Licence coach**

'Who could forget that famous cup final banner, Paul Mariner vs Arsenal centre-half Willie Young: 'Our featherlite Mariner will slip around your Big Willie'' – **Stephen Pepper**

'One of the club's all-time greats, on and off the pitch' – **Matt Holland**

'Very good player and decent man. When I spent some time with Paul, we talked a lot about football but even more about his love of hard rock music. He'd even sung on stage with Deep Purple who, on occasion, had dedicated 'Smoke on the Water' to him' – **Danny Kelly**

'I had the pleasure of playing with him in the 1982 World Cup in Spain. A great gentleman and terrific player' – **Peter Shilton**

'I feel so fortunate to call him a friend' – **Taylor Twellman**

'It is heart-breaking news to me [that Paul has died]. We roomed together in the England team. You will always be with me and remembered fondly' – **Gordon Hill**

'Sad to hear the loss of Paul Mariner. It was always a challenge to play against him' – **Kevin Ratcliffe**

'As fantastic a man as he was a footballer' – **Rob Palmer**

'My only experience with Paul Mariner was accosting him for a chat as part of a group of annoying 17-year-olds after a pre-season friendly at Truro. Far from brushing us off, he enjoyed our enthusiasm and chatted to us with charm and warmth' – **Sam Down**

'I'll never forget him and his kind words to me. DM'd me a

lot when I was having a hard time post C4 documentary. One of England's best all-round centre-forwards' – **John Sitton, former Chelsea, Millwall, Gillingham and Leyton Orient player**

'Anyone who earned compliments from Sir Bobby Robson deserves special recognition, and Paul's goal tally tells you everything you need to know about his ability as a striker. Having faced his teams as a manager, I remember Paul as a tough opponent and a great team player. His enthusiasm and passion for the game was apparent throughout his performances. Paul's contribution to football, both for club and country as a player and a coach, was enormous" – **LMA Chairman Howard Wilkinson**

Ipswich fans pen some poignant messages following Paul's death

Paul Mariner

'Paul came into management following an outstanding playing career. At Ipswich, he was part of Sir Bobby Robson's FA Cup winning side in 1978 and he lifted the 1981 UEFA Cup. For his country, he made 35 appearances for England, scoring against France at the 1982 World Cup. Paul was very highly respected as a player and a manager, and we particularly remember him for his kindness and generosity to his fellow coaches. He was always keen to welcome colleagues who wanted to learn from his experiences coaching overseas' – **LMA Chief Executive Richard Bevan**

'Gutted. As a wide-eyed 11-year-old watching my first England World Cup in '82, seeing Paul, socks down, arms straight in the air after scoring filled me with joy' – **Stan Collymore**

'Paul Mariner was a striker of the highest class who mixed old-fashioned virtues of physical presence and aerial power alongside a complete all-round game' – **Phil McNulty, BBC sport chief football writer**

A Farewell Note

by Steve Nicol

To my other half,

I was asked what I'll miss most about you. Well, the answer is everything. I suppose if I had to pick something specific it would be all the carry-ons we had. I don't remember a single time over the years when there wasn't laughter involved at some point when we were together, going all the way back to that initial meeting in the Irish pub in Massachusetts. Messing around like a couple of big kids was everything, and most of the time we didn't even know we were doing it.

Growing old might not be a choice but being daft, arranging pranks and having fun with you most certainly was.

The pair of us going on a scouting trip to Argentina is one of my favourite stories; heading down there with a list of twenty potential signings but the only decent performance we saw came courtesy of Sting during The Police concert in Buenos Aires!

Then there was that time in Seattle when, as head coach of New England Revolution, I was serving the second of a two-game touchline ban and wasn't allowed any communication whatsoever with players or coaches once we were in the stadium.

That meant you, as my assistant, had full responsibility for everything during the game while I was sitting in the stand. So what happened? You got fucking sent off and ended up sat beside me. There was nothing else to do except burst out laughing!

Paul Mariner

Life's not the same without you, Jim, but I'm thankful to have so many memories to look back on and smile.

Love,
Jim

Players and fans at the Gillette Stadium in Massachusetts pay their respects to someone who was fondly remembered by everyone at New England Revolution

Thanks

Mr Jonathan Pollock, Neurosurgeon, Queens Hospital, Dr Jenny Collins, Clinical Oncologist, Natalie Wheatley, Nurse Specialist, Radiotherapy staff and all the extraordinary team at Colchester Hospital.

Dr Maria Parsons my favourite GP and friend, you acted so quickly and no doubt bought me more time.

Nayland Doctors Surgery and Dispensing staff for your compassion and help.

SinglePoint and Bluebird Carers, especially to Heather, Victoria, Nicola, Adam, Shannon, Gina, Jess, Emma, Jenny, Joy and any I have forgotten! Your help and care was invaluable.

Night Owls for waking me up at 1am each morning! Also thanks to Alistair and Sue Bartlett for many visits and providing essential equipment in my hour of need.

My mum Peggy, who at 90 years old was by my side throughout, keeping me positive and raising my spirits, and loving me as only a mum could.

Val for loving me and saving my life several times, for being there for me all the way, my very own Florence Nightingale, my rock, my soulmate.

Paul Mariner

My sons, Dan, Joe and especially George for staying with me every fortnight throughout, keeping me entertained and upbeat. I couldn't be prouder of you.

Ellie, Tom, Parker, Rachel Bish and Poppy, for your many visits, chocolates, banter and hugs.

My Ipswich Town FC teammates for your kind gifts, well wishes and visits, you brightened my days with your banter and stories.

Stevie Nicol, Julian Rose, Tom Byers, Leo Chapel and Joe Corrigan for your calls and texts and all my wonderful friends for their kind messages.

New England Revolution and ESPN, your banter is second to none!

Tash, a good friend and nurse who pulled all the stops out to help get supplies and support for us.

This book would not have been possible without the talent, patience, and hard work of Mark Donaldson. I cannot thank you enough.

**The Mariner family's nominated charity is
The Brain Tumour Charity.
You can donate here:
www.thebraintumourcharity.org/donate**